D1602372

CATTLE COUNTRY COOK BOOK

Cattle Country Cook Book

Basic Recipes from East of the Cascades

By

Nancy Strope

BINFORDS & MORT, *Publishers*

Portland   •   Oregon   •   97242

Cattle Country Cook Book

LIBRARY OF CONGRESS CATALOG CARD NUMBER: 74-140123
ISBN: 0-8323-0219-8

Printed in the United States of America

FIRST EDITION

SECOND PRINTING 1973

PUBLISHERS' PREFACE

"Cattle Country Cook Book" embodies ideas we have long had in mind regarding a needed book in the world of cookery, one geared to regional use in the Pacific Northwest—with adaptability to any part of the world where the person in the kitchen is looking for:

Recipes that get down to facts and show you how you can gain a reputation for being a gourmet cook with simple staples found on most pantry shelves. . . .

Recipes that refer to foods by their real names and don't attach some exotic name to a dish to confuse the issue. . . .

Recipes that are told simply, with eagerness to communicate rather than to impress. . . .

Recipes that make you want to cook because they are described with enthusiasm and warmth, and make you hungry just reading them. . . .

Recipes that have been used successfully many years by the author, who reports that the recipes in this book are ones that her family has enjoyed and thrived on. . . .

Recipes that prove all recipes are merely variations of a comparatively few simple, basic ones. . . .

Recipes that catch the flavor and zest of the outdoors through regional photographs, cattle-country anecdotes, and cattle-country foods. . . .

Recipes that include a handy checklist of ingredients which you can quickly scan, and if you don't have what is needed, go on to a recipe that calls for what you do have. . . .

Recipes that are printed in large, clear type, so you don't have to hold them under a bright light to see them . . . and

Grandma can read them over the tops of her spectacles. Besides, not everybody has 20-20 vision. . . .

Recipes that require a minimum of cooking equipment. If you lack the equipment suggested, use the next best thing available. The recipes are not that technical, and that's why we think you will like them. They leave plenty of room for venturing on your own. . . .

Recipes that take care of those occasional desperate moments when you have too much of this and not enough of that. A whole chapter is given to coping with such times. . . .

Recipes that are easy to find. They are even numbered. Look up your favorites by page or by number. Not only are they numbered, indexed, and cross-indexed — but there's a Recipe Guide at the beginning of each section, whether it be Beef, Lamb, Pork, Pies, Vegetables, or others. . . .

Recipes that make good use of what nature provides . . . foods like wild berries, game birds, venison, and mountain trout. Here too, basic, simple recipes show how easy it is to make the most of what is at hand, whether the result be sourdough, Indian Bread, or Camp Biscuits. . . .

Recipes that call for simple meat seasonings like salt and pepper, but also lead the reader into more venturesome worlds of spices. . . .

Recipes collected since childhood, when Nancy Strope's love affair with cooking began . . . born in her mother's kitchen where she spent many hours watching her mother cook. Later it was only natural that she should wish to share her recipes with others, as she has in her newspaper columns, her radio programs, and now in this book.

Nancy Strope has worked in test kitchens and been widely praised for her ability as a foods demonstrator . . . and always requests have flowed in for "more information." The result has been this unique collection of recipes which we believe could aptly be summed up as the "We Love to Cook" Cook Book . . . and we hope you will too.

This book is dedicated to all the wonderful people who so faithfully listened to my "two cents worth" on Radio Station KBND, and to my husband, without whose patience and cooperation it would never have been written.

CONTENTS

CATTLE COUNTRY COOK BOOK

RECIPE GUIDE

BEEF

〰〰〰〰〰〰〰〰〰〰〰〰〰〰〰〰〰〰〰〰〰〰〰〰〰〰〰〰〰

You will find the recipes in this book, like Eastern Oregon living, simple, plain, and uncluttered. Beside each recipe, in the right-hand margin, is a quick checklist of ingredients needed. Items in parentheses are optional.

These first few recipes, all made from ground beef, can be lifesavers if your budget is in a depressed state. On the other hand, I have served them proudly to company many times, because ground beef maintains its reputation for being economical and tasty in Cattle Country too. The popular name of hamburger can refer to patties, patties in a bun, or to the bulk ground beef displayed in meat cases.

When a recipe calls for ground beef, a decision must be made as to the quality desired. If ground entirely from a certain part of the beef carcass, it usually costs a little more, and the name may be added, as Ground Chuck. Ground Chuck, generally a good buy, is made from the chuck or shoulder. The resulting ground beef has just enough fat to be juicy and full of flavor, with very little shrinkage.

Ground Round, as the name implies, is made from the "round of beef," the meat between the leg and rump. Since the round is a very lean cut of meat, the resulting ground beef is very lean, with only enough fat to give flavor and substance.

Ground beef made from scrap beef has the highest fat content and is usually lowest in price—though it is not always an economical buy, considering the amount of shrinkage during cooking and the need to drain off large amounts of fat. This waste fat often actually raises the cost to that of Ground Chuck.

For a very special occasion and truly superb "Hamburger Steak" or patties, select a good piece of boneless rump or top sirloin, and have your butcher grind it for you. . . . With these thoughts in mind, only you can decide which is the best purchase for your particular needs.

1. Beef Hash

This first recipe is one my mother used to make. You can make it with a pound of ground beef—or a half pound. It is up to you and the present state of your budget. We just simply called it Hash. It is best served with either toast or hot biscuits, a green salad, and a bit of fruit.

½ to 1 pound of ground beef
½ medium onion, chopped fine
4 medium potatoes, diced
1 teaspoon Worcestershire sauce
1 teaspoon salt
¼ teaspoon pepper

GROUND BEEF
ONION
POTATOES
WORCESTER-
  SHIRE SAUCE
SALT
PEPPER
FLOUR

Crumble the ground beef into a heavy skillet. Brown gently over medium heat until rich brown in color. Add the minced onion and continue to brown until the onion is transparent. Add the diced potatoes, salt, pepper, and Worcestershire sauce. Add just enough water barely to cover the ingredients. Simmer gently until the potatoes are tender (about 15 minutes). Don't hurry the simmering, for the slow cooking is what gives a delicious flavor.

Make a paste of 2 tablespoons of flour and ½ cup of water. When the potatoes are tender, add flour-and-water thickening. Stir until the mixture thickens and starts to bubble again. Serve with hot, buttered toast or biscuits. Serves 4.

2. Meat Loaf

I have tried out more Meat Loaf recipes than I would care to mention, only to go back—always—to my old standby method. It is very basic, easy to make, tender, and moist. What more can you ask?

1 pound ground beef	
2 slices bread	GROUND BEEF
½ cup canned milk, undiluted—or ½ cup water and ½ cup powdered milk	BREAD MILK ONION
½ small onion (minced very fine)	SALT
1 teaspoon salt	PEPPER
¼ teaspoon pepper	

The secret is in the mixing. Lay the bread in a large bowl. Pour the milk over the bread and let stand until it absorbs the milk. Add salt, pepper, and onion. Mix with a fork until the bread falls apart into a light, fluffy mixture. Mix in the ground beef, shape into a loaf, and bake at 400 degrees for 1 hour. Serves 4.

You'll notice that this Meat Loaf recipe does not call for an egg. If you want to include an egg, there is no harm, but the meat loaf will not be so tender. A light touch in handling ground beef—whether you are making patties, meat balls, or meat loaf—is half the secret of tenderness.

For a taste change that has eye appeal, add a small jar of stuffed olives, well drained, to the ground beef mixture. When the loaf is ready to serve, the slices are very eye-catching with their pretty red and green polka dots.

———◆———

I like to make Meat Loaf on busy days because it takes only a few minutes to mix. Place the loaf in the center of a 9 x 13-inch baking pan, surround with peeled potatoes that have been cut in half, and bake in the oven for 1 hour at 400 degrees. Baste the potatoes with the juice from the Meat Loaf a couple of times during the baking and that's all there is to it. Leaves you free for other things. Served with buttered corn and a bit of dessert—you'll need no more.

3. Meat Loaf Topping

A tasty topping that is easy on the budget can give your Meat Loaf a whole new flavor. This is the best one I know:
Mix together:

3 tablespoons brown sugar	Brown Sugar
¼ cup catsup	Catsup
¼ teaspoon nutmeg	Nutmeg
1 teaspoon dry mustard	Dry Mustard

Spread on top of Meat Loaf and bake as usual.

4. Meat Balls

Meat Balls can be a time-saver as well as a money-saver. Use the same recipe as in making Meat Loaf. Shape into little balls about the size of a walnut and let stand on a cookie sheet at least an hour before cooking. Two hours is still better. This gives them a chance to swell and is the difference between juicy, tender Meat Balls and tough ones.

Meat Loaf (Recipe No. 2)

Meat Balls are best of all when browned on all sides, barely covered with water, and simmered until tender (about 2 hours). At this point, remove the Meat Balls to a serving platter and thicken the broth with a mixture of cornstarch and water, allowing 1 tablespoon of cornstarch for every cup of broth used. For example, if you have a quart of broth, mix 4 tablespoons of cornstarch in just enough water to make a liquid paste and add gradually to the boiling liquid, stirring constantly as it thickens. Let the broth simmer for a couple of minutes to blend the flavors. Season with salt and pepper. Pour over the Meat Balls and serve with either noodles, mashed potatoes, or rice.

For an entirely different taste treat don't brown the Meat Balls, just drop them into boiling water, turn the heat low and simmer until tender (about two hours). They can also be simmered in spaghetti sauce and served with either rice or spaghetti. Or, simmer them in brown gravy, place in a casserole, top with unbaked biscuits, and bake in a 400-degree oven for 15 to 20 minutes, or until the biscuits are a golden brown.

5. Freezing Meat Balls

The next time ground beef is on "special," buy 5 pounds extra and make a supply of Meat Balls for the freezer. For 75 to 100 Meat Balls, it will take:

5 pounds of ground beef	GROUND BEEF
10 slices of bread	BREAD
2 large onions, minced fine	ONION
2½ cups canned milk, undiluted	MILK
5 teaspoons salt	SALT
1¼ teaspoons white pepper (black loses its flavor in the freezer)	WHITE PEPPER

Shape into Meat Balls and place on a cookie sheet. Let stand a couple of hours to allow time for swelling; then freeze.

After they are frozen, put the Meat Balls into a large plastic bag. Secure the bag with a pipe-stem cleaner (makes for easier opening) and you are in business. There is no end to the quick meals you can prepare with them.

In cooking for a family, there just isn't always time to get out the recipe books and create a gourmet dish. By memorizing a few basic recipes, such as the Meat Loaf Recipe (No. 2), you will soon find yourself able to prepare any number of dishes just by changing the sauce or method of preparing the mixture. This is what gains you a reputation for being a Gourmet Cook . . . . and it is really very simple!

6. Beef Spaghetti Sauce

I'm not much for making **Casserole Dishes** *and freezing them. While it certainly can be done, the reheated casserole isn't always what it's cooked up to be. Let's face it.* **Macaroni and spaghetti products just don't freeze well.** *Besides, they are very easy to cook. The trick to serving them at their best is to make up the sauce in larger amounts and freeze in meal-size portions . . . . then combine them at the very last minute with the freshly prepared macaroni, spaghetti, or noodles. Beef Spaghetti Sauce is such a sauce. Following is the one we like the best:*

In a large, heavy skillet, sauté (fry lightly in a small amount of hot fat, turning frequently):

    2 large onions, chopped very fine
    2 minced cloves of garlic
    4 tablespoons olive oil
Add:
    2 pounds ground beef and cook until nice
       and brown. Break up with a fork as it
       cooks.
Stir in:
    3 teaspoons salt
    ½ teaspoon pepper
    4 teaspoons sugar
    ½ teaspoon oregano
    2 bay leaves
    4 cups tomatoes, canned
    2 (6-ounce) cans tomato paste
    1 cup water

GROUND BEEF
ONION
CLOVE OF GARLIC
OLIVE OIL
OREGANO
BAY LEAVES
TOMATOES, CANNED
TOMATO PASTE
SUGAR
SALT
PEPPER

Simmer for about 1½ hours, stirring occasionally to prevent sticking. Cool and freeze in ice-cube trays. After the cubes are frozen, pop them into a plastic freezer bag until needed. When ready to use, take as many cubes as needed and thaw over low heat or in a double boiler. Pour over spaghetti, prepared according to the directions on the package, and sprinkle with Parmesan cheese. That's it!

7. Lasagna

This next recipe is a simplified form of Lasagna. It makes a good company dish to serve to a large crowd. It you should make too much, it can be frozen, for even though it contains noodles, it does take well to a return performance.

Prepare an 8-ounce package of Lasagna (very broad noodles) according to the directions on the package. While the noodles are cooking—

Brown:
    1 pound ground beef in one tablespoon shortening
Stir in:
    2 (8-ounce) cans tomato sauce and remove from the heat
Drain the cooked noodles, rinse with cold water and drain again. While the noodles are draining, combine:
    1 cup cottage cheese
    8 ounces cream cheese, crumbled
    ½ cup sour cream
    ⅓ cup chopped green onions
    1 tablespoon green pepper, chopped
    1 teaspoon salt
    ¼ teaspoon pepper

LASAGNA NOODLES
GROUND BEEF
TOMATO SAUCE
COTTAGE CHEESE
CREAM CHEESE
SOUR CREAM
GREEN ONIONS
GREEN PEPPER
QUICK MELTING CHEESE
SALT
PEPPER

In a buttered baking dish, 9 x 13 x 2 inches, spread half the noodles, cover with the cheese mixture, then add the remaining noodles. Spread slices of quick-melting cheese over the noodles. Cover the cheese with the ground-beef and tomato-sauce mixture. It isn't as complicated as it sounds—simply alternate layers of noodles and cheese topped with the ground-beef and tomato-sauce mixture.

Bake in a moderate 350-degree oven until hot and bubbly . . . or about half an hour. The cheese bubbles up through the ground beef sauce and the sauce runs down through the noodles and cheese. Serves 4 generously.

8. Hamburger Stroganoff

Hamburger Stroganoff is easy on the budget and also very tasty. . . . Cook approximately 4 ounces of noodles according to the directions on the package. While the noodles are cooking, melt 2 tablespoons of shortening in a skillet and brown together:

¾ cup diced onion
1 pound ground beef

Remove from the heat and blend in:

¼ cup flour
¾ teaspoon salt
¼ teaspoon pepper
¼ teaspoon oregano (optional)
½ cup catsup
1 can cream of mushroom soup or cream of chicken or left-over pan gravy
½ cup milk

GROUND BEEF
ONION
MUSHROOM SOUP
(OR CREAM OF CHICKEN SOUP OR LEFT-OVER PAN GRAVY)
NOODLES
CHEESE
MILK
SALT
PEPPER
(OREGANO)
FLOUR
CATSUP

Mix well and simmer together for a minute or two. Add the cooked, drained noodles. Pour into a buttered casserole and bake 25 to 30 minutes (325-degree oven). You might grate a bit of cheese over the top about 10 minutes before it is finished baking. Serves 4.

9. Cowpoke Casserole

Like the Hamburger Stroganoff, Cowpoke Casserole is both a thrifty and a tasty recipe. . . . Mix and brown together:

1½ pounds lean ground beef
1 teaspoon salt
¼ teaspoon pepper
¼ teaspoon oregano

GROUND BEEF
POTATOES
ONIONS
BACON
SALT, PEPPER
CHILI SAUCE
OREGANO

When the meat and seasonings are browned, stir in ¾ cup chili sauce and set to one side. Peel, and slice thinly, 3 medium-sized potatoes and 2 medium-sized onions. In a large casserole dish, make layers of the meat sauce, onions, and potatoes, starting with the meat and ending with the potatoes. Lay strips of bacon over the potatoes. Cover and bake in a moderate oven (350 degrees) for a good 40 minutes, or until the potatoes are tender. Remove the cover and bake 20 minutes longer. Serves 4 very hungry people.

Cattle country is usually a composite of bunchgrass, sagebrush, rimrocks, and acres and acres of sky.

10. Porcupines

The busier I get the better I like recipes that require oven cooking because it is so carefree. . . . Porcupines can be prepared in the oven. A large green salad and hot biscuits complete the menu easily, for you can use prepared biscuits if you are too busy to make your own. You might just as well utilize that oven heat!

GROUND BEEF
RICE
ONION
CELERY SEED
TOMATO SOUP
CINNAMON
WHOLE
    CLOVES
WORCESTER-
    SHIRE
    SAUCE
SUGAR
SALT, PEPPER

Mix together:

    1 pound ground beef
   ½ cup rice, uncooked
    1 small onion (minced fine)
    1 teaspoon salt
   ¼ teaspoon pepper
   ¼ teaspoon celery seed

Divide and shape the mixture into 16 little round balls. They will swell in cooking, so you don't want to get them too large. Place the meat balls in a deep baking dish.

In another bowl, mix together:
    1 can tomato soup
    1 cup water
   ¼ teaspoon cinnamon
    2 whole cloves
    2 tablespoons Worcestershire sauce
    1 tablespoon sugar

Pour the sauce over the meat balls, cover the baking dish with a tight-fitting lid and bake at 350 degrees for 1 hour. Be sure your baking dish is deep enough to allow for the expansion of the meat balls as they will double in size. Serves 4.

11. Beef Mexicana

Beef Mexicana is a simple dish to make and the Mexican people do have a way of taking a lowly pound of ground beef and making it into something very special.

When I used to cook on a wood range, I kept Beef Mexicana on the back of the range and let it simmer all afternoon. That's when it is really good, for the meat and tomatoes blend together and take on an entirely different flavor. You can get the same effect by letting it simmer in a slow oven (300 degrees). You might try it sometime when you are baking beans and have the oven on anyway.

Brown together in a large, heavy skillet:

1 pound ground beef	GROUND BEEF
1 large onion, cut in thin slices	ONION
1 teaspoon salt	CANNED TOMATOES
¼ teaspoon pepper	SALT
½ teaspoon mild chili powder	PEPPER
	CHILI POWDER

When well browned, stir in 4 cups canned tomatoes. Simmer until the meat-and-tomato mixture becomes quite thick. Serve on buns to 4 hungry people.

———◆———

Instead of serving it on buns, you can add 1½ cups whole-kernel corn (well drained), simmer 15 minutes longer, and serve with corn-bread squares. (For Corn Bread see Recipe 215.)

You can also leave out the corn and serve the Beef Mexicana with rice. Beef Mexicana is just one of those down-to-earth recipes that can be the basis of many a good meal.

12. Budget Burgers

Sunday night supper is one time we like to fix something simple and at the same time filling, as everyone has usually "thought up" a good appetite. When the family calls for hamburgers and catches you without enough ground beef to go around, here is a way to make a little go a long way:

Mix together:

1½ pounds ground beef	GROUND BEEF
⅔ cup canned milk (small can)	CANNED MILK
½ cup bread crumbs	BREAD
½ cup chopped onion	CRUMBS
½ teaspoon salt	ONION
	SALT

Shape into patties and broil or pan-fry. Makes 8 large Budget Burgers.

13. Crusty Beefburgers

Blend together:

1½ pounds ground beef	GROUND BEEF
1½ teaspoons salt	EGG
¼ teaspoon pepper	BREAD
	CRUMBS
	SALT, PEPPER
	FLOUR

Shape into 6 patties, ¼ inch thick. Dip the patties first in egg (beat 1 egg well) . . . then in flour. Use the flour sparingly—3 tablespoons will take care of the 1½ pounds of ground beef. Dip in the egg again and last of all sprinkle with a very fine coating of bread crumbs. Fry in a small amount of hot fat until they are golden brown on each side. Serves 4 with extras for the hungry ones.

An electric blender will make quick work of producing bread crumbs, but on the other hand, it is a simple matter to place the dry bread in a large plastic bag, and with a rolling pin, crumble the bread. You won't have the usual mess and you can leave any extra bread crumbs right in the bag until the next time you need crumbs.

14. Coriander Beefburgers

Coriander, a member of the parsley family, is usually used in pastries, salads, and with pork and poultry. Contrary to popular opinion, it can develop flavor in beef. Coriander Beefburgers are a tasty way to test your family's point of view.

Combine:

1 pound ground beef	GROUND BEEF
1 tablespoon minced onion	ONION
2 teaspoons parsley flakes	PARSLEY FLAKES
1 teaspoon salt	CORIANDER
½ teaspoon coriander	SALT

Shape into 4 patties and broil. (Do not add any pepper when using coriander.)

15. Meat Pie Shells

Meat Shells can be prepared quickly and easily. The variation is in the filling.

Mix together:

1 pound ground beef	GROUND BEEF
½ cup fine crumbs	CRUMBS
¼ cup chopped onions	ONIONS
¼ cup chopped green pepper (if you don't have fresh green peppers, use dehydrated pepper flakes—works fine!)	GREEN PEPPER (OR DEHYDRATED PEPPER FLAKES)
1 teaspoon salt	TOMATO SAUCE
¼ teaspoon pepper	SALT
¼ cup tomato sauce	PEPPER

Pat and spread mixture into a greased 10-inch pan. (Don't forget to grease the pan!) Then add either Cheese & Rice Filling, or Kidney Bean Filling, which follow.

Cheese & Rice Filling:

Make a mixture of:
  2 cups cooked rice
  ½ cup grated cheese
1½ cups tomato sauce
  1 teaspoon seasoned salt
  ¼ teaspoon coarse ground pepper

RICE
CHEESE
TOMATO
  SAUCE
SEASONED
  SALT
COARSE
  PEPPER

Place the mixture in the unbaked shell . . . sprinkle generously with additional cheese and bake at 350 degrees for 35 to 40 minutes, or until the meat is done.

Because rice expands during cooking to about 3 times its original size, ⅔ cup of raw rice cooked in 5 cups of water will be needed to obtain 2 cups of cooked rice.

If your family likes this type of Meat Pie, you can come up with all sorts of variations. One of the best fillings for Meat Shells is made with kidney beans.

Kidney Bean Filling:

Mix together:

  2 cups canned kidney beans
  1 minced clove of garlic
  1 teaspoon chili powder (mild)
  ½ cup (8-ounce can) tomato sauce
  ½ teaspoon salt
  ¼ teaspoon pepper

KIDNEY
  BEANS
  (CANNED)
CLOVE OF
  GARLIC
CHILI POWDER
  (MILD)
TOMATO
  SAUCE
GRATED
  CHEESE

Pour into the Meat Shells (Recipe No. 15) and top with grated cheese. Bake at 350 degrees for 35 to 40 minutes, or until the meat is done. Makes 4 generous servings.

16. Chili

Chili is another good basic to make and keep in the freezer. Chili, pure and simple, can be made in this way—

Brown together:
    2 pounds ground beef
    1 cup diced onions
Drain off the excess fat and add:
    4 cups canned red beans, (do not drain)
    6 cups canned tomatoes
 1¼ teaspoons salt
  ½ teaspoon pepper
 1½ teaspoons sugar
    2 teaspoons chili powder

GROUND BEEF
ONIONS
RED BEANS
TOMATOES
CHILI POWDER
SALT
PEPPER
SUGAR

An easy way to cook Chili, especially if you are using the baking unit for your main course, is to simmer the Chili in a covered casserole dish in the back part of the oven for 2 hours. Oven temperatures ranging from 300 to 375 degrees are best for simmering.

17. Chili Pie

Chili Pie can be made as quick as you can wink an eye with prepared Chili.

Place prepared Chili in a casserole dish and top with corn-bread batter (See Recipe 215). Bake in a 375-degree oven until the bread is done. Corn bread is done when a toothpick inserted into the bread comes out clean. Served with chopped onions, olives, and a green salad,

PREPARED CHILI
CORNBREAD BATTER
CHOPPED GREENS

it is a good cold-weather meal that will satisfy the heartiest of appetites.

18. Chili Mac

Chili Mac is a good, impromptu meal—

Mix together:

  2 cups macaroni and cheese (canned)
  2 cups chili (canned)

MACARONI &
CHEESE
(CANNED OR
LEFT-OVERS)
CHILI
(CANNED OR
LEFT-OVERS)

Bake until bubbly and hot in a 350-degree oven 15 to 20 minutes.

19. Coney Islands

Coney Islands, another "quickie," are always popular with teenagers:

Place piping-hot weiners on split buns and top with heated Chili. It's practically a meal in itself.

HOT DOGS
BUNS
CHILI
(CANNED)

20. Savory Shepherd's Pie

When a hearty meal is needed and you're not in the mood to cook, canned soups are real helpers. Savory Shepherd's Pie, made with vegetable soup, is such a dish:

Brown together:

  1 pound ground beef
  ¼ cup chopped onion
  ¼ cup chopped green pepper

Drain off excess fat and add:

  1 can condensed vegetable soup
  1 teaspoon salt
  ¼ teaspoon pepper

GROUND BEEF
ONION
GREEN
  PEPPER
VEGETABLE
  SOUP
POTATOES (OR
  INSTANT
  MASHED
  POTATOES)
SALT
PEPPER

Spoon mixture into a 1-quart casserole and place mounds of mashed potatoes around the edge of the casserole. Bake at 425 degrees for 12 minutes, or until the potatoes are a delicate brown. Serves 4.

21. Cabbage Rolls

Cabbage Rolls, made easily with tomato soup, can be an entirely different taste treat from the usual everyday fare.

Mix together:

1 pound ground beef	GROUND BEEF
1 cup cooked rice	RICE
¼ cup chopped onion	ONION
1 egg	EGG
1 teaspoon salt	TOMATO SOUP
¼ teaspoon pepper	CABBAGE
2 tablespoons tomato soup	SALT
	PEPPER

Cook 6 large cabbage leaves in boiling water a few minutes to soften. Drain well. In the center of each leaf, place a portion of the hamburger mixture. Roll up and fasten with a toothpick. Place side by side, in a single layer, in either a heavy skillet with a tight-fitting lid or a Dutch Oven. Pour the rest of the tomato soup over all. Cook over low heat for about 40 minutes, spooning sauce over the cabbage rolls often. Use as low a heat as possible because they should cook gently. Serves 4.

22. Spanish Rice with Beef

Spanish Rice with Beef is another thrifty favorite.

Crumble and brown:

1 pound ground beef	GROUND BEEF
Add:	ONION
1 cup diced onion	GREEN PEPPER
¾ cup diced green pepper	MUSHROOMS
1 (4-ounce) can mushrooms, do not drain	CELERY
1 cup diced celery	RICE
¾ cup uncooked rice	TOMATOES, CANNED
1½ cups tomatoes, canned	SALT
1 teaspoon salt	PEPPER
¼ teaspoon coarsely ground pepper	

Cover with a tight-fitting lid and simmer until the rice is tender. Takes 20 to 30 minutes. Serves 4. In this case, you can double the recipe without allowing extra time for simmering.

23. Cheese-Beef Filled Pancakes

It's very frustrating to start to prepare a meal and find you are out of bread. While hot biscuits are always good, something different is often welcome. Cheese-Beef Filled Pancakes can prove to be a real wife-saver. Besides, they are tasty enough to serve any time to anybody.

Brown together:

   1 pound ground beef
  ⅓ cup minced onion
   1 teaspoon salt
  ⅛ teaspoon pepper
   1 slight pinch of garlic salt

Add:

  ½ teaspoon Worcestershire sauce
  ¼ cup catsup

GROUND BEEF
ONION
PANCAKES
CHEDDAR CHEESE
(PARMESAN CHEESE)
GARLIC SALT
WORCESTERSHIRE SAUCE
CATSUP
SALT
PEPPER

Remove from the heat to cool while you prepare 6 large pancakes. Use a prepared mix or your own. Spread each pancake with a generous amount of meat mixture and sprinkle with ¼ cup of Cheddar cheese. Roll and secure with a toothpick. Place the roll in a baking dish and sprinkle with more Cheddar cheese and a little grated Parmesan cheese. Place under the broiler 5 to 7 minutes until the cheese is bubbly. Serves 4 or "seconds" for two.

A gelatin fruit salad goes well with this, as does a big green salad. At any rate, it's a tasty meal and it doesn't matter if you are out of bread.

———◆———

Thoughts on Entertaining: *Entertaining doesn't need to be expensive or burdensome. Some of the most delightful meals are those where, come eating time, you announce dinner simply by saying, "Help yourselves, everybody!" Simple food, served buffet-style, means that you, as hostess, can relax and enjoy the evening right along with everyone else.*

Managing on a broken shoestring has been the downfall of

more than one marriage and it's a shame. Thriftiness—aside from being a real challenge—can be lots of fun. Instead of apologizing for a lack of this and that . . . . serve the meal prettily . . . . and that needn't cost a dime!

The spirit in which something is served and the companionship of people you enjoy are generally far more important than what you are serving. It is much better to serve something your budget will allow and have fun in the process, than to serve something expensive that you can't afford. If your guests are the type you can't share your "usual" with, they aren't going to be impressed anyway.

24. Beef 'n Beans

I've served considerable "this 'n that" to a lot of unexpected company over the years and they all come back for more. I suppose you might say my theory is "guest-tested"! Here is a thrifty favorite:

In a large skillet, sauté lightly:

   1 pound ground beef

Add:

   ¼ cup diced green pepper

   ½ cup minced onion

   ½ cup diced celery

When the vegetables are tender, add:

   ½ cup tomato sauce (8-ounce can)

   ½ cup water

   1 clove of garlic, minced fine

   1 teaspoon dry mustard

   2 tablespoons wine vinegar

   1 tablespoon brown sugar

   1 teaspoon salt

   ¼ teaspoon pepper

   1 large can kidney beans (30-oz. can)

GROUND BEEF
GREEN PEPPER
ONION
CELERY
TOMATO SAUCE
GARLIC
WINE VINEGAR
DRY MUSTARD
BROWN SUGAR
KIDNEY BEANS (CANNED)
SALT
PEPPER

Place mixture in a 1½-quart casserole and bake at 375 degrees for 45 minutes. Serves 4. If you double the recipe to accommodate more people, bake in a 3-quart casserole—in which case you may need to increase the baking time by about 15 minutes. Doubled casserole recipes often need additional baking time because of the greater quantity of food to be cooked.

―――――――

Because there is no end to the tasty things you can do with ground beef, let's just call ground beef and "fixings" good, and go on to other things.

―――――――

25. Basic "Stew Beef"

Stew Beef *is the main ingredient of many outstanding recipes. It is an economical purchase, for there is little or no waste and the beef cubes are taken from the less tender cuts of beef, such as the beef round, beef chuck, neck, and shank. I like to prepare 4 to 5 pounds of Cubed Stew Beef at one time and divide it into meal-size portions, allowing 1¼ pounds for each portion. Three of these portions are then packaged for the freezer and frozen to be used when I'm not so ambitious, or just simply too busy to cook. The fourth portion is used to prepare the meal at hand. To prepare four meal-size portions of Stew Beef—*

Mix together:
1 cup flour
4 teaspoons salt
1 teaspoon pepper

CUBED STEW BEEF
FLOUR
SALT
PEPPER
SHORTENING

Dredge 4 to 5 pounds of cubed Stew Beef with the seasoned flour. Melt shortening in the bottom of a Dutch Oven or a heavy skillet to a depth of ¼ inch. Brown the dredged beef cubes in the hot shortening over medium heat. Do not over-crowd. There should be room to turn each cube easily. As the cubes are browned to perfection on all sides, remove them to a platter while browning the next portion. When all cubes have been browned, remove the remaining fat from the Dutch Oven. Add water to a depth of ⅛ inch in the bottom of the Dutch Oven or skillet. Add the browned beef cubes, cover with a tight-fitting lid, turn the heat to its lowest position, and simmer until the meat is fork-tender. This will take anywhere from 1 to 3 hours, depending on the quality of beef used. You may need to add water to prevent sticking. Do be careful, however, to add as little water as possible.

26. Beef Stew

For the meal in the making, a simple Beef Stew—prepared from one of the portions of the Basic "Stew Beef"—always meets with approval. Into a large kettle with a tight-fitting lid, place:

1¼ pounds browned stew meat (see Recipe No. 25)	STEW BEEF (RECIPE No. 25)
4 medium potatoes, quartered	POTATOES
4 carrots, one-inch thick chunks	CARROTS

Cover with water and simmer until the vegetables are tender. Don't hurry the stew, for the slow cooking brings out the flavor. I suggest you leave the final seasoning to each individual, for the browned "Stew Meat" contains enough seasoning to bring out the flavor during cooking.

Needless to say, you can add onions, tomatoes, green beans, corn, turnips . . . . whatever you prefer. If your family complains when you make stew, as mine used to do, you might try using potatoes and carrots only. It's just plain old country cooking, which is hard to beat.

27. Dumplings

Dumplings are always good with Beef Stew. The secret to good dumplings is to turn the heat low, put the lid on tight, and never peek. They will be done in 15 minutes. If you peek, they will certainly fall.

Mix together and drop by teaspoonfuls on top of the simmering stew:

1 cup pre-sift flour	FLOUR
1 teaspoon baking powder	BAKING POWDER
¼ teaspoon salt	SALT
⅔ cup milk	MILK

Cover with a tight-fitting lid and simmer 15 minutes. Makes 6 nice big dumplings.

28. 5-Hour Oven Stew

The following Oven Stew recipe came to me by way of one neighbor to another. These word-of-mouth recipes are the best recipes, always. You can put this particular stew in the oven, be gone 4 or 5 hours, and return home to the delightful aroma of a stew that is ready to serve.

Into a casserole dish or roaster that has a tight-fitting lid, put:

1 pound stew beef, cut in small cubes, (do not brown the meat)	STEW BEEF
3 large carrots, diced	CARROTS ONION
1 can drained peas (we prefer to leave the peas out and add 2 tablespoons dehydrated pepper flakes)	CANNED PEAS (DEHYDRATED PEPPER FLAKES)
3 small potatoes, diced	POTATOES
1 can cream of tomato soup, or 1 large can tomatoes	TOMATO SOUP (OR CANNED TOMATOES)
½ cup water	SALT
1 teaspoon salt	PEPPER
¼ teaspoon pepper	
1 onion, diced	

Put the lid on and place it in a 275-degree oven and forget it for 5 hours. Everything cooks in its own juice, and strange as it seems, the vegetables keep their firm texture. It's that low, low oven heat. The stew is delicious, and since this does make just enough for 4 hearty servings, you may want to double the recipe.

29. Beef Pot Pie

Mix together:

1¼ pounds browned stew meat (Recipe No. 25)	STEW BEEF (RECIPE No. 25)
1 (10-ounce) package mixed vegetables (frozen)	MIXED VEG-ETABLES (CANNED OR FROZEN)
1 cup water	READY-MADE BISCUITS

Place in a 1½-quart casserole dish. Top with ready-made biscuits and bake at 325 degrees for 20 to 30 minutes. Be sure the biscuits are not only nicely brown on top but baked throughout. The only way I know to be sure is to gently lift the top off one of the biscuits. If they do need additional baking time, place a sheet of foil loosely over the top of the biscuits to prevent further browning. With a large green salad, this will not only be a hearty meal but one that is quick to prepare. Serves 4.

———◆———

30. Cattle Country Goulash

Mix together and simmer until vegetables are tender (30 minutes):

1¼ pounds browned stew meat (Recipe No. 25)	NOODLES STEW BEEF (RECIPE No. 25)
1 cup canned tomatoes	TOMATOES
¼ cup finely diced celery	CELERY
½ green pepper, chopped	GREEN PEPPER
2 tablespoons minced onion flakes	ONION FLAKES
1 cup diced carrots	DICED CARROTS
2 whole cloves	CLOVES
1 tablespoon minced dried parsley	DRIED PARSLEY
½ teaspoon salt	SALT
⅛ teaspoon pepper	PEPPER
1 cup water	

Serve with noodles which have been cooked according to the directions on the package. A practical mode of measurement for pasta products is to allow 1 ounce per serving plus 1 for the pot. This Goulash serves 4.

31. Beef Stroganoff

Simmer together for 10 minutes:

1¼ pounds browned stew meat (Recipe No. 25)

1 (2-ounce) can sliced mushroom buttons, drained

1 tablespoon minced onion flakes

1 cup water

Gradually add:

1 cup sour cream

Cook over low, low heat for 5 minutes. Serve with rice or noodles.

STEW BEEF
(RECIPE No. 25)
MUSHROOM BUTTONS
ONION FLAKES
SOUR CREAM
RICE OR NOODLES

———◆———

Buying a Prime Beef Roast: *It is unwise to let price alone be your guide in purchasing meat. There is a brand or grade to suit your individual needs. You alone know the limits of your grocery budget. To acquaint you briefly with the various government grades of meat—the round purple stamp on fresh meat is your guarantee that meat is from animals free of disease and processed under sanitary conditions. Some stores use their own brand names to denote the quality of the meat; however, government grades will appear as U. S. Prime, U. S. Choice, U. S. Good, U. S. Commercial, and U. S. Utility. Compare prices between grades, consider the recipe you have in mind (some recipes lend themselves to economy cuts of meat with gourmet results) and then make the choice that is right for you.*

When buying a roast, look for one that is dull red in color. This indicates aging—which means greater tenderness. The fat should be white to light cream in color. A good covering of fat is needed to insure moistness in roasting. There should be streaks of fat, called marbling, throughout the lean.

For best results the roast should weigh at least 4 to 5 pounds. It is far better to prepare a large roast, cut it in half, serve one portion, and freeze the other for another time. To eliminate a "warmed over" taste when preparing a second meal from the frozen roast, place the roast on a rack in a heavy skillet or in a Dutch Oven. Add just enough water to cover the bottom of the utensil. Place lettuce leaves over the top of the roast, put the lid on, and cook over low, low heat until the meat is piping hot throughout. This is an old trick used by expert chefs. Ten minutes per pound of frozen meat, plus 5 for the pot, usually allows sufficient heating time.

Choosing a Rib Roast of Beef *can be somewhat confusing for the homemaker. I'll try to be as basic as possible in sharing "know how" . . . . Rib roasts from the same set of ribs usually sell for at least three different prices.*

The choicest are called "first" ribs in most markets; however, in some sections of the country they are referred to as "eleventh and twelfth rib" roasts. This is where it pays to be on a conversational basis with your butcher. He is always eager to help.

The "sixth and seventh ribs" are cut from the section near the shoulder pot roasts (see Chart, page 44) and are less tender; consequently, they are lower in price.

The cost of a "center rib" roast usually falls somewhere between the cost of the "first" and the cost of the "sixth and seventh."

Trimming and shaping, needless to say, affects the price of any of the roasts. A Standing Rib Roast that has not been trimmed is usually less per pound than a Standing Rib Roast with the Short Ribs removed. A Rolled Rib Roast, boned, rolled and tied, will be more per pound; on the other hand, the Rolled Roast may be the economy buy, for there will be little or no waste.

32. Prime Beef Roast

Low cooking temperatures bring out the best in meat cookery. In preparing a fine Rib Roast, this rule-of-thumb is a "must": set the oven at 325 degrees and leave it there. At this temperature, there will be only 15 to 20% shrinkage. If set at 400 degrees, the shrinkage actually doubles.

RIB ROAST
RUMP OR
  SIRLOIN
SALT
PEPPER

Seasoning a fine roast is a matter of choice. Most chefs prefer to leave a fine roast unseasoned, letting all the natural flavors come forth.

Place the Rib Roast, fat side up, on a rack in an open pan. Any pan with a 2-inch rim will do. A true roast is never covered. If you prefer to season, sprinkle with salt and pepper, allowing 2 teaspoons salt and ½ teaspoon pepper for every 4 pounds of meat.

That's all there is to it! It will baste itself and brown in the process. Do not sear or brown in a hot oven first. This will only dry out the meat.

Plan on 25 minutes per pound of meat to bring it to the basic "rare" stage. For a 5-pound roast, this would be 2 hours. After the roast reaches the "rare" stage, it takes only another 30 minutes for "medium" and 1 hour for "well done."

As a guideline, following is the timing for a 5-pound roast prepared at a temperature of 325 degrees:

2 hours = rare
2½ hours = medium
3 hours = well done

Nutritionists suggest ¼ pound per serving. A 5-pound roast will serve 4 generously and still allow ample meat to be wrapped in foil or plastic wrap and frozen to be used at a later date.

33. Country Pot Roast

When buying a Pot Roast, *keep in mind that ⅓ pound of bone-in roast is usually allowed for the average serving. Some families eat heartier than others because ages and occupations are determining factors. A homemaker soon learns to buy and prepare meals with her particular family in mind. When planning for "extras," basic rules are helpful.*

Brown a 4-pound Pot Roast on all sides in its own fat. Use a deep, heavy kettle or Dutch Oven and take your time about browning. Medium heat seals in the natural meat juices and browns the outside to perfection. Add 1 cup of hot water and scrape and work loose all the meat particles. Place the Pot Roast on a rack to hold it up out of the liquid and prevent burning. Add the following:

1 celery stalk, diced	POT ROAST
1 large carrot, sliced	CELERY
1 onion, minced fine	CARROTS
	ONION
1 teaspoon salt	SALT
¼ teaspoon pepper	PEPPER

Cover with a tight-fitting lid, turn heat on low, and simmer 3 to 4 hours—depending on whether you like your meat rare or well done. If necessary, add more water. There should be around ½ to 1 inch of water in the bottom of the kettle to form steam.

The celery, carrot, and onion will add a subtle flavor to the Pot Roast. If you care to venture still further, add a mixture of ⅛ teaspoon each of ground thyme, mace, and allspice; a few peppercorns and ½ bay leaf. Bay leaf, strong in flavor, should always be used discreetly.

———◆———

As a menu suggestion, Country Pot Roast served with Potato Pancakes is always sure to please. At the same time, it pleases the cook who likes to venture and get away from the "mashed potato and gravy bit."

34. Pot Roast Marinade

Pot Roast can be from the very toughest meat and still go to the table, tasty and tender. Tenderizers do a wonderful job of breaking down the enzymes in the meat, making it more tender . . . . and any recipe that calls for a marinade (or pickle) made with vinegar will also do the trick. For a good Pot Roast Marinade—

Make a mixture of:

2 cups cider	POT ROAST
1 tablespoon brown sugar	CIDER
¼ teaspoon cinnamon	BROWN SUGAR
¼ teaspoon ginger	CINNAMON
2 whole cloves	GINGER
	CLOVES
	ONION
	SALT, PEPPER

Fit the roast in a crock or dish which leaves only a minimum of space around the meat. Pour the cider mixture over it. Cover tightly and let stand in the refrigerator for 24 hours. Remove from the Marinade, drain and pat dry. Brown on both sides in a small amount of fat. Dice an onion very fine. Sprinkle the onion, along with a little salt and pepper, over the top of the Pot Roast. Cover tightly and cook at the lowest heat you have, until tender.

For an entirely different taste treat in a Marinade—

Mix together:

2 tablespoons vinegar	POT ROAST
½ cup chopped onion	VINEGAR
1 clove of garlic, minced fine	ONION
2 teaspoons salt	GARLIC
¼ teaspoon pepper	SALT
2 tablespoons salad oil	PEPPER
	SALAD OIL
	TOMATO
	SAUCE

Let the Pot Roast stand 24 hours in the Marinade, turning from time to time. Save the Marinade.

Brown the meat on both sides in a small amount of fat. Place the roast in a shallow baking dish. Mix together the Marinade and 2 (8-ounce) cans of tomato sauce. Pour this over the roast and bake in a 325-degree oven until tender. Place a tent made of foil loosely over the roast to prevent too rapid browning. Baste with the Marinade from time to time. After the first hour of baking, turn the roast. Continue cooking and basting until the meat is tender.

35. Short Ribs

Economy cuts of meat can make some of the best eating of all—Short Ribs, for instance. The average Short Rib weighs 4 to 6 ounces. Because of the ribbons of waste fat, you will need to allow 2 to 3 Short Ribs per serving. This large amount of fat surrounding the meat and bone is one of the factors that make Short Ribs so tasty—but not many of us want all those calories! Actually, the way to eliminate the excessive calories and at the same time retain the wonderful flavor is as easy as " A B C"—

Place the Short Ribs in a 2-inch-deep baking dish. Spread them out in the pan, allowing plenty of space for browning and turning. Bake in a 400-degree oven until they are an even caramel-brown on all sides. You can put them in the oven frozen, if you like. As they thaw, spread them about. In a 400-degree oven, frozen ribs take about 40 minutes on each side. Thawed ribs take only 20 to 30 minutes on each side. Drain off all the excess fat.

Now you can do all sorts of tasty things with them. The men in the family always call for "seconds" when you smother the Short Ribs with onions. Allow 1 medium-sized onion per serving. Put a tight-fitting lid on and bake in a 300-degree oven for an hour, or until tender.

36. Short-Rib Barbecue Sauce

You can baste the browned Short Ribs with a commercial barbecue sauce and bake in a covered casserole dish until tangy and tender. Best of all, do yourself up proud and make your own sauce.

For every 2 pounds of Short Ribs (8 to 10 pieces), combine:

SHORT RIBS
ONION
VINEGAR
SUGAR
(BROWN)
CATSUP
WORCESTER-
SHIRE
SAUCE
MUSTARD
CELERY
SALT

1 chopped onion
¼ cup good vinegar
2 tablespoons sugar (brown sugar gives added flavor)
1 cup catsup
½ cup water
3 tablespoons Worcestershire sauce
1 teaspoon prepared mustard
½ cup chopped celery
2 teaspoons salt

Pour sauce over the browned Short Ribs (Recipe No. 35), cover and bake, basting from time to time (325-degree oven). Serves 4.

Short Ribs are a good meal for an uncertain supper hour because you can speed them up or slow them down, as the need arises.

37. Flank Steak

Flank Steak, an economy cut of beef, tends to be tough, even from the choicest of meat, unless prepared properly. The secret to gourmet results is in slow, moist cooking.

Sprinkle a 2-pound flank steak with salt and pepper. Prepare a stuffing by browning:

FLANK STEAK
SAUSAGE
ONION
MILK
BREAD CUBES
(GRAVY
SEASONING)

½ cup sausage
Drain off all but 2 tablespoons of fat and add:
2 medium onions, chopped fine
Cook sausage and onion together until *lightly* browned. Remove from the stove and add:
¼ cup milk
2 cups soft bread cubes (this is the equivalent of 5 or 6 slices of bread)

Toss and turn the bread cubes until all the ingredients are well blended and coated. Spread the stuffing on the Flank Steak in a thin layer. Roll lightly as you would a jelly roll and fasten with a string. You can use skewers, but I seem to have better luck with string. Brown the meat gently and slowly on all sides in a small amount of fat. Place the steak roll on a rack in a roasting pan and add ½ cup of water. (A teaspoon of concentrated gravy seasoning added to the water will do wonders for the flavor.) Cover pan tightly. It is most important to have a tight-fitting lid. Bake in a 300-degree oven for about 2 hours, or until tender. Serve with a brown gravy made from the drippings. The aroma will be wonderful and so will the meal. Serves 4 generously.

38. Marinated Flank Steak

Surprisingly, Flank Steak can be broiled. It's the Marinade that makes the difference.

Mix together:
- 1 cup oil
- 1 clove of garlic, minced fine
- 1 tablespoon soy sauce
- 1 teaspoon salt
- ¼ teaspoon pepper

FLANK STEAK
OIL
CLOVE OF GARLIC
SOY SAUCE
SALT
PEPPER

Marinate a 1½-pound Flank Steak for 24 hours in the Marinade. Drain well, pat with a paper towel to remove the excess moisture, and broil 5 minutes on each side. Serves 4.

39. Beef Brisket

Beef Brisket, fresh or corned, lends itself with ease to a variety of tasty dishes and is usually a good buy economically. A good grade of Brisket is well streaked with layers of fat. This boneless cut of meat is usually available in 2 to 4 pound chunks. Corned Beef, which is brisket cured with salt or in a pickling brine, varies greatly in quality. The quality of the

Beef Brisket and the method used in corning are both contributing factors in the finished product. In the long run, it usually pays to buy a good brand in a top grade.

To prepare, cover with water and add:
  1 teaspoon salt for each pound of meat
  ¼ teaspoon pepper for each pound of meat
Simmer until tender. Allow 1 hour for every pound of brisket. *Never, never let meat boil, for this toughens it.*

Beef Brisket can be the basis for a variety of simple, savory meals. For instance, cut a head of cabbage into 8 wedges and add during the last 15 minutes of cooking time. The result will be **Corned Beef and Cabbage.**

Or, during the last half hour of cooking, vegetables such as potatoes, carrots, and onions may be added. The results will be a **New England Boiled Dinner.**

40. Horse-Radish Sauce for Beef Brisket

To further enhance Beef Brisket, serve with mustard or a Horse-radish Sauce such as the following:

Melt together in a sauce pan:
  1 tablespoon butter
  1 tablespoon flour
  ½ teaspoon salt
  ⅛ teaspoon pepper
Stir in:
  ½ cup milk
Cook and stir constantly until mixture bubbles fast. Remove from heat and stir in:
  ¼ cup horse-radish
  1 tablespoon lemon juice

BUTTER
FLOUR
MILK
PREPARED
  HORSE-
  RADISH
LEMON JUICE
SALT
PEPPER

Serve hot. If time is short, just heat ½ cup of canned white sauce and stir in horse-radish and lemon juice.

41. Barbecued Brisket

Season a 6- or 7-pound brisket with salt and pepper, allowing the usual 1 teaspoon salt and ¼ teaspoon pepper for each pound of meat. Place in a greased baking pan and cover with foil. Bake in a 275-degree oven for 5 hours. Do not, under any condition, turn the heat up, for it will toughen the meat. When the brisket is tender, slice thinly and arrange slices in a baking dish for barbecuing. Allow at least 2 slices for each serving. Wrap the remaining cooked brisket in freezer foil or plastic wrap and freeze for a quick meal sometime in the future.

BRISKET
ONIONS
BUTTER
CATSUP
LEMON JUICE
BROWN SUGAR
VINEGAR
WORCESTER-
  SHIRE
  SAUCE
DRY MUSTARD
LIQUID SMOKE
SALT
PEPPER

. . . Now for the **Barbecue Sauce.** Saute´ together until golden brown:

2 medium-sized onions, chopped
4 tablespoons butter

Add the following and simmer together for 30 minutes:

1½ cups water
2 cups catsup
½ cup lemon juice
6 tablespoons brown sugar
¼ cup vinegar
⅛ cup Worcestershire sauce
1 tablespoon dry mustard
2 teaspoons salt
2 teaspoons liquid smoke

ONIONS
BUTTER
CATSUP
LEMON JUICE
BROWN SUGAR
VINEGAR
WORCESTER-
  SHIRE
  SAUCE
DRY MUSTARD
LIQUID SMOKE
SALT

Baste the thinly sliced brisket generously with the barbecue sauce and heat thoroughly in a 350-degree oven for 30 minutes.

42. Beef Tongue

Beef Tongue can be the basis of many good meals. There is a minimum of waste and it is quite simple to prepare. Wash the Beef Tongue well in warm water. Place in a large kettle and cover with water. Add 1 teaspoon of salt per quart of water. Toss in a generous handful of pickling spices, a chili pepper, and gently simmer until tender. This takes about 1 hour for every pound of meat. Remove the meat from the liquid and cool. Next, remove the skin and roots. Cut the tongue into thick slices, about ¼ inch thick, and package for the freezer.

TONGUE
PICKLING
  SPICE
SALT
CHILI PEPPER

A Beef Tongue, all cooked and in the freezer, can be that needed last-minute meat. I like to slice it before freezing it. I package it by placing the slices in a row on a long sheet of plastic wrap, then stack them accordion-style. That way they can easily be spread out to thaw. In fact, they thaw so quickly, they can be ready in a matter of minutes—all of which makes Beef Tongue a very welcome item to have around. Cold, sliced tongue makes delicious sandwiches and can be used in any number of casserole dishes.

43. Tongue and Lima Skillet

For a quick and satisfying meal, pan-fry 2 tablespoons of finely chopped onion in a small amount of fat. Add:

TONGUE
ONION
CANNED LIMA
  BEANS
VINEGAR
CATSUP
SALT
PEPPER

   2 cups diced cooked tongue
   1 teaspoon salt
  ¼ teaspoon pepper
   2 cups canned lima beans (do not drain)
   1 teaspoon vinegar
  ¼ cup catsup

Simmer until heated through—about 5 minutes. Serve with whatever takes your fancy to satisfy 4 hungry people.

44. Fried Liver

Liver is one of the most nutritious meats available. It is so rich in iron that nutritionists recommend it be included in the menu at least once a week; they say it helps to prevent that weary feeling. Liver, however, can be ruined so easily in cooking that many people feel they don't care for it. It is really very simple. . . .

Wash the Liver well in cold water. Trim away any excessive membranes. Dip each piece in flour, coating lightly on both sides. Have the shortening in your skillet hot. Use medium heat and brown gently but quickly on each side. Season with salt and pepper. It's done! To fry Liver for a long period of time tends to toughen it.

PORK, BEEF OR CALF LIVER
FLOUR
SHORTENING
SALT, PEPPER

45. Freezing and Slicing Liver

When butchering, whether it is beef, pork, or wild game, soak the liver overnight in salt water. The next day, pat dry and place in the freezer until it starts to set up. Remove from the freezer and slice across the grain of the meat. It will slice much easier if it is firm. As in packaging any meat for a long period of time, wrap first in a clinging plastic wrap to seal out all the air, and then in freezer wrap. The meat will retain its original quality until the day you decide to use it.

46. Suet Shortening

Suet from around the kidney and loin of a beef is superior in quality and well worth saving. Chop or grind the Suet while it is still very fresh, package in recipe-size portions, and store in your freezer to be used in making mincemeat and steamed puddings.

For a shortening that is creamy and easy to work with, place the extra Suet in a heavy skillet over low, low heat and brown slowly.

SUET
SALAD OIL

Stir the melted fat frequently and let it cook very slowly until it is clear and smooth and the bits of unmelted fiber are crisp and brown. If preferred, this can be done in the oven sometime when you are making 5-Hour Oven Stew. (Recipe 28). Strain the fat through cheesecloth until it is perfectly clear (This may take several times). Measure the strained fat. To every cup of melted Suet, add ½ cup of ordinary vegetable salad oil. Chill the mixture quickly, stirring it occasionally as it hardens. Keep refrigerated until ready to use.

This Suet Shortening is especially good in making cakes and cookies. Since it is considerably richer than commercially manufactured shortening, a scanter measure should be used than the amount called for in your recipe.

47. Braised Oxtails with Vegetables

Last but not least is the oxtail! An inexpensive but bony piece of meat, it takes 1 pound to make 2 servings. Oxtails require moist heat and low cooking temperatures. Disjointed Oxtails can be used in 5-Hour Oven Stew as a substitute for the stew beef or they can be braised and cooked with vegetables. Prepared either way, the results are both tasty and economical.

Roll 2 pounds of disjointed Oxtails in flour. Saute' in a small amount of fat until nice and brown on all sides. Drain off the excess fat and add:

1 medium onion, diced
2 teaspoons salt
½ teaspoon pepper
2 cups water
1 tablespoon Worcestershire sauce

Cover tightly and simmer 3 to 4 hours. Then add:

. 3 carrots, diced
1 cup celery, diced
1 large green pepper, diced
5 small potatoes, cut in half

OXTAILS
ONION
CARROTS
CELERY
GREEN
  PEPPER
POTATOES
SALT
PEPPER
WORCESTER-
  SHIRE
  SAUCE

Continue cooking for another hour, or until the vegetables are tender. Place the vegetables and meat on a serving platter. Thicken the broth for gravy. Serve with hot biscuits and you will need to plan on very little else. Serves 4.

Steaks—*what can I say about Steaks, except, "Isn't it a shame that cost makes them prohibitive for everyday family fare?"*

Basically there are two types of Steaks, those that require braising (moist heat) and the very choice Steaks which are prepared by broiling or pan-frying. When buying Steaks for braising, a process whereby long, slow cooking with a small amount of water or liquid is necessary, allow ⅓ pound of boneless Steak per serving. The cost will depend on tenderness, amount of bone, and as always, supply and demand for that particular cut of beef. Top Round, Swiss Steak, Sirloin Tip Steaks, Flank Steak and Shoulder Steak should all be braised for best results.

The tale of woe that I hear oftenest is, "I'm so tired of fixing cheap cuts of Steak the same old way, over and over. How can I change it?"

The one basic thing you really can't change is the browning, which should be done slowly in a tablespoon or so of fat in a heavy skillet. The best flavor is obtained when the meat is seasoned and floured lightly before browning. This helps to retain the natural meat juices. Whether you flour the Steak or not is up to you, but do be careful not to pierce the meat when turning, for this allows the juices to escape.

When the Steak is well browned on both sides, add a small amount of liquid—½ to 1 cup, depending on the size of the Steak. This is where you can add variety. Instead of water, use tomato juice, or perhaps you would rather add a couple of tablespoons of wine vinegar to the water. Golden Mushroom soup makes a delightful change of flavor. Borrow a trick or two from the French and dissolve chicken bouillon cubes in the water. Use 1 cube for every ½ cup of water. One cup of Burgundy wine mixed with ¼ cup of strong coffee will tantalize taste buds beyond telling. A cup of apple juice with ¼ cup of raisins and ¼ cup of chopped celery added will result in another taste teaser. Something so simple as adding 1 teaspoon of Worcestershire sauce to the water used in braising can change and enhance the flavor of the whole meal.

Further flavor changes for Steaks can be made by adding special seasonings to the liquid around them. One of the most popular methods is to smother the Steak with sliced onions. Chopped celery and green pepper slices, with or without sliced or cooked tomatoes, offer still another treat. You can daringly or sparingly use such seasoning as horse-radish, catsup, chili sauce, mustard, or chili powder. It even changes the flavor to add carrots and potatoes during the last ½ hour of cooking.

48. Swiss Steak

How much you venture when cooking usually depends on those you are cooking for. Creating and adding your own little touches is half the satisfaction and fun of cooking; and to me, braised steaks are the most versatile of all the cuts of beef.

Swiss Steak is usually one of the lower-priced braising steaks. It is a tougher cut of beef and consequently requires low heat and longer cooking time. Here's the "know how" for a tender Swiss Steak:

Measure onto a board:

⅓ cup of flour for every pound of Swiss Steak. Sprinkle seasoning on the steak. For every pound of steak, allow:

SWISS STEAK
FLOUR
SALT
PEPPER
ONION

1 teaspoon salt

¼ teaspoon pepper

Cover the steak with the flour and pound with a meat hammer, or the edge of a saucer, turning and pounding until all the flour is taken up. Melt just enough shortening in the skillet to barely cover the bottom of the skillet. Gently brown the steak on both sides. Medium heat is just right. Grate a sprinkling of onion over the top of the steak. Dehydrated onion flakes may be substituted for the fresh onion, allowing ½ teaspoon for each pound of meat. For still further flavor substitute with a sprinkling of Onion Soup Mix. Add just enough water to create a steam (½ to 1 cup) and cook over low, low heat until tender (2½ to 3 hours).

49. Baked Steak

Braised Steaks usually prove to be an economical buy, for they can be "stretched" with potatoes, carrots, and "what have you," to satisfy a hungry family. A good example is Baked Steak. In this case I'll give you the ingredients first and then tell you what to do with them.

1 slice (about 2 pounds) sirloin tip steak, cut 2½ inches thick	SIRLOIN TIP STEAK
½ pound fresh mushrooms	MUSHROOMS, FRESH
3 tablespoons butter or oleo	BUTTER OR OLEO
1 large green pepper, cut into rings	GREEN PEPPER
2 large onions, sliced and separated into rings	ONIONS
1⅓ cups catsup	CATSUP
¾ cup strong coffee (this doesn't mean the kind that has set on the stove all day. It should be fresh, strong coffee)	STRONG COFFEE

Sauté mushrooms lightly in butter, push to one side of the skillet, and add green pepper and onion rings. Cook until soft but not brown, then mix with the mushrooms. Add catsup and coffee and simmer for about 5 minutes.

Place the steak under the broiler and broil 3 to 4 minutes on each side, just long enough to brown and seal in the natural juices. Transfer to a shallow baking pan.

Spoon ½ the sauce over the steak. Save the rest of the sauce to serve with the steak. Bake at 350 degrees for 15 to 20 minutes for a rare steak. If you prefer it medium, or well done, add 5 to 10 minutes for the baking time. Serve in thin slices by slicing against the grain on the diagonal.

50. Broiled Steaks

Choice Steaks, *such as Beef Tenderloin, T-Bone, Club, Boneless Loin, Pinbone Sirloin, Wedge-bone Sirloin, Chuck, and Rib are always broiled or pan-fried. To do otherwise would be a great waste.*

Broiling Steaks should be cut ¾ to 2 inches thick—but this is strictly a matter of personal preference. Filet Mignon, or the Beef Tenderloin, is the most expensive, whereas the Pinbone Sirloin is the lowest in price, for it contains a large amount of bone and fat. Other steaks are priced in between. When buying bone-in steak, allow ⅓ to ¾ pound per serving.

In order not to ruin the Broiled Steak in the cooking, here are a few little do's and don'ts one should adhere to:

1. Before broiling, slash the fat edges every inch or two to prevent the steak from curling while broiling.

2. Pre-heat the broiling oven and the broiling pan.

3. Oil the broiler pan lightly with cooking oil, or run a small piece of trimmed-off fat over the surface of the pan. This prevents sticking. The flavor of beef is all the better for being a little fat, so do not trim steaks before broiling.

   To pan-broil: preheat heavy skillet, oil lightly. Brown meat by turning from time to time to insure even cooking. Drain off any excess fat that accumulates.

4. If you like steak Rare or Medium Rare, lay the steaks on the hot broiler pan and adjust racks so that steaks are just exactly 3 inches from the heating source. This creates a cooking temperature of 350 degrees. For Well-Done steaks, lower the rack to allow 4 inches between the steaks and the source of heat. Broil steaks indicated amount of time on each side.

5. Seasoning is such an individual matter that it is far better simply to pass a tray of seasonings and sauces at serving time.

6. Following is a Broiling Guide for 1-inch-thick steaks.

TIMETABLE FOR COOKING COLD STEAKS
(REFRIGERATOR TEMPERATURE):

RARE ....5 MINUTES
MEDIUM RARE ....6 MINUTES
WELL DONE ....7 MINUTES

TIMETABLE FOR COOKING PARTIALLY
FROZEN STEAKS:

RARE ....8 MINUTES
MEDIUM RARE ....9 MINUTES
WELL DONE ....10 MINUTES

For every additional ½ inch of thickness add another 5 minutes broiling time.

51. Pan-Fried Steaks

Chuck Steak and Rib Steak are best for pan-frying. They should be cut ½ to ¾ inch thick for this purpose. There's nothing like a cast-iron skillet for pan-frying meat, and a heavy skillet is almost a must. Heat the skillet until a drop of cold water dropped on the skillet will form a bead and run around over the surface. Adjust your burner to maintain this heat; medium heat usually does the trick. Add enough shortening to cover the bottom of the skillet about 1/16 inch.

Flour the steaks well on both sides. Brown first on one side and then the other. Turn only once in cooking. Do not salt and pepper until you start browning the second side. Fried in this manner, the steaks will be crusty on the outside and juicy on the inside. Seasoning last of all prevents the salt from making the meat bleed.

———◆———

Volumes have been written about Beef Cookery. So much, in fact that there is a tendency to think of it as something requiring great skill. Actually, as you can see, with staples for ingredients and a little basic "know how," you, too, can have the fun of creating economical meals with gourmet results.

BEEF CHART

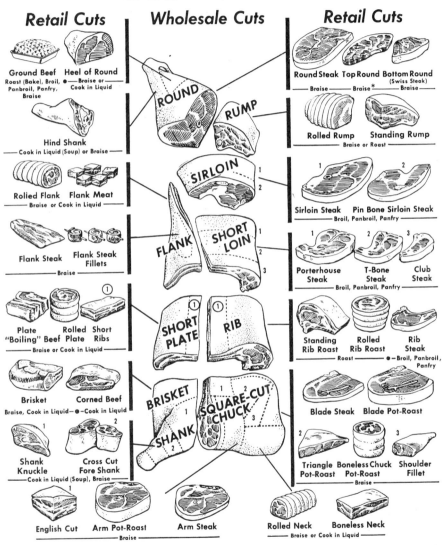

*Prime and choice grades may be broiled, panbroiled or panfried

Buying Beef in Quantity: *The decision to buy beef in quantity is always a major one in any household. As to whether it is wise for you to invest in a quarter of beef, one of the best ways to check is to take the following weights and price the same cuts of meat over the counter, where the cuts are priced individually. Figure it all up on a 100-pound basis and then compare the results with the price of beef, cut and wrapped for the freezer. Don't forget to include the cost of the waste bone and fat. This way you know exactly what you are gaining.*

Whenever the butcher asks me how I want the beef cut up, I've always wished I had the nerve to say, "Make it all steaks, please." Since I've never said it—and he couldn't do it anyway—my favorite butcher tells me that the following cuts are about what I will end up with:

A 100-Pound Hind Quarter Basically Consists of:

  7 Pounds of hind shank. This can be split into 2 soup bones. Meat trim packaged for stew meat.

10 Pounds of heel of round. Makes a good pot roast or can be made into ground beef.

26 Pounds of round. The top round is the tender portion and can be cut into boneless top round steak, or choice 4 and 5 pound roasts. The bottom round is best for sirloin tip steak. The eye of the round is not quite so tender and is best for swiss steak. The bottom round can be either steaks or roast.

  9 Pounds of rump, making 2 or 3 rump roasts.

14 Pounds of sirloin; here again, steaks or roasts.

15 Pounds of short loin, which provides us with the deli-cious T-bone, porterhouse, and club steaks.

12 Pounds of flank. Can be cut into steaks which require special preparation, or made into ground beef.

  4 Pounds of sirloin tip. Makes an extra-special pot roast.

  3 Pounds of waste fat and bones.

A 100-Pound Front Quarter Basically Consists of:

16 Pounds of ribs for roasts and rib steaks.

8 Pounds of plate beef. Ideal for stew meat. Can be cubed and packaged for use in everything from stew to meat pie.

7 Pounds of brisket. (Usually put into ground beef.)

8 Pounds of short ribs.

28 Pounds of chuck or shoulder. Chuck steak, blade steaks, and pot roasts.

10 Pounds of neck. Usually used in stew meat or ground beef.

14 Pounds of trimming, which usually goes into ground beef.

9 Pounds of waste bone and fat.

These figures are fairly average and will give you some idea as to what to expect when buying beef in quantity. If you like lots of ground beef, just tell your butcher so. If you want a quantity of stew meat, with less ground beef, he can arrange that too. Many cuts of meat can be varied, so let your butcher know your family's preferences. The average thickness for steaks is ¾ inch. This is thick enough to broil nicely, but not so thick that it is impractical for family use. If cut thinner, it is difficult to prepare a tender steak, regardless of the quality of the meat.

52. Soup Bone Stock

When buying beef in quantity, the resulting Soup Bones are a bulky item and do take up needed freezer space. To avoid this, prepare the soup bones this way:

Place all of the Soup Bones in a large roasting pan and brown well in a 300-degree oven. Turn the bones as they brown, so they will be a nice, even brown. This heals the bone and | SOUP BONES SEASONING ONION CARROTS
prevents the gray scum which normally forms when simmering Soup Bones. It will also give the soup base a nice caramel coloring. After the bones are browned, place them in a large soup kettle and cover with water. Add your favorite seasonings, one large minced onion, and 2 or 3 carrots. Simmer

until the stock is quite concentrated. Strain the broth and freeze in ice-cube trays. When frozen, place the soup cubes in a plastic bag, fasten with a pipe stem cleaner for easy opening, and store in the freezer.

These Soup Cubes can be used as the base for soups, for seasoning in casserole dishes . . . . and they can be added to tomato juice or served as a nourishing broth for convalescents and toddlers.

Cooking Utensils

Before we go any further, I feel we should have just a word about several basic cooking utensils. My husband says I collect skillets like some women collect shoes . . . and he's probably right. Actually, I have never been able to find a utensil that was just right for everything I wanted to cook in it. I'd like to find "one" that was just right, then I wouldn't have to bother with all the others . . . but I do find that my trusty old **cast-iron skillets,** ranging in size from 4 to 12 inches, get the most use. On the other hand, if I want to simmer something for a long time, I like the **stainless steel skillets,** preferably one with a copper bottom.

Because I have such a large collection of skillets, I feel that every so often they deserve a sprucing-up, so out comes the copper polish for the copper-bottomed one and the stainless steel polish for others. Then there is my assortment of cast-iron skillets, which I can make just like new by using one of the new grease solvents. Brush it on, let it stand until the residue becomes soft, sort of work it around until it gets gooey-looking, and then simply wash it off under the hot-water faucet. I have one cast-iron skillet that we received as a wedding gift. I won't tell you how old it is, but it still looks like new in spite of the things I burned in it when first learning to cook.

If you are lucky enough to have a **teflon skillet** and find that it has become discolored, measure into the skillet one cup

of water and half a cup of household bleach. Simmer for 5
minutes. Wash, rinse, dry and wipe with salad oil. It's like
new again! If it is just a stubborn spot you want to remove,
put a little baking soda on the dishcloth and rub . . . works
like a charm and it won't scratch. You simply can't use your
regular cleaners on teflon, but they are so simple to keep you
really don't need to.

Two **saucepans** and one **double-boiler** will take care of the
stewing department. One of the saucepans should have a thick
bottom to be used in cooking puddings and sauces that stick
easily. I prefer to use my stainless steel skillet in making
puddings and sauces because they cook quicker with less
chance of sticking.

Last but not least, one of the most important utensils in the
kitchen is the **Dutch Oven.** A "must" in Colonial days, it is
still just that. Early-day Dutch Ovens were usually made of
cast-iron, shaped round and deep with tight-fitting lids in the
shape of a dish designed to hold hot coals. The Dutch Ovens
were heated by the fire, set to one side, and then the food was
placed within for slow cooking.

We recently had the fun of watching Ted Welch of Redmond, Oregon, cook in Dutch Ovens. His kitchen was a
Juniper grove on the shores of the Prineville Reservoir at the
northern edge of the Oregon Desert. Someone asked Ted why
he didn't open a specialty restaurant in the city, where such
cooking is a rare if not unheard-of treat. He smiled his shy
smile and said, "I like these wide-open spaces. I can't stand
those four walls." He calmly went back to stirring up another
last-minute batch of sourdough biscuits. These, too, were
baked in a Dutch Oven. With anything as delicious as those
biscuits, the demand is naturally greater than the supply. I
think he could have made them all night long and someone
would still have said, "Do you suppose I could have just one
more?"

Ted used handfuls of flour, scoops of this and that, and
bowls of "starter." There really isn't much time for measuring when cooking outdoors for a record crowd of 3,500 hun-

gry people. The dough was so alive you could see it rise and spring as he prepared it with a rolling pin for cutting. The biscuits were then placed in large Dutch Ovens . . . which in turn were placed among the dying coals of a Juniper log and allowed to rise.

Just as they began to rise, Ted placed hotter coals on the flat surface of the lid and allowed time for browning. The results were the most beautiful sourdough biscuits I've ever seen or tasted—2 to 3 inches high, delicate brown, and as light as a feather, with a wonderful flavor. The whole process, from beginning to end, was a work of art . . . and Ted gives all the credit to the cast-iron Dutch Ovens!

Be that as it may, I have found that any time a recipe calls for long, slow cooking with a tight-fitting lid, nothing—absolutely nothing—will do the job any better than a Dutch Oven. Today's Dutch Ovens come in a variety of materials and are basically designed for "top of the stove" cooking. I happen to have three, each one made of a different material . . . and while the choice of a utensil is strictly a personal one, the use of a Dutch Oven is the "secret of success" in preparing *meats* of every kind that require long, slow cooking.

There is still lots of unconquered country in Eastern Oregon.

RECIPE GUIDE

Number

PORK

Pork, said to be richer in Vitamin B than any other meat, is a welcome change for the Main Fare, even in Cattle Country. The flesh and fat of pig or hog offers an amazing variety of cuts. In terms of human consumption, the porker is an animal of almost infinite variety. Consider the possibilities of tasty fare in just one porker: Regular Ham and Picnic Ham, Regular Bacon and Canadian Bacon, Spareribs, Pickled Pigs Feet, Salt Pork, Boston Butt, Loin Roast, Sirloin Roast, Brisket, Jowl, Hogshead Cheese, Knuckles, Chops—in fact, almost all but that curly tail offers good eating—and it probably has some use!

The particular cut of pork you select should be fine grained and firm. From a young porker, the lean meat is almost white, but from an older animal it is more a rose color. Pork fat is whiter and less firm than beef fat. Because there is plenty of this fat throughout the lean, choose pork with the least amount of visible fat.

Popular the year round, there are only two basic rules for cooking pork:

1. All pork must be well done.
2. Brown pork to improve the flavor.

Cured meats, including pork, are available in so many variations and brands that about all you can do is learn from experience which ones your family prefers. Precooked, cured ham—an all-time favorite—is usually a good buy. Preparation of a precooked ham is somewhat like coping with the family budget. Sometimes, if we take a good hard look at the use of it, we see where, with just a little different handling, we would get more for our money. The next time you purchase a precooked ham, ask the butcher to "center slice" it. This will give you a nice large roast of about 5 pounds from the butt end, some center slices, and the shank end.

When you bake the roast from the butt end, cut it in half after baking, wrap one portion in foil or plastic freezer wrap, and tuck it away in the freezer for another day. I find it best to do this before serving. If you serve with the idea of freezing what is left, that second meal won't amount to much. For generous helpings, allow ½ pound bone-in per serving. When serving cooked boneless ham, allow ⅓ pound for each person.

In yesteryear, it was always necessary to soak or parboil a ham. This was in the days when hogs weighed anywhere from 300 to 500 pounds at butchering time. Today even hogs are calorie conscious! At least their producers are, for hogs go to market at a lean 225 to 250 pounds. This progress in production methods has meant drastic changes in our ideas concerning cooking time and temperatures.

Most hams on the market today have complete directions on the wrapper for cooking. Special attention should be given to these instructions because the type of ham determines the cooking time. Care must be taken in preparing "today's" hams to avoid overcooking. Overcooked ham is dry and tasteless, with a stringy texture.

Basically, ham preparation falls into three categories . . . . the baking of a precooked ham; preparation and cooking of an uncooked whole ham, which requires simmering in water; and the roasting of smoked, or cured, ham and pork.

53. Baking a Precooked Ham

Today many hams have "water added." Meat packers will readily admit that this increases the cost to us as consumers, but at the same time they steadfastly maintain that adding water creates a tastier product. This "added water" means added cooking time. Place the precooked Ham, fat side up, on a rack in a pan with a 2-inch rim. Bake uncovered in a 325-degree oven, allowing 15 minutes to the pound (130 degrees F. on your meat thermometer).

If no water has been added to the precooked ham, here again, bake in a 325-degree oven, allowing only 10 to 15 minutes to the pound (130 degrees F. on your meat thermometer). Heating is a matter of taste and prolonged cooking will only result in the loss of natural meat juices.

When planning your meal, allow an additional 45 minutes preparation time for scoring, glazing, and resting . . . . resting the ham, that is! If allowed to rest for 15 minutes after baking, a ham will slice better.

To score a ham, cut the fat into diamond shapes with a sharp knife. Do not cut into the lean. Cover the fat-scored, hot, baked ham with a glaze (suggestions later) and bake uncovered in a 400-degree oven for an additional 20 minutes, or until a delicate brown in color.

54. Suggested Ham Glazes

1. Spread with honey and insert whole cloves, or
2. Spread with tart jelly, or
3. A mixture of 1 cup brown sugar, 2 tablespoons flour, and 1 to 2 teaspoons dry mustard (we prefer 2 teaspoons, or you might omit the dry mustard altogether and use ½ teaspoon cloves), or
4. Heavy syrup saved from canned peaches, apricots, or pineapple, plus a sprinkling of brown sugar, or
5. Make a mixture of the following . . . and spread on the ham:
   2 cups bread crumbs
   2 tablespoons molasses
   2 tablespoons brown sugar
   2 tablespoons butter
   2 teaspoons prepared mustard

55. Water-Cooked Whole Ham

It is easy to fall into the habit of buying precooked hams, but sometimes an uncooked, whole ham is the better buy. Then, too, specialty hams such as Virginia, Smithfield, and Tennessee Style Hams, as well as Home-Cured Hams, must be parboiled or simmered. When preparing this type of ham, you will need to allow ¾ pound of uncooked, bone-in ham for each serving. A ham prepared in the following manner is always moist and tender:

Wash the ham and place it in a large kettle. Cover with water and let soak for 24 hours. At cooking time, pour off the water and add fresh water. To each quart of water, add ¼ cup sugar and 2 tablespoons vinegar. Simmer until tender (allowing 25 minutes per pound). Be careful always to maintain a simmering temperature.

When the ham is tender, remove it from the fire and let it remain in the broth until cold. Remove the ham from the broth, then skin it with a sharp knife. Score and glaze the ham as explained. A water-cooked ham's crowning touch is in the glaze. Baste the ham from time to time with the broth in which it was simmered. Do not use the drippings in the bottom of the pan; they will spoil the appearance.

56. Smoked Ham

Easily prepared, this tasty choice requires no seasoning. Place on a rack in pan with a 2-inch rim, uncovered. Allowing 25 to 35 minutes per pound, in a 325-degree oven, roast to an inner temperature of 170-degrees F. (This same method may be applied to other forms of smoked and/or cured pork, such as Picnics, Cottage Butts, and Loin.)

57. Basic Preparation of the Shank End

Getting back to "making the most of a ham"—the Shank End offers a variety of tempting uses:

Simmer the Shank End in water until tender. | HAM SHANK
Remove the shank from the water (now a | END
broth) and set aside to cool. Freeze the broth |
in ice-cube trays. When frozen, store the cubes in a plastic
bag in the freezer. These can be used for flavoring in Soups,
Meat Pies, and Beans; or just make a big kettle of Split Pea
Soup and freeze in meal-size portions.

Slice the top part of the shank meat and freeze for breakfast slices. Place a double layer of wax paper between the
slices for easy removal. Ham and eggs are popular fare any
time of the day, any day of the year. A supply of "breakfast
slices" makes it an easy matter to broil or pan-fry ham slices
for a quick and easy meal. As for the scrappy pieces of ham,
grind for use in Ham Loaf, Sandwich Spreads, Croquettes, and
Casseroles.

58. Split Pea Soup

*After a day in the open air, the aroma of a kettle of Split
Pea Soup simmering on the range, with its promise of fulfill-
ment, is welcome fare indeed. Easy to prepare, it is ideal for
busy times outside.*

Place one pound of "split pea" peas, green or | SPLIT PEAS
yellow, with water to cover in a kettle. Let | SALT PORK
soak overnight. Dice and brown lightly in a | SHANK BONE
small skillet: | HAM BITS
| ONION
    ¼ pound salt pork | CARROT
Drain off any excessive fat and add: | BAY LEAF
    ½ cup chopped onion | SUGAR
    ½ cup carrots, finely diced | CREAM

Cook about 10 minutes. Add to the peas along with:
    1 shank bone, and bits of scrappy ham,
    1 very small piece of Bay leaf
Simmer gently for about 2½ hours. Remove the shank bone
and continue cooking until thick. Just before serving, add:
    1 teaspoon sugar
    ½ cup cream
Reheat and serve to 4 hearty eaters.

Split Pea Soup is actually better when reheated later.

59. Barbecued Ham Loaf

The next time someone says, "Let's make it potluck," say, "Great, I'll bring Barbecued Ham Loaf." Tasty, with a special flavor of its own, it goes well with salads of all kinds, making it ideal for Buffet Dinners and potluck affairs.

Mix together and bake in a loaf pan in a 350-degree oven for 2 hours (mixture is quite soft before baking):

GROUND HAM
GROUND PORK
TOMATO SOUP
BREAD
  CRUMBS
CELERY
ONION
EGGS
SALT
PEPPER

1 pound ground (lean) ham
1 pound ground (lean) pork
1 can tomato soup
1 cup dry bread crumbs
½ cup chopped celery
¼ cup minced onion
2 eggs, lightly beaten
½ teaspoon salt
¼ teaspoon pepper

For a complete change of taste, omit the tomato soup and celery and add ¼ cup chopped green pepper and 1 cup of milk. Serves 8.

60. Ham Croquettes

Our family likes Ham Croquettes served with mashed potatoes and creamed peas and pickled beets for that something tangy. We like to top it all off with a berry pie.

Combine the following ingredients:

HAM
EGGS
SALT
PEPPER
WHITE SAUCE
CRUMBS

2 cups finely chopped ham
½ teaspoon salt
⅛ teaspoon pepper
1 egg

Shape into croquettes by rolling 1 rounded tablespoon of the mixture between the palms of your hands. Roll to desired length and flatten the ends, then roll the croquette in dried bread crumbs. Dip in beaten egg that has been thinned with water (2 tablespoons of water for each egg). Coat the croquettes well with egg and then roll once again in crumbs. Fry in deep fat until a golden brown (390 degrees F). Drain on paper towels. Makes 12 to 15 croquettes.

61. Ham and Egg Casserole

Most women love to make casseroles—for several reasons I suppose. They can be mixed up ahead of time. Casserole meals are usually easy to clean up after, making them ideal for busy times. Besides, there is something about making casseroles that gives you a very creative feeling. Yet, in spite of all the advantages, many men get a long face when they find a casserole dish is in the making. One day I decided that, long faces or not, Ham and Egg Casserole was going to be our evening meal. As it turned out, the men in the family were happy about it and we've been having it from time to time ever since.

Saute':
    4 tablespoons butter
    1 tablespoon chopped onion
Stir in and blend together with:
    4 tablespoons flour
Add, all at once:
    2 cups milk
Stir constantly until smooth and thick. Add:
    ½ teaspoon salt
    ⅛ teaspoon pepper
    ¼ cup green pepper, chopped
      (optional, but tasty)

COOKED HAM
EGGS
BUTTER
FLOUR
ONION
MILK
GREEN
  PEPPER
MUSHROOM
  SLICES
SALT
PEPPER
BREAD
  CRUMBS

Arrange the following in layers, in a buttered casserole:
    6 hard-cooked eggs, sliced
    1 (4-ounce) can of mushroom slices, drained
    1½ cups cooked ham, finely cubed

Pour the above sauce over the top of all and cover with a layer of crumbs made by browning together in a heavy skillet:
    2 cups bread crumbs
    1 tablespoon butter

Bake at 350 degrees for 30 minutes, or until heated through, all bubbly and hot. Serves 4 generously.

62. Ham and Rice Casserole

Ham and Rice Casserole has proved very popular at our house.

To make this, you will need:

    1 cup rice
    1 teaspoon salt
    1 tablespoon butter
    2 cups ground ham
    ½ onion
    ½ green pepper
    1 (2-ounce) jar of pimento
    303-size can of tomatoes

GROUND HAM
RICE
TOMATOES, CANNED
GREEN PEPPER
ONION
PIMENTO
BUTTER
SALT
GRATED CHEESE

Boil 1 cup of rice in 2 cups of boiling water. The easiest way is to put the rice and cold water along with 1 teaspoon of salt and 1 tablespoon of butter in a saucepan. As soon as the mixture starts to boil, stir well, put on a tight-fitting lid, and let simmer gently for 15 minutes.

While all this is going on, put the ground ham into a heavy skillet. You will need to add a little shortening to prevent sticking. While the ham gently browns, add ½ onion, chopped fine, and ½ green pepper, chopped fine. When brown, add the chopped pimento and canned tomatoes. Stir in the rice. Top with grated cheese. Use a generous hand as far as the grated cheese is concerned. Bake at 350 degrees for 30 to 45 minutes. Serves 4.

63. Ham Slices

There is a trick to cooking ham slices. This simple method of preparation will assure you of the ultimate in flavor and texture.

Ham slices (preferably center cut) should be soaked for one hour in lukewarm water, HAM SLICES

drained, and patted dry with paper towels. At this point they can be prepared by broiling 3 minutes on each side, or if you prefer, floured lightly and pan-fried in a small amount of shortening.

64. Ham 'n Pineapple

For something a little different in the way of ham slices, try Ham 'n Pineapple.

Take 2 large center slices of ham and place 1 slice flat in the bottom of the roaster. Arrange drained pineapple slices or chunks on the ham slice. Put the other slice of ham on top of the pineapple, sandwich style. Baste | HAM SLICES / SLICED PINEAPPLE AND JUICE / GINGER ALE

with a mixture of 1 cup of pineapple juice and ¼ cup of ginger ale. Bake in an open pan, 30 to 40 minutes, basting every 15 minutes in a 375-degree oven. The ginger ale takes away that too-sweet taste.

Ham slices, regular bacon, and Canadian bacon—all considered breakfast meats—can be pan-fried, broiled, or baked. When cooking breakfast for a large crowd, heat the oven to 400 degrees. Arrange bacon on a wire rack, set in a baking pan. A cake rack will do fine. The bacon will brown to perfection in 10 minutes with no attention from you. This leaves you free to prepare the eggs and hotcakes. When preparing ham slices for a large crowd, slice the ham ⅛ inch thick. Slash the edges to prevent curling. Place on a broiler rack, 3 inches below the heat, and broil for 3 to 5 minutes on each side.

65. Pork Roast

There are basically three types of pork loin roasts: the Loin End contains the tenderloin and has very little bone. The Center-Cut roast is usually higher priced but is considered choice meat, and it is easily carved into chop portions. The Rib-End roast contains more bone than the Loin End and is quite often made into a Crown Roast for special occasions. Pork shoulder roasts are usually displayed and labeled as Boston Butt and fresh Picnic Shoulder roasts.

For best results in preparing any pork roast, buy at least 3 to 4 pounds and allow ⅓ pound bone-in per serving. . . . Potatoes cooked in the pan with the pork are delicious; allow about an hour's cooking time for them. And, remember, all fresh pork should be thoroughly cooked.

To prepare: Place roast fat side up on a rack in an open roaster. Rub with salt and pepper, allowing ½ teaspoon salt and ⅛ teaspoon pepper per pound of meat. Roast in a 325-degree oven until the meat is gray, with no tinge of pink. If a meat thermometer is used, internal temperature should register 185 degrees. Basically, you will need to allow 40 minutes per pound . . . if the roast is frozen, allow 20 minutes per pound additional roasting time.

PORK ROAST
SALT
PEPPER

66. Marinated Pork Loin Roast

Heat together to the boiling point:

¼ cup brown sugar
2 teaspoons paprika
2 teaspoons salt
¼ teaspoon pepper
¼ teaspoon garlic salt
1 teaspoon onion salt
1 tablespoon Worcestershire sauce
½ cup lemon juice
½ cup water
1 tablespoon soy sauce
½ cup catsup

PORK ROAST
SUGAR, BROWN
PAPRIKA
SALT/PEPPER
GARLIC SALT
ONION SALT
WORCESTER-
  SHIRE SAUCE
LEMON JUICE
SOY SAUCE
CATSUP

Let the sauce cool, then pour into a large plastic bag, one that will hold a 5- or 6-pound roast. Set the bag of sauce in a deep bowl. It is better to be safe than sorry in the event that the bag should decide to leak. Place the 5- or 6-pound roast in the marinade in the bag. Close tightly and let marinate for several hours. If the marinade does not cover the meat completely, turn it from time to time.

When you are ready to roast, place the meat on a rack in a shallow roasting pan and roast as usual in a 325-degree oven until the meat thermometer registers 185 degrees. This usually takes about 4 hours. During the last ½ hour of roasting, brush the roast with marinade at least twice.

67. Sweet 'n Sour Pork

Pork roast can be the basis not only of the meal in the making but also the needed pork for a good Chinese dish. Take any left-over roast pork, cut into 1-inch cubes and place in a plastic bag. Store in the freezer until some day when you want "something different."

Here is the way we like to fix Sweet 'n Sour Pork—which may not be a truly Chinese dish but is downright good eating.

Make a batter, by mixing together:

1 egg	PORK CUBES
2 tablespoons flour	GREEN
½ teaspoon salt	PEPPER
⅛ teaspoon pepper	PINEAPPLE
	TOMATOES

You will need 1½ pounds of cubed cooked pork. Thoroughly coat each piece of pork by dipping it in the batter. Carefully brown each piece of coated meat on all sides either in shortening or bacon drippings. Careful browning will make your creation "extra special" in appearance as well as flavor.

EGG
FLOUR
CORN STARCH
SOY SAUCE
SUGAR
VINEGAR
SALT/PEPPER

Cut 3 large green peppers into strips and place in a saucepan. Add a little water and simmer for 5 minutes.

Take the meat cubes out of the skillet and pour off all the excess fat, then put the meat back into the skillet. Drain the green peppers and add them to the skillet along with ½ cup of well-drained pineapple chunks. Cover and let simmer over low heat for 10 minutes while you make the sauce.

To make the sauce, mix together in a saucepan:

2½ tablespoons corn starch
2½ tablespoons soy sauce
¼ cup sugar
¼ cup good vinegar
½ cup pineapple juice

Cook until thick and clear, stirring constantly. Takes about 2 minutes. Pour over meat mixture in skillet and gently simmer 5 minutes. Serve with Chinese noodles or cooked rice.

We think this dish is rather special. I have even made this recipe using canned meat cut in cubes, when I didn't have good pork on hand. Made this way, it can be a real economy dish. When tomatoes are a good buy, you can give added eye-appeal, as well as flavor, by cutting 2 medium-size firm tomatoes into about 8 sections and adding to the meat at the same time you add the sauce.

68. Braised Pork Chops or Pork Steaks

Pork chops are the ultimate in pork fare as far as I'm concerned—and the thicker the chops the better, up to a point. They should never be more than 1 inch thick, nor less than ⅓ inch. For each serving, allow ¾ pound of bone-in chops or steaks.

To prepare: Wash the chops or steaks with cold, running water and pat dry with paper towels. Heat a small amount of fat in a heavy skillet. Season the chops with salt and pepper, flour lightly, and brown slowly on both sides.

PORK CHOPS
OR STEAKS
SHORTENING
SALT
PEPPER

Allow 15 to 20 minutes for this. Add 3 or 4 tablespoons of water, cover with a tight-fitting lid, and cook slowly for at least another ½ hour. Remember, never serve rare pork. It should be a pale grey in color.

The flavor of any chop or steak, be it pork, beef, or wild game, is greatly improved by washing with cold, running water and patting dry. This removes the deposits left on the meat by the saw blade. These deposits become rancid quickly and produce an "off" flavor.

69. Oven-Easy Pork Chops

Place ½ stick of margarine in a pan in the oven to melt (325 degrees). In a shallow bowl, mix together:

1 cup coarse crumbs
⅓ cup grated Parmesan cheese
½ teaspoon salt
⅛ teaspoon pepper

In another bowl, beat together:
1 egg
2 tablespoons milk

PORK CHOPS
BREAD
CRUMBS
PARMESAN
CHEESE
SALT
PEPPER

Coat pork chops with crumb mixture, dip in egg mixture, and again in the crumb mix. Place the chops in the baking pan and bake for 30 minutes. Turn the chops and bake another 30 minutes.

For a simple variation of this recipe, dip pork chops in canned milk, coat well with flour, season with salt and pepper, and bake.

PORK CHOPS
CANNED MILK
FLOUR

70. Stuffed Pork Chops

Stuffed Pork Chops is a way of making small chops satisfy a hungry, hungry family—and a mighty tasty way, I might add.

Brown the pork chops by flouring lightly and searing in a small amount of fat. Sprinkle with salt, pepper, and a wee bit of pork seasoning. Set aside while you make the dressing.

Any dressing recipe can be used for the "stuffing." If you don't have a favorite of your own, the following one is simple and tasty.

PORK CHOPS
BREAD CUBES
ONION
SALT
PEPPER
(SAGE)
(PORK
    SEASONING)

"Stuffing"

Heat ½ cup of butter or oleo (at our house, butter starts with an "o") in a large skillet. Add a medium-size onion, chopped fine, and cook over low heat until soft but not brown. Add:

  ½ cup water
  ⅛ teaspoon pepper
  1 teaspoon salt
  ½ teaspoon sage (optional)
  4 to 5 cups of day-old bread cubes

Toss lightly until the bread cubes absorb the liquid.

To make the Stuffed Pork Chops, arrange them file fashion . . . you know, put in a little dressing to prop the first pork chop against, then more dressing; another pork chop, etc., until chops are all used. Arrange any extra dressing down the side of the pan. Bake in a covered pan or roaster in the oven for about 1 hour at 350 degrees. To brown, remove the cover for the last 15 minutes. Serves 4.

If any cooked dressing is left over, pack into a loaf pan. Cover with freezer wrap and freeze. When a quick supper is needed, take the dressing from the freezer, slice, dip in beaten egg, and then in flour. Pan-fry until a delicate golden brown. Dressing is almost better this way than it was in the first place. For a quick and tasty meal, serve with scrambled eggs, a tossed salad, and a light dessert.

71. Apple-Raisin Pork

"Apple-Raisin Pork" speaks for itself . . . and very well too!

Flour, salt, and pepper either pork chops or pork steak. Brown well in a small amount of fat in a heavy skillet. An electric skillet works especially well for this dish. While the chops brown to a lovely golden color, core as many apples as you have chops. Do not peel the apples. Winesaps or Roman Beauties are good.

PORK CHOPS
OR
PORK STEAK
APPLES
RAISINS
BROWN SUGAR
SALT
PEPPER

Any apple that is a little on the tart side is best. Slice the apples rather thick and arrange over the tops of the browned chops. Sprinkle with:

⅓ cup raisins
¼ cup brown sugar

This is the right amount of sugar and raisins for 6 chops. Pour ¼ cup of water around the chops. Cover and bake in a 325-degree oven for an hour, or if an electric skillet is used, set the temperature on "low" and let cook for 1 hour. Twice during the baking, baste the chops with the liquid in the pan.

72. Tangy Spareribs

Spareribs are bony (they take 1 pound per person) but they are such good eating, no one seems to care:

Brown 4 pounds of Spareribs in a heavy skillet in a 425-degree oven. Pour off the excess fat.

In a saucepan, cook together until thick and glossy:

1 cup tomato catsup	SPARERIBS
1 (8-ounce) can crushed pineapple	CATSUP
⅔ cup light brown sugar	PINEAPPLE
1 teaspoon dry mustard	BROWN SUGAR
2 tablespoons corn starch	DRY MUSTARD
	CORN STARCH

You will need to stir this mixture constantly SALT
as it thickens . . . only takes a minute or two. PEPPER

Salt and pepper the ribs just as you would if you were getting ready to eat them. Pour the thickened mixture over the browned ribs and cook for 2 hours at 350 degrees. Serves 4.

Or, perhaps you would rather leave them plain and cook with dressing. If time is of the essence, drain the excess fat from the browned ribs, smother the ribs with sauerkraut, cover with a tight-fitting lid, and go on about your other business for a couple of hours.

Barbecued Spareribs can be easy too. After the basic browning, baste the ribs with a commercial barbecue sauce. Spoon extra sauce over the ribs 2 or 3 times during the baking. Bake uncovered during the last 15 minutes. Other tasty variations are almost endless, so let's go on to something simple and elegant with sausage:

73. Stuffed Pork Sausage Roll

All you need is:

2 pounds pork sausage	SAUSAGE
2 cups chopped tart apples	APPLES
2 small onions, chopped	ONIONS
2 cups small bread cubes	BREAD CUBES

Seasoning is usually unnecessary, as there is plenty in the sausage. Pat the pork sausage onto a piece of wax paper in the shape of a rectangle. Your layer of sausage should be about ½ inch thick. Mix together the onions, apples, and bread cubes. Spread the mix over the meat and roll up like a jelly roll. Place on a rack in a roasting pan and bake at 350 degrees for 1 hour.

PORK CHART

Retail Cuts   Wholesale Cuts   Retail Cuts

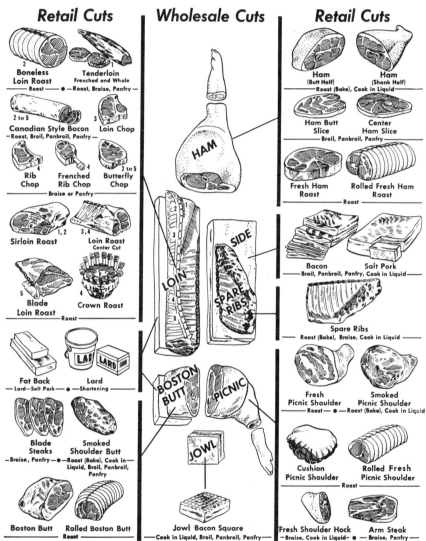

Retail Cuts (left column):

2
Boneless
Loin Roast
——— Roast ———

Tenderloin
Frenched and Whole
● — Roast, Braise, Panfry —

2 to 5
Canadian Style Bacon
— Roast, Broil, Panbroil, Panfry —

3
Loin Chop

Rib Chop
4
Frenched Rib Chop
2 to 5
Butterfly Chop
——— Braise or Panfry ———

1, 2
Sirloin Roast

3, 4
Loin Roast
Center Cut

5
Blade Loin Roast

Crown Roast
——— Roast ———

Fat Back
— Lard—Salt Pork — ●

Lard
● —Shortening

Blade Steaks
— Braise, Panfry — ●

Smoked Shoulder Butt
—Roast (Bake), Cook in—
Liquid, Broil, Panbroil, Panfry

Boston Butt

Rolled Boston Butt
——— Roast ———

Wholesale Cuts (center):

HAM

LOIN

SIDE

SPARE RIBS

BOSTON BUTT

PICNIC

JOWL

Jowl Bacon Square
— Cook in Liquid, Broil, Panbroil, Panfry —

Retail Cuts (right column):

Ham
(Butt Half)

Ham
(Shank Half)
— Roast (Bake), Cook in Liquid —

Ham Butt Slice

Center Ham Slice
— Broil, Panbroil, Panfry —

Fresh Ham Roast

Rolled Fresh Ham Roast
——— Roast ———

Bacon

Salt Pork
— Broil, Panbroil, Panfry, Cook in Liquid —

Spare Ribs
— Roast (Bake), Braise, Cook in Liquid —

Fresh Picnic Shoulder
— Roast — ●

Smoked Picnic Shoulder
● —Roast (Bake), Cook in Liquid

Cushion Picnic Shoulder

Rolled Fresh Picnic Shoulder
——— Roast ———

Fresh Shoulder Hock
— Braise, Cook in Liquid— ●

Arm Steak
● — Braise, Panfry —

National Livestock and Meat Board

Buying Pork in Quantity

The decision to buy a whole hog and freeze for home use isn't always a wise one because of the high fat content. When figuring cost per pound, you have to take into consideration that you are also paying that same price for lard. Then, too, pork should be kept for only about three months. Pork never really freezes as solid as heavy-textured lean meats do. Because of this, there is a tendency for the pork to take on a rancid flavor if kept for too long a period. But, if your family can use a whole hog in this length of time, it can prove to be a good buy. If not, talk to your butcher about buying just the portions that meet your family's needs the best—such as a side of bacon, a ham, and a loin. To help you in making a decision—a 225-pound hog on the hoof will weigh about 175 pounds dressed.

A 225-pound hog basically consists of:

32 Pounds of Ham. Can be cut with center slices, end roasts. The Hock Ends can be split and knuckles removed for small roasts and to provide grinding meat.

26 Pounds of Bacon . . . some to be cured and perhaps some left fresh for sliced side pork.

8 Pounds of Spareribs. This will make 2 packages for barbecuing for the average family.

32 Pounds of Loin. To me, this is the choice part—those delicious pork chops and loin roasts.

28 Pounds of Shoulder. This, like the Hams, can be cut to your specifications.

20 Pounds of Back Fat to make into sausage.

6 Pounds of Jowl. This is frequently served as heavy bacon.

10 Pounds of trimmings and extra fat. Can be ground and made into old-fashioned Corn Meal Scrapple.

13 Pounds Lard.

To figure the real savings in buying a hog, figure on a 100-pound basis and then compare with the price of pork, cut and wrapped for the freezer.

RECIPE GUIDE

LAMB

An abundance of good lamb is available to Eastern Oregonians. Over 200,000 of the animals are shipped to market each year from this area. Government land-leases and wide-open spaces combine to make it ideal country for grazing. To come suddenly upon a band of 1,000 or more grazing sheep is an unforgettable experience—and you probably will startle the sheep just as much as they will you. To see the ever-faithful sheep dog get everything under control again in mere minutes is an awesome sight indeed.

Sheep play an important part in the economy of Eastern Oregon.

Lamb Cookery

Lamb Cookery is basically much the same as that for any other meat, and the same government grades and brands used in denoting quality in beef are used on lamb. Here, too, cost is determined by the quality and amount of bone-in. Slow cooking keeps the shrinkage to a minimum and brings out the flavor. Cold or hot lamb is delicious, but it should never be served in a tepid state. The "fell" of lamb (the thick white membrane surrounding the meat) need not be removed for cooking; however, removal does make for easier slicing and serving.

There are many retail cuts of Lamb Roast. A full Leg of Lamb weighs around 8 pounds. If this is too much for your family, the butcher can cut about 3 pounds from the fleshy end, making a choice Sirloin Roast—or he can trim the "leg end" and furnish you with a 4- to 5-pound roast. You can choose a Shoulder Roast or a Crown Rib Roast. All of these roasts may be purchased with the bone removed and the meat rolled and tied—or with the bone in.

The accompanying chart will help you become familiar with the various types. Allow ½ pound bone-in and ⅓ pound boneless per serving.

LAMB CHART

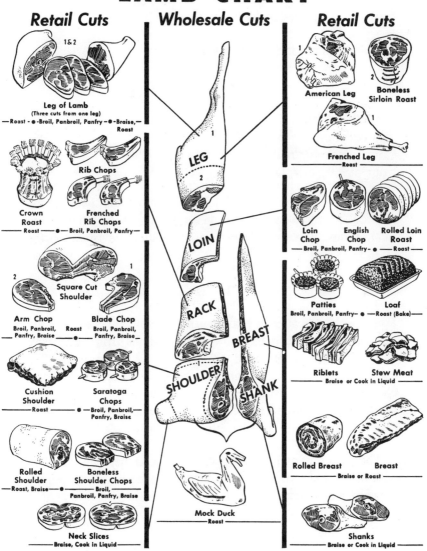

Retail Cuts

1 & 2

Leg of Lamb
(Three cuts from one leg)
—Roast - ● -Broil, Panbroil, Panfry –●-Braise,—
Roast

Rib Chops

Crown Roast
— Roast —
Frenched Rib Chops
● — Broil, Panbroil, Panfry—

2
Square Cut Shoulder
1

Arm Chop
Broil, Panbroil, Panfry, Braise
Roast
Blade Chop
Broil, Panbroil, Panfry, Braise—

Cushion Shoulder
— Roast —
Saratoga Chops
● —Broil, Panbroil,—
Panfry, Braise

Rolled Shoulder
—Roast, Braise—●
Boneless Shoulder Chops
— Broil, Panbroil, Panfry, Braise

Neck Slices
— Braise, Cook in Liquid —

Wholesale Cuts

LEG

LOIN

RACK

BREAST

SHOULDER

SHANK

Mock Duck
— Roast —

Retail Cuts

1
American Leg
2
Boneless Sirloin Roast

1
Frenched Leg
— Roast —

Loin Chop
English Chop
Rolled Loin Roast
— Broil, Panbroil, Panfry - ● — Roast —

Patties
Broil, Panbroil, Panfry– ●
Loaf
—Roast (Bake)—

Riblets
Stew Meat
— Braise or Cook in Liquid —

Rolled Breast
Breast
— Braise or Roast —

Shanks
— Braise or Cook in Liquid —

National Livestock and Meat Board

74. Lamb Roast

I have always found that guidelines in the following recipe will give gourmet results to the Lamb Roast of your choice.

Salt, pepper, and sprinkle with flour. Place on a rack in a roasting pan, fat side up. If the fat layer is thin, cover with strips of bacon. Roast at 325 degrees, allowing 30 minutes per pound. If a meat thermometer is used . . . 175 degrees indicates rare and 182 degrees well-done. Baste the roast from time to time. Take your pick of basters:

LAMB ROAST
BACON
SALT
PEPPER
WORCESTER-
  SHIRE SAUCE
TOMATO JUICE
  OR
(MINT JELLY)
  OR
(GRAPE
  JELLY)

1. Tomato juice flavored with Worcestershire sauce
2. Mint jelly dissolved in an equal amount of hot water
3. Grape jelly dissolved in an equal amount of hot water

75. Stuffed Shoulder of Roast Lamb

Have the blade removed from the shoulder. Fill the pocket with dressing (Recipe No. 70). Add 1 teaspoon chopped celery and 1 teaspoon chopped mint leaves to the dressing. Sew edges to hold the dressing in place and roast at 325 degrees, allowing 30 minutes per pound of meat.

SHOULDER OF
  LAMB
DRESSING
CELERY
(MINT
  LEAVES)

76. Broiled Lamb Chops

Use same suggestions given for Broiling Steaks (Recipe No. 50.) Serve at once. For a taste treat, lay an orange slice on each chop during the last 2 or 3 minutes of broiling time —or, if this does not appeal, rub each lamb chop with a clove of garlic before broiling.

LAMB CHOPS
(ORANGE
  SLICES)
(CLOVE OF
  GARLIC)

77. Breaded Lamb Chops

Season chops with salt and pepper, dust with flour, dip in beaten egg, and roll in cracker crumbs. Melt shortening in skillet. Saute´ chops, turning often. (12 to 15 minutes cooking time is required)

LAMB CHOPS
FLOUR
EGG
CRACKER
    CRUMBS
SALT
PEPPER

78. Lamb Shanks

Neck slices, riblets, shanks, and stew meat are retail cuts of lamb that can be transformed into economical stews and curries. Lamb Shanks prepared in a Dutch Oven are excellent. In fact, a Dutch Oven is worth its weight in gold, in preparing dishes such as this one:

Wash 4 lamb shanks well in cold water. Pat dry and brown well in a Dutch Oven. Browning is done by melting a small amount of shortening in the bottom of the Dutch Oven. Brown the Lamb Shanks well on each side, using a medium heat. Combine together in a sauce pan:

LAMB SHANKS
ONION
TOMATO SOUP
CATSUP
WORCESTER-
    SHIRE SAUCE
CELERY SALT
CLOVE OF
    GARLIC
SALT
PEPPER

1 medium onion, chopped
1 can of tomato soup
1 cup catsup
1 teaspoon Worcestershire sauce
1 clove of garlic, minced
1 teaspoon celery seed

Simmer for 5 minutes. Pour the sauce over the browned shanks. Season with salt and pepper. Cover tightly and cook over low heat for 2 hours. I prefer to slip my Dutch Oven into a 325-degree oven and let it cook on its own for the allotted 2 hours. Serves 4.

79. Baked Lamb Chops

Brown 4 lamb chops in a small amount of shortening. Place the browned chops in a baking dish. Garnish the top of each chop with 1 slice of onion and several green pepper rings. Pour 1 cup of tomato juice over and around the chops. Season the garnished chops with salt and pepper. Cover with a tight-fitting lid and bake at 325 degrees for 1½ hours. Check during the last ½ hour of baking time. You may need to add just a bit of water. Serves 4.

LAMB CHOPS
ONION
GREEN
  PEPPER
TOMATO JUICE
SALT
PEPPER

————◆————

Lamb Stews and Curries are best when made with good lean meat. Water-cooking is generally preferred for tougher portions of meat (the meat cooks in liquid at a low simmer until fork tender). Before simmering, brown meat in a small amount of shortening to seal the juices in. This also provides a tasty brown broth. Most people prefer pre-browning the meat.

80. Irish Stew with Dumplings
(the easy way)

Irish Stew with Dumplings is a tasty example of stew prepared without pre-browning the meat.

Into a large roaster with a tight-fitting lid, put:

LAMB CUBES
ONION
CARROTS
TURNIPS
POTATOES
SALT
PEPPER
DUMPLINGS
(RECIPE NO. 27)

  3 pounds cubed lamb
  1 onion, sliced
  1 cup diced carrots
  1 cup diced turnips
  3 cups diced potatoes
  1 teaspoon salt
  ¼ teaspoon pepper

Cover with water. Cook in the oven at 275 degrees for 5 hours. Just before serving, thicken the broth with flour mixed into a paste in cold water. Serve with dumplings (Recipe No. 27). Serves 4 with "seconds" for everyone.

81. Curry of Lamb

A true Curry, as it is known in the Orient, is a combination of at least 16 different spicy ingredients. In India, Curry condiments are prepared fresh each time they are used. In America, we simplify matters by using a prepared Curry Powder. While the results are not the same, the results are tasty. Curry Powder is often used in the preparation of lamb. The following is a very simple Curry of Lamb recipe—one that I think you will enjoy:

Cut 2 pounds of lean lamb into 1-inch cubes. Make a seasoning mixture of:

LAMB STEW
MEAT
ONION
CELERY
GREEN PEPPER
SALT
PEPPER
ROSEMARY
CURRY POWDER

   1 teaspoon salt
   ¼ teaspoon pepper
   ⅛ teaspoon Rosemary

Work the spices into the meat and dredge the meat cubes with flour. Brown the cubes in a small amount of fat. Here, too, the use of the faithful old Dutch Oven is almost indispensable. When the meat cubes are browned, add:

   1 medium onion, diced
   1 cup diced celery
   ½ green pepper, diced
   Just enough water to cover the meat cubes.

Simmer until the meat is fork-tender. Make a thickening by mixing together 2 tablespoons flour and ½ cup of water. Add slowly to the meat and broth, stirring constantly. Cook until the mixture thickens and begins to bubble. At this point, add and stir in well:

   ⅛ to 1 teaspoon of Curry Powder. (This is strictly a matter of taste and should be used discreetly if you are a first-time user.)

Serve to 4 hungry people on fluffy mounds of rice.

RECIPE GUIDE

POULTRY AND GAME

Chicken, or fowl of any kind, makes a wonderful meat to freeze and have on hand for one delicious meal after another. If you buy your chickens already frozen, slip them into a plastic freezer bag before putting them into your own freezer. It makes for added protection in the event there is a small break in the package caused by handling. This takes only a minute and will assure you of the same eating quality that you bought and paid for when "eating time" comes—whether it's next week or six months from now.

Scalding, Picking, and Packaging for Freezer: If you buy chickens "on foot" and dress your own, here are two suggestions that might help:

1. When scalding and picking the chickens, add a tablespoon or two of soda to the water in which you scald the chicken. The pin feathers will slip right out. The soda emulsifies the little fat deposits which hold the pin feathers, allowing them to slip out easily.

2. To package, slip the chicken—either cut up or whole—into a freezer bag and immerse the bag in warm water, being careful not to let any water get into the bag. This forces all the air out, giving you a vacuum-type seal. Secure the end of the bag tightly and then, just for good measure, place in a second freezer bag.

82. Scotch-Side Chicken

In most families of any size, it usually takes at least two chickens to make enough fried chicken to fill the bill. You can stretch the food budget if you will fry the "choice" pieces and make Scotch-Side Chicken for another time with the bony pieces.

Place the bony pieces, along with the hearts, livers, and gizzards, in a saucepan. Cover with water. Add:

BONY CHICKEN
SALT
PEPPER
ONION
PEPPER FLAKES
(POULTRY SEASONING)
CREAM OF CHICKEN SOUP

1 teaspoon salt
¼ teaspoon pepper
a bit of onion
1 tablespoon dehydrated pepper flakes
1 teaspoon poultry seasoning (optional)

Simmer until the chicken falls off the bone. Set aside to cool. Remove the bones and slice the gizzards and livers. To all of this, add 1 can of cream of chicken soup (gives it a richer, creamier flavor).

———◆———

At this point you can do all sorts of things with the chicken. For a quick meal, serve with noodles. If you have a little more time, make a Chicken Pie. Place the Scotch-Side Chicken in a baking dish. Top with little round biscuits. Put a cheese cube on top of each biscuit and bake until the biscuits are nice and brown. . . . Usually takes 15 to 20 minutes for biscuit centers that are fluffy and tender. ⁓

It is better to add the cheese cubes about 5 minutes before the biscuits are done; then the cheese doesn't get too brown.

In making the most of all this chicken, instead of preparing the rich gravy, you can separate the chicken from the broth— then freeze the broth to have on hand for seasoning casseroles. Chop the chicken and use in making summer salads, sandwiches, or croquettes that are "irresistible."

83. Chicken Croquettes

Make a thick white sauce like this: In a small flat-bottomed saucepan, melt:

COOKED
CHICKEN
SALT
CELERY SALT
ONION
BUTTER
FLOUR
MILK

    4 tablespoons butter

Stir in and blend until smooth:

    4 tablespoons flour

All at once add:

    1 cup of cold milk

Stir constantly until the mixture bubbles and the lumps smooth out. When the white sauce is completely cooled, add:

    2 cups chopped cooked chicken

    ½ teaspoon salt

    ¼ teaspoon celery salt

    A wee bit of grated onion, or for quickness' sake, use a few drops of onion juice.

Shape the mixture into croquettes. Roll in fine bread crumbs and deep-fat fry until crusty and golden brown on the outside and bubbling hot on the inside. Makes 10 to 12 Croquettes which are a delightful addition to any buffet dinner.

84. Chicken 'n Chips

This recipe is a trick my mother-in-law taught me. Every time I fix it, our son comments, "This is what I call real eating."

For one chicken, mix together in a paper bag:

CHICKEN
POTATOES
SHORTENING
SALT
PEPPER
FLOUR
PAPRIKA

    2 cups flour

    1 teaspoon salt

    ¼ teaspoon pepper

    1 teaspoon paprika

Place chicken pieces in the bag and shake until coated with flour and seasoning. Melt enough fat in a heavy skillet to make about one inch of fat. Brown the chicken first on one side and then the other. After the chicken has browned on the one side, place quartered potatoes on top of the chicken. Cover the skillet with a tight-fitting lid. As the chicken browns on the second side, the potatoes will become tender from the steam.

When the chicken is done, put the chicken on top and the potatoes on the bottom for about 10 minutes. They will become crisp and crunchy and tender. The chicken crumbs will stick to the potatoes, giving them an extra special flavor. A large fruit salad is an ideal way to complete this meal.

85. Pan-Fried Chicken

Nearly everybody likes good old family style Pan-Fried Chicken. . . .

In a paper bag place:
  2 cups flour
  2 teaspoons salt
  1 teaspoon black pepper
  1 teaspoon paprika

FRYING
  CHICKEN
FLOUR
SALT
PEPPER
PAPRIKA

Have chicken cut into frying pieces. Wash well with cold water. Coat the chicken with the seasoned flour by placing several pieces of chicken in the bag at a time, and sealing the bag by folding at the top; shake several times until the chicken is well-coated. In a heavy skillet (your Dutch Oven is perfect for this) melt fat to a depth of ½ inch. When the shortening is hot, place the meaty pieces of chicken into the hot fat and brown to perfection on both sides. This will take 20 to 25 minutes. The smaller pieces of chicken can be done in a shorter length of time.

In browning the chicken—if you like your chicken crusty with lots of crumbs—be careful not to over-crowd the skillet. When all the pieces are browned to your liking, cover with a tight-fitting lid and cook over low heat an additional 30 to 40 minutes, or until tender. Remove the lid during the last 10 minutes to recrisp the skin.

86. Chicken Fricassee

My own family has mixed emotions about Chicken Fricassee. It is an old-fashioned recipe that my mother always served with golden-brown biscuits that would melt in your mouth. We thought it very fine eating.

Prepare chicken as you would Pan-Fried Chicken (Recipe No. 85). Drain off all excess fat. Cover the chicken with rich milk, then with a tight-fitting lid and continue to cook at a very low temperature for another hour. This is a total of approximately 2 hours' slow cooking—almost 1 hour in its own steam and an additional hour in the milk. An old hen can be prepared in this manner and arrive at the table all tender and good. (If you don't have time to keep an eye on it simmering on top of the stove, bake in a 325-degree oven for the same length of time. Remove the lid during the last 10 minutes of baking and allow to brown lightly.)

CHICKEN
FRYER
FLOUR
SALT/PEPPER
PAPRIKA
MILK

87. Oven-Fried Chicken

For easy, tasty fried chicken, preheat the oven to 425 degrees. Dip cut-up chicken in milk, coat with flour, and season with salt and pepper. Melt ½ cup of shortening in a 13-by-9-by-2-inch pan or baking dish. Place the chicken skin-side down in a single layer in the melted shortening. Reduce the oven heat to 375 degrees and bake the chicken, uncovered, for 30 minutes. Turn the chicken and continue baking for 30 more minutes.

CHICKEN
SHORTENING
FLOUR
MILK
SALT
PEPPER
(BISCUITS)

At this point you can serve as usual, or push the drippings and chicken to one end of the pan, place biscuits in the other end, and pop the whole thing back into the oven until the biscuits are done . . . about 12 minutes.

If you want gravy for the biscuits, there are enough drippings in the pan to do the job nicely and I can't think of an easier way to prepare a hearty meal.

88. Oven-Barbecued Chicken

A change from just plain fried chicken is Oven-Barbecued Chicken:

For one broiler chicken, make a marinade by combining:

1 cup salad oil	BROILER CHICKEN
¼ cup lemon juice	SALAD OIL
1 teaspoon salt	LEMON JUICE
⅛ teaspoon pepper	SALT
Either one clove of garlic or sprinkle the chicken "oh so lightly" with garlic salt.	PEPPER CLOVE OF GARLIC

Cut broiler chicken into serving pieces. Marinate in the sauce for at least 12 hours. One hour before eating time, remove the broiler from the sauce and arrange in a shallow baking pan. Bake in a 375-degree oven for 1 hour. From time to time, baste the broiler pieces with the marinade.

89. Basic Broiled Chicken

Mention Broiled Chicken, and nine times out of ten someone will give you a recipe for a favorite sauce with which to brush the chicken. The important thing is to know the "basics" and then have fun experimenting. . . . Herbs may be rubbed into the chicken before broiling, lemon juice may be brushed over the chicken during broiling, or you may baste it with barbecue sauce. . . .

To prepare: Wash the broiler chicken thoroughly. Split in half along the backbone and through the breastbone. Break all the joints by bending, but do not cut them. Sprinkle with salt and pepper and brush with melted butter.

BROILER CHICKEN
SALT
PEPPER
BUTTER

Place on a broiler pan without a rack. The pan should be 6 to 7 inches from the source of heat. Every 10 or 15 minutes, turn the chicken and brush with melted butter (or the sauce of your choice). Most broilers are done to perfection in 40 to 50 minutes. There should be no trace of pink color in the meat.

90. Roast Chicken

Clean and stuff a 4- to 5-pound roasting hen with dressing (Recipe No. 70). Fasten legs and wings close to the body with skewers or by tying. Spread butter over the breast and legs. Sprinkle with salt, pepper, and flour. Place chicken on its back in the roaster.

ROASTING HEN
DRESSING
(RECIPE
No. 70)
SALT
PEPPER
BUTTER
FLOUR

Put in a 425-degree oven for 15 minutes. Lower the temperature to 325 degrees and cook until tender. Baste occasionally, adding a little water to the drippings in the pan if needed.

Sprinkling with flour 2 or 3 times during cooking will result in a luscious crust. If a glazed surface is wanted, omit the flour. Allow 40 minutes per pound for roasting.

91. Roast Duck

When roasting a 4- to 5-pound duck, better remember that ducks are quite fatty . . . which makes stuffing in the usual manner impractical. I like to place a quartered apple and sliced orange in the cavity of the duck . . . which I discard after the baking, but the subtle flavor given is delightful. Sprinkle the duck with salt, pepper, and flour, and place on its back in a covered roaster. Bake in a 325-degree oven, allowing 30 minutes per pound. Do not add any water—and plan on 1 pound per person.

92. Roast Turkey

A turkey prepared in the following manner is moist inside, golden brown outside, and the aroma is superb.

Wash, scrub and clean the turkey. Rub generously, inside and out, with butter. Sprinkle salt over the entire surface of the turkey. Stuff

TURKEY
BUTTER
SALT

the cavities of the turkey lightly with stuffing (Recipe No. 93). Do not pack the dressing tightly, for it will expand as it cooks. Close the stuffed turkey with skewers and lace tightly with a strong string. If you don't have skewers, sew the opening together with a darning needle and clean string.

Place the stuffed turkey on a rack, breast side up, in a large roasting pan. Cover with a tent made of heavy duty foil. Do not tuck the foil over the edges of the roaster. The idea is to protect the turkey while it roasts and contains its own juices. If you seal the roaster, it will steam and the turkey will lose its natural meat juice, making it dry. Allow 30 minutes per pound cooking time in a 325-degree oven. Maintain this temperature to prevent shrinkage and dryness of meat.

Brush the surface of the turkey with butter and sprinkle with salt on the average of once each hour. When the turkey is done (192 degrees) the leg joints will move freely. Remove the turkey from the oven, and allow to stand for 20 minutes before slicing. The turkey will reabsorb its juices.

93. Turkey Stuffing

Heat 1 cup butter in a large skillet. Add 2 medium-sized onions, chopped fine. Cook over low heat until soft, being careful not to brown. Add:

WHITE BREAD
BUTTER
ONION
SALT
PEPPER

1½ cups water
1 tablespoon salt
1 teaspoon pepper

Pour over bread cubes made from a large loaf of white bread. Toss lightly, using 2 forks, until the bread cubes absorb the liquid. Stuff the cavities of the turkey and place the extra dressing in a well-buttered casserole. Baste the extra dressing with pan drippings, cover tightly, and bake for 1 hour.

94. Baked Turkey Broiler

This recipe is ideal for preparing turkey for buffet dinners where a variety of "side dishes" make up the main fare—and there are only about 200 calories to each generous serving.

Split a 4- to 5-pound turkey broiler. Sprinkle with salt, pepper, and a generous dredging of flour. Dot with butter and place on a rack in a roasting pan. Add ½ cup of water to the bottom of the roasting pan. Bake in a 325-degree oven until tender . . . about 2½ hours. Baste frequently with the pan drippings. Serves 4.

TURKEY
BROILER
BUTTER
SALT
PEPPER
FLOUR

About Game Birds...

Game Birds are usually prepared and eaten just the same as domestic birds. However, for Game Birds, proper care in the field is important. The oldest method of caring for the birds in the field, and one that is still the best, is to carry the birds on a loop on your belt. This allows the air to circulate through the birds until they are cleaned and ready to go in the freezer. Even meat that has been purchased in the store and placed in the refrigerator will keep longer if wrapped loosely and allowed to breathe. When wrapped tightly it sweats, creating a breeding ground for bacteria.

Scald, pluck, and clean Game Birds as soon as possible. In plucking, it helps to add a tablespoon or two of soda to the boiling water in which they are scalded. Let the water cool about 10 degrees or pour in 1 cup of cold water before scalding the birds. This keeps the skin from breaking. The soda emulsifies the fat pockets that hold the pin feathers . . . and they slip out more easily.

95. Roast Wild Duck — Rare

Roasting a wild duck is such a controversial subject, I hesitate even to mention it. There are those who feel it should be well-done, and there are those who feel it should be rare. I suppose the diplomatic thing to do is give you both basic methods. Following is for Roast Wild Duck — Rare:

Allow 1 pound of duck per person being served. Wash the duck well, clean carefully and remove all pinfeathers. Fill the cavity with unpeeled, quartered apples — the tarter they are the better. Sprinkle the outside of the duck liberally with salt and pepper. Cover the breast with slices of thin salt pork. Bake the average duck 20 to 30 minutes in a 450-degree oven. Baste with the drippings in the pan several times during baking. Remove the salt pork during the last 5 minutes' baking to allow the duck time to brown. Discard the apple stuffing before serving. This method of cookery eliminates the gamy flavor.

DUCK
SALT PORK
APPLE
SALT
PEPPER

96. Roast Wild Duck — Well-Done

For a well-done duck, follow the directions in Recipe No. 95, with the exception of time and temperature. Instead, place the duck in an open roaster in a 425-degree oven for 15 minutes. Lower the temperature to 325 degrees and cook until tender. Allow 30 minutes per pound cooking time. Baste occasionally, adding a little water to the drippings in the pan if needed. Basting with orange juice is a happy variation.

DUCK
SALT PORK
APPLE
SALT
PEPPER
(ORANGE JUICE)

97. Roast Wild Goose

My idea of a perfect Roast Goose is to prepare it exactly as you would a Roast Chicken. (Recipe No. 90).

GOOSE
DRESSING
SALT
PEPPER
BUTTER
FLOUR

98. Gourmet Breast of Wild Goose

The Goose Hunter in our family feels the following recipe is an elegant ending for geese he brings home:

Wash the goose breast in cold water. Pat dry and cut into thin slices. Fry in butter, being careful not to over-cook. Real butter is a "must" in this recipe. When the slices of goose are done, transfer them to a hot platter. Add ½ cup white wine to the pan drippings. When thoroughly mixed, remove the pan from the heat and slowly stir in ½ cup thick cream. Stir until smooth. Add 1 fresh tomato, diced, ½ teaspoon salt, and ¼ teaspoon pepper. Cook over low heat for 2 minutes. Pour over the goose steaks and garnish with canned mushroom slices.

GOOSE BREAST
BUTTER
WHITE WINE
CREAM
FRESH TOMATO
SALT
PEPPER
MUSHROOM SLICES

99. Baked Pheasant

Cut the pheasant into serving pieces. Season lightly with salt and pepper. Dredge each piece with flour and brown in a small amount of fat, just as you would pan-fried chicken. Place the browned pieces in a casserole dish or Dutch Oven. Cover the pheasant with a can of cream of chicken soup. Cover with a tight-fitting lid and bake in a 325-degree oven until tender. This usually takes about an hour, depending on the age and size of the pheasant. Thirty minutes per pound of meat is a fairly accurate guideline.

PHEASANT
CREAM OF CHICKEN SOUP
FLOUR
SHORTENING
SALT
PEPPER

100. Sage Hen Steaks

Soaking Sage Hen in salt water for several hours before cooking helps to remove some of the sage flavor. This dish is best left unseasoned, permitting the individual to season to taste.

Remove the meat from the breast and soak in a solution of 1 teaspoon salt to 1 quart of water for at least 4 hours. Rinse and pat dry. Pound in flour just as you would a Swiss Steak. Fry gently until a golden brown on each side.

SAGE HEN
FLOUR
SALT
SHORTENING

101. Fried Quail

Scald, pluck, and clean. Cut into serving pieces and place in a small bowl with deep sides. Sprinkle with a mixture of:

1 teaspoon salt
¼ teaspoon pepper
A tiny pinch of each of the following:
dried parsley
thyme
bay leaf, crumbled
Add:
1 small onion, sliced
juice of 1 lemon
2 tablespoons olive oil

QUAIL
SALT
PEPPER
PARSLEY
THYME
BAY LEAF
ONION
LEMON
OLIVE OIL
BREAD CRUMBS
BUTTER

Marinate the Quail in this mixture for several hours, then

drain and roll in bread crumbs. Brown gently on all sides. As the Quail browns, moisten with drops of butter.

102. Chukar

This popular bird is one of the tastiest of all the Game Birds. It can be prepared just as you would chicken. They are "extra special" when prepared according to the directions in Recipes No. 85, 86, or 90.

About Venison . . .

Venison, a highly sought-after game meat, can be used in any recipe as a substitute for beef. Proper preparation of Venison for the freezer can determine whether your family enjoys and makes the most of this wonderful meat.

It is very important that the deer be bled and dressed immediately, and doubly important that it be cooled as quickly as possible and aged a week to ten days in a cold place. This "aging" process is what makes the meat tender. The minute the meat is frozen, the action of the enzymes stops. If the deer is not aged properly, the meat will be tough and there isn't a thing that can be done about it.

Venison will be tasty all winter long if you are careful to trim away as much of the fatty tissue as possible before freezing. Fat never really freezes solid and will become rancid if stored over a long period of time. The trimming is well worth the extra time it takes. . . . Package the Venison in meal-size portions, label carefully and freeze quickly.

In the event, that because of the age of the animal you feel the Venison might have a tendency to be tough, sprinkle it with a commercial tenderizer before wrapping. The result is tender meat and only you are the wiser.

A quick and easy way to cut venison liver into meal-size portions is to partially freeze, then slice and package for the freezer. This is much easier than trying to hang onto the slippery meat and slice it at the same time.

Neck, shoulders, shanks, and other bonier parts are better if ground and made into "Venisonburger." Venison tends to be too dry alone. Mix a good sausage with the ground Venison in a proportion of 2 parts of Venison to 1 part sausage. Do not add salt. Pepper and other seasonings may be added at this time if you like, but salt would make the meat bleed, creating a dry and tasteless ground meat.

In preparing Venison roasts and steaks, thawing in a marinated sauce will safeguard against toughness. Any marinade which contains a good portion of vinegar is satisfactory, depending on your preference. It's fun to try some of the different vinegars on the market. Each one adds a subtle something of its own to the flavor of the meat.

103. Making the Most of a Deer Heart

It is amazing how much meat there is in a Deer Heart, though I am afraid I have never had much enthusiasm for cooking Heart of any kind . . . just one of those squeamish notions most of us have of one kind or another. Being a frugal soul, however, I always feel I should do something with the Heart, only to find again that it is really very good eating. For any other squeamish cooks, perhaps you would like to try my method:

Wash and clean thoroughly, being sure that the cavity is clean. Place in salted water and | HEART
SALT

let simmer until tender. After the cooked heart has cooled, slice and remove any membrane. Package the slices of heart and freeze to be used at a later date. By cooking and freezing Heart, I find the meat looks more tempting all the time.

104. Fried Deer Heart

Slice the Deer Heart in ¼-inch-thick slices. Dip in flour, brown on both sides, and serve piping hot with a big platter of scrambled eggs. | COOKED
HEART
FLOUR
SHORTENING
EGGS

105. Sunday Night Supper Dish

Brown together in a small amount of shortening:

1 heart, precooked and cut in cubes	HEART
1 medium-sized onion, diced	ONION
Add:	BROWN SUGAR
	VINEGAR
2 tablespoons brown sugar	CATSUP
¼ cup vinegar	WORCESTER-
½ cup catsup	SHIRE SAUCE
1 cup water	SALT
2 teaspoons Worcestershire sauce	CHILI POWDER
1 teaspoon salt	
½ teaspoon chili powder	

Let simmer about 30 minutes until the flavors are well blended. Serve with rice or cooked noodles.

106. Venison (or Beef) Jerky

This section wouldn't be complete without a jerky recipe. This is the way Great Grandpa did it and I can't see where you would want to change it any—

Into a stone jar (you could use a plastic bucket), mix a brine of:	VENISON OR BEEF
	SALT
1 pound salt	MOLASSES
½ cup molasses	BROWN SUGAR
⅓ cup brown sugar	CAYENNE PEPPER
A dash of cayenne pepper	"SMOKE
1 gallon water	HOUSE"

Cut lean strips of Venison, 1 to 5 inches long and ¼ inch thick. Place in the brine. Weight down with a heavy bowl and let stand for at least 12 hours. At the end of this period, rinse with cold water, drain well, and pat dry. Arrange in the smokehouse or smoker on racks that allow ventilation for a period of 1 to 2 weeks.

Smoking Jerky . . .

If you live in town, your neighbor might not appreciate your "smoke," so here is a method that anyone can use successfully—even apartment dwellers.

Follow the above directions for Jerky up to "smokehouse time." Then brush the meat with liquid smoke, sprinkle with pepper, and lay the strips of meat on racks from your oven. Arrange the meat in such a way that there is plenty of room for circulation. Place the racks in the middle grooves of the oven so that the meat is as far from the elements as possible.

VENISON OR BEEF
SALT
MOLASSES
BROWN SUGAR
CAYENNE PEPPER
LIQUID SMOKE
PEPPER

Place aluminum foil on a rack near the bottom to catch any drips. Set the oven at 150 degrees and let the meat dry for 12 hours. Cool completely and store in jars. Poke holes in the lids of the jars to allow room for ventilation.

Old Broken Top Crater, as seen from the Green Lakes Trail. Soil is of a pumice nature.

RECIPE GUIDE

Number

107. Fish Croquettes
108. Fish Sandwiches
109. Fish Fillets
110. Broiled Fish
111. Fish Cakes
112. Tartar Sauce
113. New England Chowder
114. French-Fried Shrimp
115. Creamed Shrimp
116. Clam Chowder
117. Crab Meat Patties
118. Oyster Stew
119. Tuna Bites
120. Baked Salmon
121. Steamed Fish
122. Canned Mountain Trout

FISH AND SHELLFISH

There is nothing our family would rather do for relaxation than fish; it's a good excuse for being just plain lazy, soaking up sun (or freezing to death), and doing lots of "thinking." As a result, we have a sizable amount of fish to prepare. There are many ways of preparing it, but most of our fish ends up "pan-fried," because that is the way we like it best.

107. Fish Croquettes

When frying fish, it is hard to fry just the right amount. Because I'm always afraid there won't be enough, I tend to fix too much. Then there is the problem of what to do with the leftover fish. I hate to throw it out; still, no one at our house gets very excited about cold fish except the cats. However, if I make Croquettes, that's another story. There are rarely any leftovers and croquettes can be frozen for the time when a quick meal is needed and fishing is not so good.

While leftover Trout is usually the basis for Croquettes at our house, Salmon or Halibut is equally good.

Make a white sauce. You will need:

COOKED FISH
BUTTER
FLOUR
MILK
SALT
PEPPER
EGG
BREAD
  CRUMBS

- 2 tablespoons butter
- 2 tablespoons flour
- 1 cup milk

Melt the butter in a saucepan, add flour; cook until it bubbles well; add milk all at once and stir constantly until it thickens. Quickly stir in 1 beaten egg and 3 cups of cooked, flaked, boned fish. (This recipe can be used for salmon, ham, chicken, or anything else you might want to make croquettes of.) Spread mixture on a platter to cool. When cool, shape into croquettes. Roll croquettes first in flour, then dip in beaten egg, and last in fine bread crumbs. At this point the croquettes can be packaged and frozen. When ready to use, just deep-fat fry.

Freezing Fish . . .

Fish is a luxury meal, if you were actually to figure the cost per pound of catching your own. On the other hand, if you are "fishin' fools" like us, it is better not even to worry about the cost. Just have fun and make the most of your catches.

The secret to good frozen fish is absolute freshness, so a little care is essential. Whenever possible, fish should be frozen the same day they are caught. Since this isn't always possible, the next best solution is to pack the fish in ice. If you can't do this, clean them, wash well, pat dry, and then take a tip from the Indians—don't put them in water to become water-soaked. It is better to keep them in a cool, dry place until you can get them home for proper care.

Lean fish may be dipped in a salt solution (one cup of salt to one gallon of water) for a few minutes. This will prevent leakage in thawing and make for a tastier fish.

Fatty fish is improved by dipping in ascorbic acid solution (1 tablespoon of ascorbic acid powder to ½ gallon of water). This is the same product used to prevent fruit from darkening and is found in your favorite supermarket with the canning supplies. While freezing fish in water does take up more space in the freezer, the quality of the fish come eating time, plus the practical, easy processing, is so superior to other methods, it is worth the lost space. To freeze fish in water, simply place the cleaned fish in a pan, covering completely with water, and freeze. Encased in the ice, the fish will keep for many months with no chance of freezer burn. In fact, this is the only method I would ever personally recommend for "long-term" freezer storage.

108. Fish Sandwiches

Cod, Haddock, Halibut, and Trout are easily boned. For a tasty change, try this:

Prepare 2 good big cups of boned fish. Then blend together:

BONED FISH
BUTTER
ONION
MUSTARD
(NUTMEG)
(GARLIC SALT)
SALT
BUNS
FOIL

½ cup butter
2 tablespoons minced onion
1 tablespoon prepared mustard
(¼ teaspoon nutmeg)
(¼ teaspoon garlic salt)
¼ teaspoon salt

Spread the mixture over the fish. Wrap individual servings of the fish mixture in heavy-duty aluminum foil and seal the edges tightly. Place on a grill over hot coals for 10 to 15 minutes. Meanwhile, be toasting wiener buns. Place the heated mixture on the buns—and you'll know what to do next!

This is a good camp menu. Served with either potato chips or potato salad and plenty of good hot coffee . . . you won't mind the leftover fish at all.

109. Fish Fillets

For Fish Fillets, allow ½ pound of fish per serving. Popular choices are Sole (Flounder), Haddock, Halibut, Red Snapper, Cod, Perch and Pike.

Sprinkle 1 pound of fish fillets with salt and pepper. Beat together:

FISH FILLETS
EGG
MILK
CRACKER CRUMBS
SHORTENING
SALT
PEPPER

1 egg
1 tablespoon milk

Dip fish in egg mixture and then in crumbs. (Make a crumb bag by placing crackers or dry bread in a heavy plastic bag and rolling with a rolling pin. This keeps the crumbs from scattering.)

Heat ½ cup shortening over medium high heat. Add fish fillets and brown on both sides. Drain on paper towels and serve.

Variations for crumb or meal mixture:
1. Corn meal or half corn meal and half flour.
2. Cracker crumbs for New England fried fish.
3. Crushed corn chips. (Leave the salt off the fish, if you do this.)
4. Fine, dry bread crumbs seasoned with ½ teaspoon garlic salt and ¼ teaspoon oregano.

When adventuring with new seasonings, use sparingly in order to enhance the fish flavor rather than consume it. Generally speaking, ¼ teaspoon of spice will season fish for 4 people.

110. Broiled Fish

A number of fish are delicious when broiled. Cod, Salmon, White fish, Halibut, Mackerel, and Red Snapper become taste tempters.

Arrange fish steaks on the broiler pan. Brush with lemon juice, season with salt and pepper, and spread with sour cream. Broil until a golden brown, turn, and repeat the process on the other side. Salmon steaks are especially good prepared in this manner.

FISH STEAKS
LEMON JUICE
SALT
PEPPER
SOUR CREAM

111. Fish Cakes

For every 4 cups of boned fish, add:
- 1 egg white
- 1 cup soft bread crumbs
- 1 cup boiled potato, grated (can use instant mashed potatoes)
- 1 teaspoon salt
- ¼ teaspoon pepper
- ¼ teaspoon herb seasoning

BONED FISH
SHORTENING
BREAD
  CRUMBS
POTATO
EGG
SALT
PEPPER
HERB
  SEASONING

Form into cakes. If necessary to make them "form" into cakes, add just a bit of water. Dip the cakes in a mixture of 1 egg yolk plus one whole egg. Cover with dry bread crumbs and gently fry until a light brown in color. Use just enough shortening to keep the cakes from sticking.

112. Tartar Sauce

Tartar Sauce does things to my taste buds, just thinking about it:

Chop or grind fine:
   3 dill pickles
   1 small onion
Add:
   ¼ cup dried parsley
   1 teaspoon celery seed
Mix:
   1 cup mayonnaise
   ½ cup milk
   Juice of 1 lemon
Blend in the pickle and onion mixture.

DILL PICKLES
ONION
PARSLEY
CELERY SEED
MAYONNAISE
MILK
LEMON

If you hesitate to cook fish because of the "fishy smell" it leaves in the kitchen, put a couple of pieces of celery in the skillet. It doesn't affect the flavor of the fish and for some strange reason it does help absorb the fish odor.

General Patch Bridge over the Deschutes River, southwest of Bend, Oregon. It is always pleasant fishing here.

113. New England Chowder

Fish chowder is a good meal to have if you don't know when the family will show up for supper, for the longer it waits, the better it gets . . . and that kind of meal is hard to come by.

A truly good chowder is not a chowder if you put tomatoes in it; at least not in chowder country. To be at its best, it should be made ahead of time and set on the back of the stove to age to allow the flavors to blend. Since the days of cooking on a wood range are over for most of us, you can get the same effect by placing in the oven and setting the control on "warm."

Simmer a 3-pound Haddock until the bones are easily removed. You can use Cod . . . or do the way we "inlanders" do and use canned clams. While simmering is going on, fry ¼ pound of diced salt pork in the kettle in which you are planning to make the chowder. Remove the diced pork and save.

HADDOCK OR
COD
POTATOES
ONIONS
SALT PORK
MILK
BUTTER
SALT
PEPPER

Into the kettle, put:
    3 cups raw diced potatoes
    3 medium sized onions, sliced *very* thin
Cover with the water in which the fish was boiled and cook until the potatoes are tender, but not mushy. Add:
    Boned fish, keeping the pieces as large as possible
    Crisp pork giblets
    1 teaspoon salt
    ¼ teaspoon pepper   ◄ *Add more if you like*
    1 tablespoon butter
    1 quart whole milk, the richer the better

Let stand and blend at least 1 hour—longer if possible. Reheat and serve. This makes 4 very generous servings.

To Freeze Shrimp

If you should be so lucky (and I hope you are) as to be in a position to buy shrimp in quantity and freeze, there are a few do's and don'ts that should be kept in mind. Cooked shrimp has a tendency to toughen when frozen and there just isn't that much advantage in having it precooked.

Fresh shrimp are easily cleaned under cold, running water. Remove the shell and run the tip of a sharp, pointed knife along the edge of the black intestinal vein. Rinse well and pat dry. The shrimp are now ready for packaging tightly in rigid freezer containers.

114. French-Fried Shrimp

Clean under cold, running water, remove the shell and black intestinal vein, rinse well, then drop into rapidly boiling water and simmer until just a rosy pink. (If frozen, separate under cold running water and drop into boiling water.)

SHRIMP
SEASONING
PANCAKE
  BATTER
SHORTENING

Remove as soon as pink and drain well. For extra flavor add salt—and any other seasoning you might like—to the water. Dip in a very thin pancake batter. Drain off all excess batter. This is important for the batter will puff up in the deep-fat frying, and you want just enough crust on the shrimp to make them crunchy tasting, not doughy. Prepared this way, it's like eating popcorn: you don't know when to quit.

115. Creamed Shrimp

In a saucepan, melt:
  ¼ cup butter
Add:
  1 (8-ounce) can of shrimp
  1 pint light cream
  2 tablespoons bottled Chinese Oyster
    sauce (available in most supermarkets)

CANNED
  SHRIMP
LIGHT CREAM
BUTTER
CHINESE
  OYSTER
  SAUCE
RICE

Stir to blend well. Heat just to the boiling point. Serve on fluffy mounds of rice to 4 hungry people.

116. Clam Chowder

Recipes such as this come in handy at noon, when a quick and hearty lunch is needed. Combine:

½ cup chopped onion
½ cup chopped celery
3½ cups milk
⅛ teaspoon pepper
2 teaspoons salt

Bring to the boiling point. Just before serving, add:

1 (4-ounce) can minced clams
1½ cups instant potato flakes
1 tablespoon butter

CLAMS
(CANNED)
ONION
CELERY
MILK
INSTANT
POTATO
FLAKES OR
LEFT-OVER
MASHED
POTATOES
BUTTER
SALT
PEPPER

117. Crab Meat Patties
(a "quickie")

Chop 1 small onion very fine.
Cook in 3 tablespoons butter until a light
    brown.
Remove from heat and add 1 cup soft bread-
    crumbs.
Stir until well blended.
Drain, flake, and add 2 (7-ounce) cans of crab-
meat. Add:

2 beaten eggs
1 tablespoon chopped parsley
Salt and pepper to taste
Just enough cream to moisten lightly

CRAB MEAT
ONION
BUTTER
BREADCRUMBS
EGGS
PARSLEY
SALT
PEPPER
CREAM

Mix together and shape into flat patties. Coat lightly on both sides with flour. Fry in a small amount of butter or shortening until golden brown on both sides.

118. Oyster Stew

For Oyster Stew with a "different" flavor, add ½ cup chopped dill pickles. It's made like this:

Melt ½ cup butter in a large sauce pan.
Add 2 (7-ounce) cans of well-drained oysters.
Cook in butter until the edges curl.
Add:

OYSTERS
BUTTER
MILK
CREAM
SALT
PEPPER
(DILL
   PICKLES)

   3 cups milk
1½ cups heavy cream
1½ teaspoons salt
  ¼ teaspoon pepper
  ½ cup chopped dill pickles (optional)

Stir and heat to serving temperature. Do not let boil.

119. Tuna Bites

Tuna Bites served with a zesty tomato barbecue sauce will add welcome variety to meals—or they can be used as "Snacks." They are similar to Swedish Meatballs in that they are tiny. They may be shaped ahead of time and refrigerated. Baked instead of fried, they are quick and easy:

Mix together:

TUNA
BREAD
   CRUMBS
CELERY
ONION
SALT
PEPPER
EGG
MILK
LEMON JUICE
WORCESTER-
   SHIRE
   SAUCE

  2 cans (6½-ounce size) drained
     flaked tuna
  1 cup dry bread crumbs
  ½ cup finely chopped celery
  ¼ cup finely chopped onion
  ¾ teaspoon salt
  ¼ teaspoon pepper
  1 beaten egg
  ⅓ cup milk
  2 teaspoons lemon juice
  1 teaspoon Worcestershire sauce

Shape into tiny balls using a teaspoon. It's easier if you dip the spoon into cold water occasionally. Place the Tuna Bites on a lightly buttered cooky sheet and bake in a 350-degree oven for 15 minutes, or until lightly browned. Serve hot with a Tomato Barbecue Sauce.

120. Baked Salmon

Baked Salmon, Sturgeon, Bass, and large Trout are simple to prepare. Clean a 4- to 5-pound fish. Dry well and sprinkle with salt, inside and out. Since there is always danger of salting the fish to the point where even the cat won't eat it, pre-measure the salt, allowing ¼ teaspoon per pound of fish. This amount brings out the natural flavors and leaves no "salt" taste. Further seasoning should be left to the individual at serving time. Stuff loosely with a Bread Stuffing. Stuffing Recipe No. 70 is just dry enough to be right for fish. Fasten the opening with skewers or by sewing edges together. Place on a well-buttered sheet of foil in the bottom of a baking pan. With a very sharp knife, slit the skin in several places to prevent the fish from curling. Brush generous amounts of butter over the top of the fish and into the slits. Bake in a preheated, 400-degree oven, allowing 12 minutes to the pound. Take care not to over-bake. When done, the fish flesh separates easily from the bone. If you prefer to bake without stuffing, 10 minutes per pound is usually sufficient.

121. Steamed Fish

Steamed fish can be prepared without a lot of special equipment. Pour about 1½ inches of water into the bottom of your oven broiler pan. Place the rack in position. Lay the cleaned fish on the rack. Drizzle lemon juice into the cavity. Add seasonings, but keep them subtle. Using aluminum foil, make a roomy tent covering pan and all. Seal the edges of the foil by pleating and pinching foil. Place on the bottom rack in a preheated, 400-degree oven. Allow 12 to 15 minutes for the water to start simmering in the pan, plus 12 minutes per pound for the fish. . . . We like to skin the fish when it is done, then serve the tender, moist chunks of meat with Tartar Sauce (Recipe No. 112).

Salmon Loaf from leftover Baked or Steamed Salmon is easy. Just to show how basic and simple gourmet cooking can be, use Meat Loaf Recipe No. 2, substitute 4 cups of flaked

Salmon or similar fish for the ground beef, add ¼ teaspoon of celery salt, put together with 1 beaten egg and bake 35 to 40 minutes in a 350-degree oven. Serve with Tartar Sauce or Chili Sauce for some very good eating.

122. Canned Mountain Trout

We like to can at least half of our catches. Canned mountain trout is delicious and can be used in any recipe calling for tuna fish or canned salmon. This is how it is done:

Clean fish and cut into pieces about 1 inch shorter than a pint jar. Soak the fish in a salt water brine (1 cup of salt to 1 gallon of water) for 1 hour. Drain well. Pack the fish in the jars. Add 1 tablespoon of cooking oil to each jar. Seal tightly. Process for 90 minutes at 10 pounds of pressure. Use in any recipe calling for tuna fish or canned salmon . . . or just enjoy "as is."

TROUT
SALAD OIL
SALT

Mackinaw trout make Odell Lake interesting fishing.

RECIPE GUIDE

VEGETABLES

〰〰〰〰〰〰〰〰〰〰〰〰〰〰〰〰〰〰〰〰〰〰〰〰

There are times when I believe that the homesteaders who cleared and tilled the soil in Central Oregon must have felt as though the Good Lord used this area for a rock disposal. Man, being the energetic soul he is, has cleared and made some mighty fine fields in portions of it, but for the greater part it is best left "as is" and enjoyed for what it is—one of the most popular recreation areas in the Northwest. This is much the way it is with vegetables. Generally they are best cooked and served "as is," with a bit of butter and seasoning to taste; or served with a cream sauce, either plain or touched up with a grating of cheese. For more energetic souls, following are some interesting things you can do with vegetables.

123. Artichokes

Remove the large outside leaves and cut off the stem close to the base. Clip the hooked tips of the leaves and remove the prickly choke at the center of the head. Then tie the head with a string to help retain its shape. Plunge it into boiling salted water and cook 30 to 45 minutes—or until tender. Cooking time depends on size and tenderness of the vegetable itself. Remove the string and drain well. It is now ready to serve with butter, etc., or you could chill, fill the bottom with crab meat, and serve with French dressing or mayonnaise.

ARTICHOKES
BUTTER
(CRAB MEAT)
(FRENCH
  DRESSING)
(MAYON-
  NAISE)

124. Creamed Asparagus

In the spring, I always think of my mother and her fondness for asparagus. Her cherished asparagus bed gave us many delicious meals, as well as beauty for our home. As the season progressed, a lovely bouquet of roses and daisies, interlaced with asparagus ferns, graced our table daily; and our supper often consisted of creamed asparagus on toast, garnished with egg slices—if the hens were doing their bit. We always lingered over a cup of tea; Mother humored our children's game of "reading" each other's tea leaves. We shared the events of the day as we sat around the old oak table with its faded oil cloth. From the kitchen window we could see the sun set serenely behind a field of corn. As the light went out of the sky, we would light the old kerosene lamp and go about our kitchen chores.

Creamed asparagus made the way my mother made it was a simple dish, but food simply prepared is usually the best. To begin with, we made the toast, buttering the bread well and placing it on a cookie sheet in the oven of the wood range. We burned cobs for a quick heat, and they were easily available at that time in the Midwest. The nearest thing I can do now to obtain the flavor of that toast, is to make toast with the broiler. As for the creamed asparagus . . . it was really very simple:

Wash the fresh asparagus well, being careful to remove all soil from the tips. Peel the stalk below the tips if the outer skin is tough. Snap the tougher portion off. In a heavy skillet or saucepan, place just enough water to cover the bottom of the utensil. Place the tougher stalks carefully in the skillet. Lay the delicate spears on top so they will cook in the steam. Season lightly with a sprinkling of salt. Cover with a tight-fitting lid and cook over medium heat until the stalks are tender. Do be careful not to over-cook; 15 to 20 minutes is usually sufficient. You may need to add more water, but use it sparingly. When the stalks are tender, there should be very little water left. For every 2 cups of cooked asparagus, add:

2 cups of milk
2 generous tablespoons of butter
⅛ teaspoon black pepper
Make a thickening by mixing together until smooth:
⅛ cup of flour
¼ cup of water

Asparagus
Milk
Butter
Salt
Pepper
Flour

Bring the milk and asparagus to a boil and add the thickening gradually, stirring constantly. Let the mixture simmer gently for just a minute or two. Serve on triangles of toast, and perhaps you, too, will want to garnish with egg slices.

————◆————

Tender, delicate spears will cook to perfection if prepared this way: Do not snap the stalks off. Tie the stalks in a bunch and place upright on a rack in the bottom part of a double boiler. Add water to the depth of the stalks only. Invert the top part of the double boiler and use as a deep lid to cover the stalks. The delicate spears will cook in the steam.

Following is the quickest way I know to make Creamed Asparagus. Simmer together:

1 (15-ounce) can of asparagus, drained
½ cup of the water drained from the asparagus
1 can of Cream of Celery Soup
Serve on hot, buttered toast squares.

Asparagus
Cream of
  Celery
  Soup
Toast
Butter

125. Dried Beans

There is something about a pot of beans simmering on the stove that makes a house seem like a home. I don't know why; it just does!

Dried beans, such as kidney beans, black-eyed beans, lima beans, and navy beans, are all high in protein and make an excellent substitute for the meat course. Easy to prepare, they are basically all prepared in the same manner.

First wash the beans in cold water. Then:
  1. Soak overnight in cold water. This cuts down on cooking time.

2. Pick over carefully to remove any bits of stone or pod.
3. Cook over moderate heat to retain the vitamins.
4. Cook until just tender not mushy (generally takes 1½ to 2 hours).
5. For tender beans in a hurry, add the seasonings and bacon fat during the last half hour of cooking. Fat tends to cling to the beans and will prolong cooking time if added too soon.

Such things as green pepper strips, salt pork, onion, and tomatoes just naturally go hand in hand with dried beans of all kinds. However, the combinations and amounts are strictly a matter of family preference. For example, we like Red Beans and Salt Pork prepared this way:

126. Red Beans and Salt Pork

Prepare the red beans according to the basic instructions in Recipe No. 125. When the beans are tender add 1 teaspoon sugar for every 2 cups of red beans. Dice and brown gently ¼ pound of salt pork. To the beans, add:

RED BEANS
SALT PORK
SUGAR
ONION

1 small onion, minced fine
¼ cup fat from the salt pork
salt pork giblets

Continue cooking until the beans are quite tender and the water is mostly absorbed. Serves 4, even with requests for "more."

You might prefer to add a can of tomatoes to Red Beans and Salt Pork, or use navy beans instead of red beans.

127. Creamed Fresh Lima Beans

Shell the lima beans (frozen ones may be used) and cook them in slightly salted boiling water just until the beans are tender. This usually takes about 20 minutes. When the beans are tender, the liquid should be absorbed.

FRESH LIMA
BEANS
CREAM
SALT
PEPPER
BUTTER

Season with salt, pepper, and a lump of butter. Add ½ cup of rich milk or cream to every 10 ounces of lima beans. Heat just to the boiling point and serve immediately.

128. Green Beans

No matter what the experts say about being careful not to overcook vegetables, I like green beans the way we had them when I was a little girl, and an electric skillet is the ideal pan to use.

Slice and brown an onion in a small amount of bacon fat. Add frozen or fresh green beans and 4 or 5 slices of bacon. Put the lid on, set the control on low heat, and cook 3 to 4 hours. About once every hour, add ½ cup of water. During the last hour of cooking, add whole small potatoes and season with salt and pepper. At this point, the green beans, onions, and bacon have begun to make a rich brown sauce of their own juices.

GREEN BEANS
ONIONS
BACON FAT
BACON
POTATOES

You'll just have to try it sometime to know how good it is. It's a meal in itself and because of requiring very little attention, it makes ideal busy-day fare.

———◆———

129. Pickled Green Beans

Put 4 cups of canned green beans (drained well) into a large jar. Bring the following ingredients to a boil:

1½ cups cider vinegar
¼ cup brown sugar
¼ teaspoon salt
⅛ teaspoon pepper
¼ teaspoon allspice
small stick of cinnamon
1 teaspoon whole cloves

GREEN BEANS
  (CANNED)
VINEGAR
BROWN SUGAR
SALT
PEPPER
ALLSPICE
STICK
  CINNAMON
WHOLE
  CLOVES

Pour the mixture over the green beans and store in the refrigerator for at least 12 hours before using. Can be served "as is" with slices of fresh onion or in a combination salad.

130. Fresh Beets

In this "time-saver" day and age, most of us use canned beets. Cooking fresh beets, however, is simply a matter of boiling them. Wash the fresh beets well and cook with the skins on and at least 2 inches of the stem on. Add a tablespoon of vinegar to the water in which they are cooked. This helps to retain their color. Cover the beets with water and boil until they are tender. It takes about 40 minutes for young beets but as much as 2 hours for winter beets. When the beets are tender, plunge them into cold water and "slip" the skins. They are now ready for use.

131. Pickled Beets

Pickled beets are quick and easy if you save the pickle vinegar from a jar of sweet pickles, bring to a boil and pour over drained, canned, sliced beets. Stored in the refrigerator in a covered container, they will keep 3 to 4 weeks.

CANNED BEETS
SWEET PICKLE
VINEGAR

If you want to make your own vinegar solution, a tasty combination is:

COOKED OR CANNED BEETS
VINEGAR
SUGAR
SALT
CINNAMON
ALLSPICE
VINEGAR

½ cup sugar
½ teaspoon salt
stick of cinnamon
½ teaspoon allspice
½ cup vinegar
1 cup water

You may need to dilute with beet juice. Bring just to the boiling point to dissolve the sugar. Never boil for this will make the vinegar strong. This amount of pickling solution will cover 3 cans of sliced beets.

132. Broccoli with Lemon Butter

Fresh broccoli stalks or "little trees" as our children used to call them, should be washed well and the tougher bottoms of the stems re-

BROCCOLI
BUTTER
LEMON

moved. Tie the broccoli stalks in bunches; stand them upright on a rack in a pan with a tight-fitting lid. Cook in a small amount of water with the stems cooking in the water and the flowerheads cooking in the steam . . . takes 20 to 30 minutes, depending on the age of the broccoli. Serve with lemon butter made by whipping together until fluffy:

¼ cup butter

Few gratings of lemon rind

2 teaspoons lemon juice

Many times, vegetables are literally ruined in the cooking. Basically, without going into much detail about vitamin loss, there are only four things you need to remember:

1. *Serve unpeeled as often as possible.*
2. *Do not leave vegetables standing in water (the vitamins actually dissolve).*
3. *Use the least water necessary, cooking in steam when at all possible.*
4. *Salt just before serving. When salt is added during the cooking time, vitamins and juices are drawn out and lost.*

133. Brussels Sprouts

Wash Brussels sprouts, removing any discolored leaves. Cut off stems and cook quickly in a small amount of water until tender. It takes 10 to 20 minutes, depending on the age of the sprouts. There are many easy and tasty ways to serve Brussels sprouts, such as:

1. Saute´ equal amounts of Brussels sprouts and chestnuts in butter. . . . Makes a good vegetable dish for holiday fare.

2. Serve with Lemon Butter (Recipe No. 132) and garnish with crisp bacon bits.

3. Season with salt, pepper, and butter. Sprinkle generously with grated cheese. Place under the broiler just long enough to start the cheese melting.

4. Yes, Brussels sprouts can even be deep-fat fried. Dip in beaten egg, roll in fine bread crumbs and fry in deep fat until a delicate brown. Sprinkle with Parmesan cheese.

134. Sweet & Sour Cabbage

In the winter months you can't be too careful about seeing to it that your family's diet includes plenty of Vitamin C. Orange juice and tomato juice are excellent sources, but it takes 2 glasses of tomato juice to obtain the same amount of Vitamin C as there is in 1 glass of orange juice. An often neglected source of Vitamin C is cabbage. Cabbage is not only high in Vitamin C content, it is low in calories—only 15 per cup—which all adds up to making it worth while to find ways that your family will enjoy it. We like it this way:

Shred a medium-size head of cabbage into a heavy saucepan. Add just enough water to prevent sticking, put the lid on, and simmer until tender. The cabbage will have a transparent look when done. Drain and keep hot.

Mix together:

1 teaspoon brown sugar
½ teaspoon salt
dash of pepper
¼ teaspoon paprika
¼ teaspoon dry mustard

CABBAGE
BROWN SUGAR
SALT
PEPPER
PAPRIKA
DRY MUSTARD
VINEGAR
BACON

Dice 8 strips of bacon and fry until nice and crisp. Add:

The brown sugar and spice mixture
3 tablespoons vinegar
1 tablespoon water

Heat to the boiling point and pour it over the hot, cooked cabbage. Serve at once to 4 hungry people.

135. Sauerkraut Salad

This salad recipe is "extra special." It was given to me by my sister-in-law, who got it from our other sister-in-law, who got it from her son-in-law's mother. Now that's what I call a real test! It's a simple salad to make and I think you would like it even if you didn't like sauerkraut:

Mix all together:
1½ cups chopped celery
1½ cups chopped onions
  1 (2-ounce) jar of pimento (chopped
    fine)
  1 cup sugar
  2 (1-pound) cans of sauerkraut
Let stand 12 hours to blend the flavors.

SAUERKRAUT
CELERY
ONION
PIMENTO
SUGAR

It's wonderful with hamburgers and makes a good salad when serving pot roast. It is ideal to take camping. In fact, it's a very special salad. It is not only unusual; it is also colorful—and just as good to eat as it is to look at. As I mentioned . . . it is what you would call In-law tested, and that is good enough for me.

136. Steamed Carrots

Wash and scrub the carrots. In the top part of a double boiler, place:
1 pound of sliced carrots (may be left whole
  if they are young and tender)
¼ cup water

CARROTS
SALT

Cover with a tight-fitting lid and cook over boiling water for 10 to 15 minutes, or until tender. Add:
½ teaspoon salt
Carrots are very versatile. At this point they can be served any number of ways, such as:
1. Seasoned with Lemon Butter (Recipe 132).
2. Sprinkled lightly with sugar and simmered in a small amount of butter until glazed.
3. Added to a thin white sauce, or if it is a "hurry-up affair," added to Cream of Celery Soup diluted with milk.
4. Mix with Cream of Cheese Soup for quick Carrots au Gratin.
5. Mint Butter? . . . just add 1 tablespoon of finely chopped mint leaves to Lemon Butter.

137. Baked Carrots

Preparing vegetables by coating lightly with cooking oil and baking in a covered casserole dish is highly recommended for there is very little loss of vitamin content. The following recipe is a tasty example:

Wash and scrape 1 pound of small carrots. Place in a baking dish. Dot with butter and sprinkle with salt. Cover with either 1 cup of canned apricot or peach syrup from canned fruit. Cover with tight-fitting lid and bake in a 375-degree oven until tender . . . normally takes about 30 minutes. Uncover during the last 10 minutes of baking to give them that golden-brown glow.

CARROTS
CANNED APRICOT OR PEACH SYRUP
BUTTER
SALT

138. Pickled Carrots

Next time you are busy washing and freezing endless rows of carrots, and want to do something different with them, make carrot pickles. Cook small carrots until tender in a spiced syrup just as you would pickled peaches. Be careful not to overcook, for you want the carrots to retain their firmness.

Cook 1 pound of small whole carrots until crisply tender. While the carrots are cooking, make a syrup by mixing together:

6 cups sugar
1 cup vinegar
1 cup water

CARROTS
SUGAR
VINEGAR
WHOLE MACE
WHOLE ALLSPICE
STICK CINNAMON
WHOLE CLOVES

Tie the following spices together in a cloth bag and add to the syrup:

2 teaspoons whole mace
1 teaspoon whole allspice
3 sticks of cinnamon
1 teaspoon whole cloves

Bring just to the boiling point. Add the cooked, drained, carrots to the spicy syrup and simmer together for 5 minutes. Using kitchen tongs, pack the carrots into ½-pint jars. Ladle the boiling syrup over the carrots and seal.

139. Cauliflower

1. Soak cauliflower head-down in heavily salted water for 30 minutes to drive out any insects.
2. Add 1 tablespoon vinegar or lemon juice to the cooking water. This keeps the cauliflower from turning yellow.

CAULIFLOWER
VINEGAR
OR LEMON
JUICE

3. Cook whole heads 15 to 20 minutes. Be careful not to overcook.
4. If divided into flowerets, only 8 to 10 minutes' cooking time is required.
5. Cauliflower is best when cooked in a tightly covered container in a very small amount of water.
6. Simple seasonings are best, such as:
   A. Butter, salt, and pepper.
   B. A simple cheese sauce or grating of cheese.
   C. Lemon Butter. (In fact, we like Lemon Butter with all vegetables.)

140. Cauliflower Salad

Cauliflower doesn't *have* to be cooked. Toss together lightly:

½ head cauliflower, divided into flowerets
2 Roman Beauty apples, unpeeled and diced
1 cup celery, diced
1 green pepper, cut into slices
1 small onion, thinly sliced

CAULIFLOWER
ROMAN
 BEAUTY
 APPLES
CELERY
GREEN
 PEPPER
ONION
SUGAR
VINEGAR
SALAD OIL
DRY MUSTARD
CELERY SEED
SALT
COARSE
 PEPPER

Serve with a dressing made like this: beat together until well blended:

½ cup sugar
1 teaspoon dry mustard
1 teaspoon salt
¼ teaspoon coarsely ground black pepper
⅓ cup vinegar
⅔ cup salad oil
1 teaspoon celery seed

141. Creamed Celery

I always think of celery as being crisp and crunchy, served in salads, or as appetizers. This doesn't really do the flavorful vegetable justice though, for it can also be boiled, creamed, or baked. Many vegetables are "still better" when creamed and served on toast. Following recipe is one of the best of this type that I know of:

Cook 2 cups of sliced celery until tender, in a small amount of water. This takes 10 to 15 minutes. While the celery is cooking, saute:

2 tablespoons butter	
2 tablespoons finely minced onion	
1 large green pepper, diced	CELERY
When the celery is tender, add:	ONION
the hot onion and green pepper	GREEN PEPPER
1 tablespoon pimento, diced (Pour a small amount of sweet pickle juice or vinegar over any remaining pimento . . . It will keep indefinitely in the refrigerator.)	PIMENTO BUTTER CREAM OF MUSHROOM SOUP
1 can Cream of Mushroom Soup	MILK
1 cup milk	

Bring just to the boiling point and serve on buttered toast.

142. Corn Casserole

A vegetable casserole is usually just right when the main fare is light. . . .

Combine the following ingredients and place in a buttered casserole dish:

2 cups milk	WHOLE-KERNEL CORN
½ green pepper, chopped or sliced	
1 tablespoon chopped onion	MILK
½ pimento, minced fine	GREEN PEPPER
½ teaspoon salt	ONION
⅛ teaspoon pepper	PIMENTO
2 eggs, well beaten	EGGS
1½ cups well-drained whole kernel corn	SALT/PEPPER

Place casserole dish in a pan of hot water and bake in a 375-degree oven about 30 minutes, or until custard is set.

143. Corn Fritters

Sift together:
  1 cup flour
  ½ teaspoon baking powder
  ¼ teaspoon salt
  1 tablespoon sugar
Mix together and add to the dry ingredients:
  2 eggs, well beaten
  ½ cup milk
Fold in:
  1 cup whole kernel corn (well drained).
Drop by teaspoonfuls on a hot, well-greased griddle or pan. Brown on both sides and serve with pot roast, or perhaps baked ham. Served with fruit jelly they are delicious.

WHOLE KERNEL CORN
FLOUR
BAKING POWDER
SALT
SUGAR
EGGS
MILK

144. Succotash

Saute':
  2 tablespoons finely minced salt pork
Add:
  1½ cups canned lima beans, drained
  1½ cups canned whole kernel corn, drained
  ⅔ cup milk
  ½ teaspoon sugar
  ¼ teaspoon salt
  ⅛ teaspoon black pepper
Simmer together for about 5 minutes. Serves 4.

WHOLE KERNEL CORN
LIMA BEANS
SALT PORK
MILK
SUGAR
SALT
PEPPER

145. Marinated Cucumbers and Onions

Cucumbers can be boiled until tender and seasoned with cream, salt, and pepper. For that matter, they can be fried by dipping thick slices, first in beaten egg, then in crumbs, and fried quickly in deep fat. But when it's all said and done, they

*are at their best when served raw with things like tomatoes,
green peppers, radishes and onions.*

*Marinated cucumbers and onions will keep well in the re-
frigerator for 7 to 10 days. Good with meat of any kind, they
are made like this:*
Clean and peel:
    6 large cucumbers
    6 large onions
Slice thinly into a ½ gallon jar. Cover with a
solution of:
    1 cup vinegar
    3 cups water
    4 teaspoons salt
    1 teaspoon seasoned pepper (can be omitted)

CUCUMBERS
ONIONS
VINEGAR
SALT
PEPPER

Let stand in the refrigerator for at least 12 hours before serving. Drain the cucumbers and onions as needed.

146. Southern Style Eggplant

*When buying an eggplant, choose one that is heavy, firm,
smooth, and a dark purple in color. Eggplant, tomatoes, green
pepper, and onions complement each other in a way that tanta-
lizes the taste buds when prepared in this way:*
Dice into small pieces and fry until crisp:
    2 slices bacon
Remove the bacon and drain on absorbent
paper. In the bacon fat, sauté:
    1 small onion, diced
    1 green pepper, diced
Add:
    ½ teaspoon salt
    ¼ teaspoon pepper
    1 cup canned tomatoes

EGGPLANT
BACON
ONIONS
GREEN
    PEPPER
CANNED
    TOMATOES
SALT
PEPPER

    1 medium sized eggplant, cut into ½-inch cubes (If the
        eggplant is tender and young, it is not necessary to peel)
Simmer together 15 minutes, or until the eggplant is tender.
Add the bacon pieces and serve at once. Serves 4.

147. French-Fried Eggplant

It's all a matter of opinion, of course, but frying seems to bring out the flavor in eggplant.

Peel and cut the eggplant into ¼-inch sticks just as you would French-fried potatoes. Dip the sticks in beaten egg and roll them in crumbs. Fry in hot fat, 2 to 4 minutes. The eggplant sticks will be delicate, brown, and crisp. Serve hot with a sprinkling of salt and pepper.

EGGPLANT
FAT
EGGS
CRUMBS
SALT
PEPPER

148. Hominy, Ham, and Cheese Timbales

Hominy, seasoned with meat drippings, salt, and pepper, is often used as a substitute for potatoes. A starchy vegetable, hominy can almost be the main fare:

Beat until thick and foamy:

   2 eggs

Add:

   2 cups drained hominy

   1 cup milk

   ⅔ cup grated cheese

   1 cup diced ham, pre-cooked

   1 teaspoon salt

   1 small green pepper, diced

   1 ounce pimento, diced

HOMINY
EGGS
HAM
CHEESE
MILK
GREEN
  PEPPER
PIMENTO
SALT
CHILI SAUCE

Pour into individual baking dishes. Place in a pan of hot water and bake in a 350-degree oven for 30 minutes or until firm. Serve with chili sauce.

149. Kale

This vegetable dish is one that makes good use of the left-over ham bone and giblets from a baked ham. If necessary, a ham bone can be purchased. Just ask the butcher if you do not find one on display. Cook the ham bone (or you could use pork hocks) until tender and use like this:

Buy 1½ pounds of kale that is dark bluish-green in color. Strip the leaves from the tough middle ribs. Discard any yellowed leaves. Put in a kettle with a tight-fitting lid and add:

3 cups water (use the ham broth if you cooked the ham bone)	KALE HAM BONE
1 ham bone and giblets from a baked ham	HAM GIBLETS
2 whole cloves	CLOVES, WHOLE
1 small onion, grated fine	ONION
1 teaspoon salt	SALT
¼ teaspoon pepper	PEPPER

Cover and simmer together gently for about ½ hour. Serve liquid and all, with corn bread. The men of the house will usually ask for just a wee bit of vinegar.

150. Mushroom Puffs

Canned mushrooms, drained and sauteed in butter just long enough to heat them through, add immeasurably to Main Fare such as scrambled eggs, rice, spaghetti, and meat sauces; and they can be used without reservation to add a touch of the "gourmet" to beef.

Fresh cap mushrooms, available the year round on the market, can and should be prepared quickly. Peel the skin from the caps and cut off the tough end of the stems. Large ones can be sliced and small ones are best left whole. Whether you elect to saute' or boil in a small amount of water, only 5 to 10 minutes' cooking time is needed, for overcooking toughens mushrooms.

Hot Mushroom Puffs can be that "talked about" something special for a Buffet Dinner:

Cook together:	MUSHROOMS EGG
2 tablespoons flour	MILK
2 tablespoons butter	CRACKER CRUMBS
½ teaspoon salt	FLOUR
⅛ teaspoon pepper	BUTTER
Quickly add:	SALT
½ cup milk	PEPPER
Cook until thick. Cool completely and add:	

1 egg, beaten
1 cup chopped mushrooms, canned or fresh
¼ cup fine cracker crumbs
Form into small balls and roll in fine cracker crumbs and
deep-fat fry. Drain and serve while hot. Mushroom Puffs can
be prepared in advance and reheated for 5 minutes in a 400-
degree oven at serving time. This recipe makes about 24
hors d'oeuvres, but there are never enough to satisfy those who
enjoy them.

151. Shaggy Mane Mushrooms

*We like to seek our own mushrooms. This is a project in
which it is better to have someone who "knows" go with you
the first few times.* Some Edible Mushrooms and How to Cook
Them *by Nina Lane Faubion is a good book for the novice. It
will help you identify the "good" from the "bad." Shaggy
Mane Mushrooms look like little droopy umbrellas. They
grow in bunches and seem to abound in the red cinders along
mountainous roads. Once you find them, they are easy to
process.*

To freeze: Wash and pack in freezer containers. Cover with water to which you have added 2 teaspoons of ascorbic acid powder for every quart of water. That's it!
Plan on a maximum of 3 months' storage.

SHAGGY MANE
MUSHROOMS
ASCORBIC
ACID
POWDER

They are a very delicate mushroom and tend to darken if kept
for a longer period of time. Once they begin to darken, they
turn black quickly and form an inky substance—which the
homesteaders of yesteryear used for ink. I always try to keep
ours either in the quick-freeze section of the freezer or directly
on the shelves which contain freezer coils.

To cook: These delicate mushrooms are best dipped in beaten egg, coated with flour, seasoned with salt and pepper, and carefully fried to a golden brown on each side.

MUSHROOMS
EGG
FLOUR
SHORTENING
SALT
PEPPER

152. Morel Mushrooms

Another favorite with us is the Morel Mushroom. They look like sponges. In Eastern Oregon, they are found in the early spring along the snow line as you leave the plateau and start up into the mountains. They are easy to store for good eating all year round. Just use the old Indian method of drying:

To store: Soak freshly gathered Morel Mushrooms in a solution of salt water (1 tablespoon salt to a gallon of water) to remove the insects and soil from the crevices. Drain, pat dry, and string them as you would popcorn. Hang in the open air to dry. Store the dried mushrooms in a paper bag in a cool, dry place until needed.

MOREL
  MUSHROOMS
SALT

Dried mushrooms may be grated with a nut grater and used in seasoning, or you can soak the dried mushrooms in water for 8 to 10 hours to restore them to their original moist state. Use in any recipe calling for mushrooms.

To cook: We like to slice the Morel Mushrooms in half, dip in beaten eggs, then in fine cracker crumbs. Fry until a golden brown on each side.

MOREL
  MUSHROOMS
EGG
CRACKER
  CRUMBS

153. French Onion Soup

French Onion Soup served with toasted, well-buttered slices of French bread adds gusto to any meal:

Slice 1 pound of onions into very thin slices. Brown the onions slowly in ½ cup butter.

Stir in:
  1 tablespoon flour
  1 teaspoon salt
  ¼ teaspoon coarse ground pepper
Add, all at once:
  8 cups beef stock (if no beef stock is available, you can substitute with canned consomme)

ONIONS
BUTTER
FLOUR
BEEF STOCK
  OR CANNED
  CONSOMME
SALT
COARSE
  PEPPER

Stir until the beef stock begins to bubble. Turn the heat on low and let simmer for 30 minutes.

154. Creamed Onions

Cook 6 to 8 small onions in just enough water to prevent sticking. When the onions are tender but firm, add:

1 cup milk
½ teaspoon salt
⅛ teaspoon pepper
⅛ teaspoon paprika

Simmer gently until the milk is partly absorbed. Serves 4.

SMALL
  ONIONS
MILK
SALT
PEPPER
PAPRIKA

155. French-Fried Onion Rings

There is no need to go to all the fuss of batters. These are simple to do and are everything they should be.

Cut peeled onions into thick slices. Separate into rings and dip in cream or canned milk. Drain off excess milk, dip in flour, and deep-fat fry. Drain on absorbent paper and season with salt. It's as easy as that!

ONIONS
MILK
FLOUR
SHORTENING
SALT

———◆———

Leftover onions can be sliced and dried in the oven heat that is left after baking. Let the slices dry to a golden brown. Store in a tightly covered jar for use in soups and stews . . . and, to remove onion odor from your hands: wet your hands, sprinkle with baking soda, and then rub your hands together as you would to lather soap. Rinse in warm water. The soda emulsifies the skin's natural oils which hold onto those odors. When you rinse your hands, the odor rinses away.

156. Fried Parsnips

Peel and grate tender young parsnips with
a coarse grater. Fry in a small amount of
butter or bacon fat until tender, brown, and tasty. Delicious
with baked ham.

| PARSNIPS |
| BUTTER |

*Parsnips should always be steamed, never boiled. Place
parsnips on a rack in a kettle with a tight-fitting lid. Pour a
small amount of water in the bottom of the kettle and cook
over medium heat until the parsnips are tender. When they
are tender, peel and split them lengthwise. If the centers are
tough and woody, they should be removed with the tip of a
knife. At this point, they can be seasoned with butter, salt
and pepper. For that matter, they can be creamed, scalloped,
or baked.*

157. Creamed Peas

*Peas lose their natural sweetness quickly after being picked.
They should be kept cool and cooked as quickly as possible.
A pound of fresh peas will yield a good rounded cup of shelled
peas. Cook in as little water as possible. Usually takes about
15 minutes for peas to become tender. Creamed peas are easy
to prepare when made this way.*

Cook 1 cup of shelled peas until tender in a
small amount of water. Add:

    1 cup milk
    1 tablespoon butter
    ½ teaspoon salt
    ⅛ teaspoon pepper
    ¼ teaspoon sugar

| PEAS |
| MILK |
| BUTTER |
| FLOUR |
| SALT |
| PEPPER |
| SUGAR |

Bring to a boil and thicken by adding slowly, a flour and water
paste, made by mixing together 1 tablespoon flour and ¼ cup
water. Stir constantly until the creamy sauce bubbles and
thickens. Makes 4 servings.

158. Baked Potatoes

*We natives of Eastern Oregon who take this land of the
big, blue sky and majestic snow-capped Cascades for granted
also take Roy Bradetich and his famed Eastern Oregon potatoes for granted. Just meeting Roy, a native of Austria, can
prove to be quite an experience.*

*Roy's arrival in Eastern Oregon as a boy of fourteen in
1923, his struggles and triumphs with the language barrier,
the sand, sagebrush, and water, make an interesting story—but
here it is enough to applaud his contribution to the potato
industry. A second helping of his famous Eastern-Oregon-
grown potatoes is as hard to resist as the twinkle in his eyes
and his broken dialect. As for his preference in cooking
methods, Roy says he and his wife like them best baked:*

Scrub long, medium-sized potatoes with a
metal pot cleaner or a good stiff brush, then
rub shortening on the potatoes. This is a good
| POTATOES
| SHORTENING
| BUTTER

way to use the bacon drippings that seem to accumulate so
quickly. Place on a baking sheet and bake at 400 degrees for
½ hour. At this point, prick each potato with a fork to allow
the steam to escape. Continue baking for 30 more minutes, or
until tender. Cut a gash crosswise in the top and insert a piece
of butter. Serve at once.

For tasty Main Fare, cut a large gash crosswise in the
baked potato. Top with quick-melting cheese. Place under the
broiler just long enough to melt the cheese. For that matter,
Baked Potatoes served with fried eggs and a tossed salad do
make a meal—and a good one too!

If you prefer to serve Baked Potatoes "stuffed," cut the
baked potato in half. Scoop out the insides. Mash and add
2 tablespoons of milk, 1 teaspoon butter, and ¼ teaspoon salt
for each potato. Beat together until fluffy. You can add bits
of green pepper, diced onion . . . maybe you would prefer
chopped mushrooms or really adventure and add chopped
anchovies. Refill the potato shells and place under the broiler
for just a quick minute, or return to the oven, turn the heat up
to 450 degrees and let them reheat for about 10 minutes.

159. Quick-Baked Potatoes

While I'm talking about Baked Potatoes, | POTATOES
another excellent (and quick) way with them | BACON FAT
is . . . peel and quarter potatoes. Arrange the quartered potatoes in a baking dish. Brush the potato tops with melted bacon
fat. Sprinkle with salt and pepper and bake in a 400-degree
oven until tender. Takes 30 to 40 minutes depending on the
size of the potatoes. Brush with bacon fat once or twice during
the baking. Prepared this way, they are good served any time
you would ordinarily serve baked potatoes . . . for that matter,
they are good any time!

160. Boiled Potatoes

To peel, or not to peel . . . only you can | POTATOES
decide, but do serve them, well-scrubbed, in |
the skins as often as possible for greater vitamin retention.
Choose potatoes of a uniform size. Scrub them well. Cook,
using one of the following methods:

Pressure cooker...8 minutes
Steamer over boiling water......40 minutes or until tender
Saucepan with a tight-fitting lid..............15 to 20 minutes

161. Mashed Potatoes

Boil the potatoes in a small amount of water. | POTATOES
When the potatoes are tender, drain off any | MILK
excess water. Save the water to be used in | BUTTER
making breads, cakes, etc. Potato water added | SALT
to the milk in your favorite cake recipe will add moistness to
the cake. For the fluffiest potatoes ever, keep the potatoes over
low heat and whip or beat until they are fluffy. Add milk,
butter, and salt, allowing 1 tablespoon of milk, 1 teaspoon
butter, and ¼ teaspoon salt for each potato used. Beat until
creamy and fluffy and pile lightly on a pre-heated dish.

162. Fried Potatoes

I could make a meal on Fried Potatoes, a poached egg, and cole slaw. . . .

Wash, peel, and slice potatoes very thin. It is better to chill the potatoes in the refrigerator before peeling and prepare and cook them while they are still cold than it is to slice the potatoes into cold water, allowing them to stand for a long period of time. Any time you let pared vegetables stand in water, you literally wash the vitamins away.

POTATOES
SHORTENING

Melt fat in a heavy skillet to a depth of ⅛ inch. Drop sliced potatoes into the hot fat and fry over medium heat. Turn the potatoes from time to time to prevent sticking and to allow them to brown on all sides as much as possible. Season to taste.

163. Batter Potatoes

Mix together:

POTATOES
FLOUR
BAKING
   POWDER
SALT
SHORTENING

    1 teaspoon baking powder
    1 cup flour
    ½ teaspoon salt

Add just enough water to make a sticky batter. Slice potatoes very thin. Dip each slice of potato in batter and fry in deep fat until a golden brown on each side.

164. Potatoes Au Gratin

You don't need a white sauce to make good Potatoes au Gratin. Here's how:

Peel 3 medium-sized potatoes and cut in ½-inch cubes. Cook in boiling water until tender, using just enough water to keep them from cooking dry. When the potatoes are tender, cover with milk and turn the heat low.

POTATOES
MILK
CHEESE
FLOUR
SALT
PEPPER
BUTTER

Add:

    ½ teaspoon salt
    ⅛ teaspoon pepper
    1 tablespoon butter

Make a thickening with 2 tablespoons of flour and ⅓ cup water. When the milk and potatoes reach the boiling point, stir in just enough of the thickening for the desired consistency. Let the mixture bubble good, stirring constantly. Only takes a minute. Remove from the heat and stir in 1 cup grated cheese.

Serve plain or garnish with sliced, hard-boiled eggs and pimento strips. Makes a complete meal when served with a tossed salad, crisp bacon strips, hot rolls, and stewed fruit.

165. Scalloped Potatoes

Scalloped Potatoes make tasty Main Fare when baked with slices of ham or cubed cheese as a part of the arrangement. Basic Scalloped Potatoes go well with any meal:

Peel and slice potatoes in ¼-inch slices. Allow 1 potato per person. In a buttered casserole dish, place a layer of potato slices, sprinkle with flour, dot with butter, and season lightly with salt and pepper. Repeat this process at least three times, or until all the potatoes have been used. Add milk until it barely reaches the top of the potatoes. Cover and bake for 1½ hours in a 350-degree oven. Remove the lid during the last 15 minutes of baking to allow the potatoes to brown lightly.

POTATOES
MILK
FLOUR
BUTTER
SALT
PEPPER

166. Spinach and Tomato Casserole

Fresh spinach should be washed thoroughly in several waters to remove the soil which tends to cling to the leaves. Shake the leaves to remove all the excess moisture. Sprinkle the spinach with a small amount of cooking oil, just as you would in making a fresh salad. Cook in as little water as possible in a saucepan with a tight-fitting lid. This method of cooking helps to seal the vitamins within and the spinach will retain its intense green coloring. Five to 15 minutes' cooking time is required for cooking leafy vegetables, all depending on whether you have shredded the leaves.

Most families prefer spinach served simply with butter, salt, pepper, and a few drops of vinegar. A Spinach and Tomato Casserole can be tempting too. This is another dish that's served with corn bread and needs little else to finish out the meal.

Absolutely drain 3 cups of cooked spinach and 3 cups of canned tomatoes. Save the broth of both to add to soups, or just mix it and drink it—no calories to speak of and it is good for you. Now, for the recipe in the making, butter a baking dish and make layers of the following ingredients in the order listed:

Drained spinach
Drained tomatoes
¼ cup of chili sauce
1 cup cracker crumbs
1 teaspoon salt
¼ teaspoon paprika

SPINACH
TOMATOES
CHILI SAUCE
CRACKER
  CRUMBS
SALT
PAPRIKA
CHEESE
BACON

Arrange a good ½ pound of cheese slices over the top. Lay 6 or 7 slices of bacon over the cheese and bake in a 325-degree oven until the cheese melts and runs down through the tomatoes and spinach and the bacon becomes crisp.

167. Steamed Squash

It would take another book to tell you "all about" squash. There are many kinds and varieties, but basically there are two types of squash available.

Summer Squash, such as Zucchini, Pattypan, and Crookneck, are extremely high in moisture content, over 90% water, and are not meant to be stored over a long period of time.

Winter squash varieties, like Hubbard, Acorn, and Sweet Potato, have tough, roughened skins and keep well for many months in a dark cool place.

Since the moisture content of squash is high, it should never be boiled. Cooking methods recommended are baking or steaming. A pound of squash will serve 3 people generously.

Wash the squash well and cut it in half. Remove all seeds and stringy portions. Cut the squash into 1-inch cubes. If young and tender, Summer Squash does not need to be peeled.

WINTER
  SQUASH OR
SUMMER
  SQUASH

The skin, too, is eaten and enjoyed. Since Winter Squash is

difficult to peel, leave the skin on until after it is cooked and then remove. Add just enough water to prevent sticking. Cover with a tight-fitting lid and let the squash cook in its own steam. Cooking time required:

Summer Squash ....15 to 20 minutes
Winter Squash ....35 to 45 minutes

168. Baked Squash

Cut squash in half. Remove all seeds and stringy parts. Cut in generous pieces. Place a small amount of water in a 9x11x2-inch baking dish. Arrange the pieces of squash in the dish. Brush with melted butter or bacon drippings and add a sprinkling of salt and pepper. Bake in a 375-degree oven, uncovered, basting occasionally with the juices in the pan. Baking time required:

SUMMER
  SQUASH OR
WINTER
  SQUASH
BUTTER OR
BACON
  DRIPPINGS
SALT
PEPPER

Summer Squash ....10 to 20 minutes
Winter Squash ....40 to 60 minutes

169. Acorn Squash
(quick and easy)

Cut 2 Acorn Squash in half. Place them cut-side down in a baking dish containing a small amount of water. This forces them to cook in their own steam and only 20 to 30 minutes baking time is required. When the squash are tender, turn them over, brush with melted butter or bacon fat; season with salt and pepper and continue baking for 10 minutes to give them a delicate brown coloring. Serves four.

ACORN
  SQUASH
BUTTER OR
BACON FAT
SALT
PEPPER

170. Baked Sweet Potatoes

Sweet potatoes should always be cooked in their jackets to preserve their natural sweetness and vitamin content.

Wash and scrub long, medium-sized Sweet Potatoes with a good stiff vegetable brush. Rub the surface of the potato with shortening. Place on a baking sheet and bake at 350 degrees for ½ hour. Prick the surface to allow the steam to escape and then continue baking for 20 to 30 minutes longer, or until tender. Baking in this way prevents sogginess.

SWEET
POTATOES
SHORTENING

171. Boiled Sweet Potatoes

Sweet Potatoes are difficult to peel and they darken rapidly once the surface is exposed to the air. Cook with the skins on, then peel. Choose potatoes of uniform size. Scrub them well. Cover with water and cook over medium heat, just until tender. As a general rule, 30 to 40 minutes cooking time is required, all depending on the size of the Sweet Potatoes. They are delicious, served "as is," with butter, salt, and pepper—or you can peel and fry them.

SWEET
POTATOES

172. Fried Sweet Potatoes

Peel the boiled Sweet Potatoes. Cut in thick slices. Brown gently on each side in a small amount of bacon fat. Sprinkle with salt and pepper. Serve with Baked Ham, Cranberry Relish, and a Tossed Green Salad.

SWEET
POTATOES
BACON FAT
SALT
PEPPER

173. Candied Sweet Potatoes

Candied Sweet Potatoes are nearly always served as a side dish with turkey and trimmings. Peel 4 boiled Sweet Potatoes and cut in half lengthwise. Place in a baking dish and cover with a syrup made of:

SWEET
POTATOES
BROWN SUGAR
CORN SYRUP
BUTTER
NUTMEG

½ cup brown sugar
¼ cup corn syrup
½ cup water

Dot with butter. Sprinkle with nutmeg and bake in a covered casserole dish for 30 to 40 minutes in a 350-degree oven. Baste frequently with the syrup.

Raising a Garden...

Raising a garden in this land of sunny blue skies, snow showers in July, twelve inches of annual rainfall, and frost eight to ten months of the year is accomplished only by those with an abundance of patience and skill.

Anything that grows under the ground, such as potatoes, carrots, turnips, etc., is unusually sweet and good—but slow-maturing, above-the-ground vegetables have many ups and downs. If your vegetable garden is down in a protected area, chances are your efforts will be rewarded. However, if you plant out in the open or on higher ground, ninety-nine times out of a hundred the frost will nip your vegetables in the bud.

We gave up the whole idea of a vegetable garden years ago and went fishing—but I still can't resist trying a tomato plant or two. I usually put them in with the petunias. The results of last year's crops are typical. Three plants equaled 3 ripe tomatoes and 32 green ones. Final results . . . one tossed salad, one meal of fried green tomatoes, and the balance in Green Tomato Relish.

174. Fried Green Tomatoes

Fried Green Tomatoes aren't something you would want every week, but on occasion, they are very tasty:

Select well-formed green tomatoes. Wash, dry, and cut into ½-inch slices. Dip in flour seasoned with salt and pepper. Fry in a small amount of shortening until a golden brown on each side.

GREEN
TOMATOES
FLOUR
SHORTENING
SALT
PEPPER

175. Green Tomato Relish

Green Tomato Relish is a welcome addition to any meal.
This recipe makes 6 pints and you'll wish it made more!

Put the following ingredients through a food chopper using
a medium blade:

12 pounds of green tomatoes
5 red peppers
6 green peppers
6 onions

Sprinkle thoroughly with ½ cup salt. Let stand
overnight. Drain *thoroughly*. Add:

5 cups sugar
1½ quarts cider vinegar
1 teaspoon ground cinnamon

Simmer slowly for 1 hour. Mix together:

1 teaspoon turmeric
1 teaspoon mustard
2 tablespoons flour

GREEN
TOMATOES
RED PEPPERS
GREEN
PEPPERS
ONIONS
VINEGAR
SALT
SUGAR
CINNAMON
TURMERIC
MUSTARD
FLOUR

Stir into the mixture and cook 15 minutes longer, stirring from
time to time to prevent sticking. Pack into hot sterilized jars
and seal at once.

176. Frozen Tomato Sauce

*A practical method of taking care of tomatoes is to freeze
them. For the most part, tomatoes are used in the form of
sauce, catsup, or tomato juice. The following recipe for Frozen
Tomato Sauce is easy and practical . . . no cooking . . . the
flavor is that of fresh tomatoes, and you have the basis for
any recipe that calls for tomatoes or Tomato Paste. If you
prefer a breakfast drink it can be mixed with other vegetable
juices or just used "as is."*

Take the whole tomatoes after they are fully
ripened and run them through a juicer or a

TOMATOES
SALT

food mixer. This separates the skins and seeds from the delicious juice and pulp. Add ½ teaspoon salt per quart of sauce
and pour into rigid containers. Allow ½ inch head space for
expansion and freeze.

177. Ripe Tomato Preserves

Ripe Tomato Preserves adds a gourmet touch to any meal (especially a winter meal) that I don't believe money can buy. . . . At any rate, I have never found this preserves on grocers' shelves in all my meanderings.

Prepare the tomatoes by washing, then scalding with boiling water to make the skins slip off easily. Cut out the stems and hard cores and put the tomatoes through a coarse grinder. If you don't have a grinder, dice them up in small chunks.

Into a large kettle, measure:

4 tablespoons lemon juice	RIPE TOMATOES
¼ cup boiling water	LEMON JUICE
⅛ teaspoon salt	SALT
1 package of pectin	PECTIN
grated rind of 1 lemon	LEMON RIND
2¼ cups ground ripe tomatoes	SUGAR

Stir well and bring to a boil. Add 3½ cups of sugar and bring to a rolling boil. Boil for exactly 4 minutes. You must stir the preserves all the time you are making it—but the whole process takes only about 6 minutes.

178. Breaded Tomatoes
("guess and by golly" method)

To 1 quart of tomatoes, add about ½ cup of sugar and a good pinch of salt. Bring to a boil, stirring from time to time so that the sugar doesn't stick.

TOMATOES
SUGAR
BREAD

When it reaches the boiling point, turn the heat down as low as you can. Tear 3 slices of bread into small pieces and stir into the tomatoes and sugar. Cover and keep hot 5 to 10 minutes while you finish up dinner—which might be a pork roast, mashed potatoes, gravy, and a simple green salad.

179. Turnip Pancakes

Turnips, like any other vegetable, should be cooked in as little water as possible. Care should be taken to not over-cook, for this brings about vitamin loss and an undesirable strong flavor. Ten to 15 minutes cooking time at a slow simmer is usually sufficient.

Turnip Pancakes, hot roast beef slices and brown gravy, complete with Jello fruit salad, all add up to a good dinner:
Mix together:

1 cup grated turnips	Turnips
1 cup grated carrots	Carrots
2 tablespoons grated onion	Onion
2 tablespoons milk	Milk
1 egg	Egg
½ teaspoon salt	Salt
Pinch of pepper	Pepper

Drop by teaspoonfuls onto a hot, well-oiled griddle. Fry over medium heat until well browned on each side.

180. Basic Tossed Salad

Whoever measured a salad? Simply said, the success of a salad lies in its crispness. Wash ingredients for tossed salad quickly to prevent loss of vitamins. Shake off any excess water and place the greens in a large plastic bag in the refrigerator to crisp. Rules for preparing a tossed salad are very easy, but each step is vital in the making of a really good tossed salad.

Greens used in making salad should be broken rather than shredded or cut. Carrots should be grated or sliced in paper-thin slices for easy chewing. At salad-making time, toss together *any or all* of the following ingredients:

(Any or All)

Lettuce (any variety of greens that you like)	Lettuce
Thinly sliced radishes	Radishes
Thinly sliced cucumbers	Cucumbers
Thin strips of green pepper	Green Pepper
Diced celery	Celery
Thinly sliced white or red onions	Onions
	Eggs
	Cheese
	Ham
	Salad Oil

For each serving, allow 1 teaspoon of salad oil. Sprinkle the oil over the greens, tossing lightly until all the ingredients are shiny with oil. Adding the oil in this manner seals the vitamins in and keeps the greens from becoming soggy when the vinegar or lemon juice is added. Hard-boiled eggs, grated cheese, and ham should be added just before serving. At this point, leave the choice of a salad dressing up to the individual.

181. Basic Dressing

Mix together and serve with oiled greens:

⅓ cup lemon juice or vinegar

1 teaspoon salt

¼ teaspoon coarse black pepper

LEMON JUICE
OR VINEGAR
SALT
BLACK PEPPER
(COARSE)

In making simple basic dressings, keep in mind a ratio of 1 part vinegar or lemon juice to 3 parts oil. Seasoning still further is a matter of taste and it is fun to experiment.

182. Sour Cream Dressing

Blend together:

⅔ cup mayonnaise

⅔ cup sour cream

1 tablespoon grated onion

1 teaspoon Beau Monde

MAYONNAISE
SOUR CREAM
ONION
BEAU MONDE

Chill for an hour and serve with crisp salad greens.

183. French Dressing

Combine together:

¾ cup sugar

¼ cup vinegar

¼ cup water

½ cup catsup

3 tablespoons lemon juice

1 tablespoon paprika

1 teaspoon salt

1 teaspoon horseradish

1/16 teaspoon garlic salt (in other words, just show it the shaker!)

1/16 teaspoon onion salt

SUGAR
VINEGAR
CATSUP
LEMON JUICE
PAPRIKA
SALT
HORSERADISH
GARLIC SALT
ONION SALT
SALAD OIL
STUFFED
GREEN
OLIVES

Beat continuously while you gradually add:

1½ cups salad oil

When the mixture is smooth and creamy, stir in:

¼ cup chopped stuffed green olives

184. Sweet Onion Dressing

Mix together:

½ cup sugar	SUGAR
½ cup vinegar	VINEGAR
1 teaspoon dry mustard	DRY MUSTARD
1 teaspoon celery seed	CELERY SEED
1 teaspoon salt	SALT
2 teaspoons grated onion	ONION
	SALAD OIL

Beat continuously while you gradually add:
  1½ cups salad oil

185. Roquefort Dressing

Thoroughly blend together:

2 cups sour cream	SOUR CREAM
½ cup mayonnaise	MAYONNAISE
1 small onion, minced fine	ONION
Juice of 1 lemon	LEMON
¼ teaspoon salt	SALT
⅛ teaspoon coarse black pepper	COARSE BLACK PEPPER
	ROQUEFORT
	CHEESE

Break ¼ -pound Roquefort Cheese into small pieces and stir in.

186. Old-Fashioned Boiled Salad Dressing

(Good on cole slaw, potato salad, or macaroni salad)
Make a paste by mixing together the following ingredients:

1 teaspoon dry mustard	MUSTARD
1 teaspoon salt	(DRY)
1 teaspoon cornstarch	SALT
1 tablespoon sugar	CORNSTARCH
⅓ cup mild vinegar	SUGAR
	VINEGAR
Beat together:	EGG YOLK
1 egg yolk	MILK
1 tablespoon milk	

Blend all the ingredients together until smooth. Pour into a
heavy saucepan (I use a cast-iron skillet) and cook over medium heat. Stir constantly until it thickens. Cook 1 minute.
Let cool and beat in 1 tablespoon cream.

RECIPE GUIDE

EGGS AND CHEESE

Selection of Eggs: I guess you have to be "grandmother age" to remember taking eggs to the store, having them candled, and being paid accordingly. Basically this is how eggs are graded, even today—though candling is no longer done by candlelight. In a very fresh egg (Grade A), the yolk is in the center of the egg and is barely visible when held between the eye and a strong light. As the egg grows older, the white becomes thin and runny and the yolk floats outward toward the shell. The flatter the yolk, the older the egg is and consequently the lower the grade. Grade B eggs, flatter and thinner and lacking in eye appeal when fried, are used in baking and in making omelets and scrambled eggs. The United States Department of Agriculture has established specifications in most states . . . not all of them, but in most of them, requiring that certain standards be met concerning both the size and grade of eggs.

When buying eggs, note whether or not they have a shiny surface. Shiny eggs have been washed and are subject to rapid deterioration. The surface of an egg should be dull. This dull, thin film is nature's way of protecting the porous shell and its contents.

If you personally want to test your eggs for freshness:

1. Examine the egg under a strong light. If it is fresh, the yolk is in the center and barely visible. . . .Or
2. Place the egg in a basin of cold water. If it is fresh it will sink and lie "flat." If it is not fresh it will stand "on end."

As to size, the following chart makes it easy to remember required weights per dozen:

Small eggs per dozen.......................18 ounces
Medium eggs per dozen..................21 ounces
Large eggs per dozen.......................24 ounces
Extra large eggs per dozen...............27 ounces

You will note there is a difference of 3 ounces per dozen between sizes. If there is less than 7¢ per dozen between sizes, it pays to buy the larger size. And while I'm thinking about it, scientists have proved that there is no difference whatsoever in the quality of white and brown eggs. The color of the shell is determined by the breed of chicken and the color of the egg yolk itself is determined by the chicken's diet.

Eggs are one of the easiest forms of protein to prepare; there is a right way and a wrong way, even to preparing an egg. Did you know an egg really shouldn't be boiled? That's right! This is what makes the whites tough and indigestible to many—and the yolks discolored.

187. Eggs Cooked in the Shell

Place eggs in cold water to a depth of 2 inches over the eggs and bring just to the boil- | EGGS
ing point over low heat. If eggs and water are both cold to start with, the shells seldom crack in the cooking. If you are in a hurry and want to put cold eggs into boiling water, slip each egg carefully into the water with a tablespoon. When the water reaches the boiling point, simmer the eggs gently, until of the desired doneness.

Soft-cooked eggs
    (both yolk and white are runny)......................1 minute
Medium-cooked eggs
    (yolk runny, white more set).............................4 minutes
Hard-cooked eggs (yolk and white both set)......8 minutes

188. Coddled Eggs

This is an ideal way of preparing eggs for
infants and for those who are on special diets. | Eggs
They are easily digested and the method is simple. Place eggs
in a saucepan and cover with boiling water. Let the eggs stand
in the boiling water 8 to 10 minutes for soft-cooked eggs and
12 minutes for medium-cooked eggs.

189. Poached Eggs

*You don't have to own an egg poacher to enjoy Poached
Eggs. Here's how:*

Place water in a skillet to a depth of 1 inch. | Eggs
Add 1 teaspoon salt and 1 teaspoon vinegar. | Salt
The vinegar will keep the whites of the eggs | Vinegar
from spreading. Bring the water to a boil. Remove from the
hot burner. Break each egg carefully into the water. When
the white is firm and a film covers the yolk, carefully remove
from the water with slotted spoon or pancake turner. Serve
with toast.

190. Scrambled Eggs

For every egg, beat in: | Egg
   1 tablespoon milk | Milk
   few grains of salt and pepper | Salt
Skillet Method: Pour beaten egg and milk | Pepper
mixture into a well-oiled, heated skillet. Cook | Shortening
slowly, scraping the sides and bottom of the skillet as the mixture thickens.

Double Boiler Method: Allow 1 teaspoon melted fat for
each egg. Melt the fat in the top part of a double boiler. Add
the egg mixture and cook over boiling water until the eggs are
creamy and thick. Stir at the end of cooking only.

191. Fried Eggs

Serve with crisp bacon strips, jelly and hot, buttered toast for a quick breakfast. The simple addition of a side dish of buttered asparagus makes a tasty menu for Sunday night fare or a light luncheon.

"Sunny Side Up": Allow 1 teaspoon of but- | EGGS
ter for each egg, plus 1 for the skillet. Heat | BUTTER
skillet to medium hot. Coat bottom of skillet well with butter. Break eggs into a saucer and then slip the eggs gently into the skillet. Add ½ teaspoon of water for each egg. Cover the skillet with a heavy serving plate and allow to cook 2 to 3 minutes, or until of the desired doneness. The whites should be firm with a thin film over the runny yolk. Serve on the hot serving plate with slices of ham, buttered toast, Oregon Grape Jelly, milk for the children, and steaming cups of hot coffee for those who enjoy it.

"Over Easy": Here, too, allow 1 teaspoon of butter for each egg and 1 for the skillet. Heat the skillet to medium hot. Coat the bottom of the skillet well with butter. I find that just as a measure of precaution against getting a bad egg, it is wise to first break the egg into a saucer and then slip it gently into the skillet. When cooking eggs "over easy" do not cover the skillet. When the whites begin to set up, gently turn the egg with a spatula and continue cooking to the desired doneness.

192. Shirred or Baked Eggs

Use individual baking dishes such as custard | EGGS
cups. Grease the baking dishes and carefully | CREAM
break 1 egg into each cup. Add 1 tablespoon | SALT
of cream and sprinkle lightly with salt and | PEPPER
pepper. Dot with butter and bake in a 350-degree oven until the whites are set. This usually takes about 15 minutes.

This method of preparation proves to be ideal when cooking eggs for a large number of people, for the eggs can be baking while you pan-fry ham slices to perfection and make toast. On the other hand, you can make it still easier by lining the custard cups with thin slices of ham. You then break the egg into the ham cup and proceed as before. Going still further with this line of thought, a hearty supper dish can be prepared by lining the cups with mashed potatoes, placing an egg in the center, adding the cream as directed, and sprinkling with a grating of cheese. Variations are endless and limited only by your imagination.

193. Basic Omelet

For some time I have believed that the superior reputation of Souffles and Omelets is over-inflated and that is just about what they are . . . over-inflated eggs. I am a firm believer in Newton's theory that whatever goes up must come down . . . and that is what usually happens to my Souffles and "puffy" Omelets, so we'll take it from there. This is a "down-to-earth" cookbook anyway. If after trying the following basic Omelet and Souffle recipes, you find yours come "down to earth" too, don't worry about it; blame it all on Newton's theory of gravity. Just eat them and enjoy them. Our favorite Omelet is made this way:

For every member of the family, plan on:

2 eggs	EGGS
2 tablespoons milk (cream or canned milk is best)	MILK SALT PEPPER
1/16 teaspoon salt	(BACON
few grains of pepper	GIBLETS)

Beat until very fluffy. Heat a well-oiled skillet until moderately hot. (A skillet with a rounded bottom works best.) Add the egg mixture. Cook over *low* heat. As it cooks, ease the mixture very gently from the sides of the skillet so that the uncooked mixture runs under. Do not cut or stir, but cook so that it remains in one large cake. When the mixture is browned on the bottom and firm on top, sprinkle with crisp bacon giblets and *start calling everybody to the table.* Fold and serve at once while it is still a thing of beauty. All joking aside, it is a wonderful dish suggesting a variety of fillings: grated cheese, chopped and sauteed mushrooms, or almost any chopped, cooked meat.

194. Basic Souffle

Since entire books have been written about Souffles, here it is enough to have a good Basic Souffle recipe and then advise you to experiment on your own. Variation in flavor is all a matter of substituting fruit juice to your liking for the milk, leaving out the vanilla, and folding in ⅔ cup of well-drained fruit just before baking. Whenever you make Fruit Souffles, add 1 tablespoon of lemon juice to the fruit juice. Brings out the flavor!

If it's a main dish you are needing, use the Basic Souffle recipe "as is," leaving out the vanilla and folding in 1 cup of chopped, cooked meat. Anyway, here's your starter:

In a saucepan, combine:

    ⅓ cup flour

    ½ cup sugar

    ⅛ teaspoon salt

Add:

    1 cup milk (a little at a time, stirring constantly so that mixture is smooth)

FLOUR
SUGAR
SALT
MILK
EGGS
CREAM OF TARTAR
VANILLA

Cook over low heat, stirring constantly, until the mixture is smooth and thick. Remove from the heat. Beat until thick and yellow:

4 egg yolks

Fold into the milk mixture and set aside to cool. It is important that you fold the mixture together, not stir. To fold a batter, you do just that. Take a wide spatula and fold the batter up and over, cutting down through the middle of the batter and up the side of the bowl each time, putting as much air into the mixture as possible. Don't overdo it. Use this up over motion just enough to blend the ingredients. While the mixture is cooling, beat until foamy:

    4 egg whites (for best results, egg whites should be room temperature)

Continue to beat until they are stiff, but not dry. As soon as they will hold their own peaks and still have a glossy look they are ready. If you continue to beat at this point, they will lose their gloss and be too dry. Cells collapse in overbeaten egg whites during baking, so it is most important to beat the egg whites to the right consistency.

Add 1 teaspoon of vanilla to the *cooled* milk and eggs. (The trick is to have the milk mixture the same temperature as the beaten egg whites.) The next and last step is simply to *fold* the egg whites into the milk mixture, using that high, "up and over" motion. The more air you incorporate into the mixture, without deflating the "puffed" whites, the higher and prettier your Souffle will be. Pour into an ungreased casserole (1½ quarts). Bake in a 325-degree oven 50 to 60 minutes. Serve to 6 hungry people immediately.

Extra Yolks and Whites

In the daily run of cooking, extra egg yolks and egg whites need to be saved for future use. There are several ways in which to do this. I find one of the most practical ways is to drop them into a small amount of boiling water. Let stand until the yolks are firm. These hard-cooked yolks can be grated and used as a garnish on salads, creamed asparagus, and potato salad. . . .

If you plan to prepare a sponge cake soon or some other recipe which requires a large number of egg yolks, left-over yolks can be placed in a small jar, covered with water, and stored in the refrigerator for a short time. I find the big draw-back to this method is that I tend to forget about their being there . . . and you know how it goes. I prefer to place them in a waxed paper cup. I stir in a few grains of salt for each egg, fasten a piece of plastic wrap over the top of the cup with a rubber band, then freeze them. When ready to use these "extra" yolks (you can do the same with whites) put them to thaw about an hour before using. You can hasten the thawing by running cold water over the cup when you first take it from the freezer. Use the egg and throw away the paper cup container. No dish to wash!

About Cheese...

Selection of Cheese: Read labels carefully when buying cheese, for here you will find helpful information. Do not confuse true dairy products with "filled" cheese products. The latter are good and have their place, but they do contain vegetable oil in place of milk fat. . . . Be careful not to confuse brand names with the cheese itself. . . . "Age" information is always indicated on the label.

Knowing what cheese to buy can be a perplexing problem, for cheeses do have to be tried and savored to see if they are to your liking. Try experimenting a little on cheeses you have not yet tried. You may find some that will hereafter be your favorites, and you will find that most cheeses have distinct personalities and flavors.

All cheese, with the exception of Parmesan, should be kept refrigerated. After using the cheese, rub the cut surface of the remaining cheese with a little butter and cover in plastic wrap or foil to prevent drying out. Mold that develops on cheese can be cut off. This does not hurt the cheese in any way. Keep limburger or strong cheeses in a jar with a tight-fitting lid.

Freezing is not recommended for cheese for it damages the texture and causes it to be crumbly. If it is really necessary to freeze an over-supply of cheese, Camembert, Cheddar, Edam, Gouda, Provolone, Swiss, and other milder cheeses may be frozen up to six months. Cut cheese into 1-pound pieces not over 1 inch thick, wrap in saran and then in foil. Freeze quickly at zero temperature or lower. Thaw in the refrigerator when needed and use at once.

Use a **LOW temperature in cooking cheese and avoid overcooking.** I believe this is the one basic cooking rule that applies to each and every type of cheese. Grated or cubed cheese melts and blends with other foods faster. Whenever possible, add cheese to food at the last minute, for only enough cooking to melt and blend the cheese is necessary. Any more is too much, for high heat makes cheese tough and stringy and prolonged baking produces a leathery texture. Cheese appetizers—except for soft, unripened cheeses—are best served at room temperature. It usually takes about an hour at this temperature to bring out the distinctive flavors.

High in protein, cheese is popular as an appetizer served with crackers or fresh fruit. It is used to perk up what might otherwise be an uninteresting vegetable dish. Cheese cubes add flavor as well as nourishment to salads. Best of all, cheese is often used as a meat substitute. Following are some tasty, but simple ways to use cheese as the Main Fare:

———◆———

195. Baked Cheesewiches

You will need 8 slices of bread and 4 slices of cheese. Beat together:

2 eggs
¼ cup milk
⅛ teaspoon salt

BREAD
CHEESE
EGGS
MILK
SALT
BUTTER

Dip slices of bread into the mixture, one at a time, and place on waxed paper. Arrange a slice of cheese between each 2 slices of the dipped bread, making 4 cheesewiches in all. Melt ¼ cup of butter in a 9 x 12 x 2-inch baking dish. Place the cheesewiches in the melted butter. Brush tops with more butter and bake in a 350-degree oven for 30 minutes.

196. Cheese Puff

Our family enjoys Cheese Puff served with a hearty green salad and plain gelatin for dessert.

Trim the crust from 8 slices of bread. Place 4 slices of bread in the bottom of an 8-inch square baking pan. Arrange a slice of Cheddar Cheese on each slice of bread, then top with the remaining slices of bread. Beat together:

BREAD
EGGS
MILK
CHEESE
SALT
PEPPER

- 4 eggs
- ½ teaspoon salt
- ⅛ teaspoon pepper
- 2 cups milk

Pour over bread and cheese and let stand for at least an hour. Bake at 350 degrees for 1 hour or until puffed and lightly browned. Serve at once. Makes 4 generous servings.

197. Macaroni and Cheese

Cook 4 ounces (½ package) of macaroni by dropping it into rapidly boiling salted water. Allow 2 quarts of water and 2 teaspoons of salt. Boil for 5 to 10 minutes, or until tender. Do not overcook. The macaroni should still have texture to it when cut with a fork. When tender, pour cold water directly into the macaroni to cool at once and then pour into a colander to drain. While the macaroni is draining, make a thin sauce by mixing together in a small skillet:

MACARONI
CHEDDAR
CHEESE
BUTTER
FLOUR
MILK
SALT
MINCED
ONION
DRY MUSTARD
WORCESTER-
SHIRE
SAUCE

- 2 tablespoons melted butter
- 2 tablespoons flour
- 1 teaspoon salt

When well blended, add all at once:

- 2 cups milk

Continue stirring until thick and smooth. To the sauce, add:

- ½ pound grated Cheddar cheese
- 1 teaspoon minced onion
- ¼ teaspoon dry mustard
- ½ teaspoon Worcestershire sauce

Add to the macaroni. Place in a well-oiled casserole. Top with buttered crumbs and bake in a 350-degree oven about 30 minutes, or until a delicate golden brown. Serves 4.

198. Welsh Rarebit

In the top of a double boiler, melt:

2 tablespoons butter

Place double boiler insert pan over hot water and add:

2 cups shredded sharp cheese
1 teaspoon Worcestershire sauce
¼ teaspoon dry mustard

Stir until the cheese is melted. Beat together and add:

½ cup cream
2 eggs

SHARP CHEESE
BUTTER
WORCESTER-
  SHIRE
  SAUCE
DRY MUSTARD
CREAM
EGGS
ENGLISH
  MUFFINS
TOMATO
  SLICES
  (POACHED
  EGGS)

Cook until thick over medium heat, stirring from time to time. Serve on toasted English Muffins. Top each serving with a tomato slice and a bacon strip. This makes enough Welsh Rarebit to serve 4. You can omit the tomato slice and top each muffin with a poached egg for heartier eating.

199. Cheese Fritters

Beat together thoroughly:

1 cup cooked rice
1 egg
1 tablespoon milk
¾ cup grated cheese
¼ teaspoon salt

Shape into small balls. Coat lightly with flour. Beat together until well mixed:

1 egg white
1 tablespoon milk

RICE
EGG
MILK
CHEESE
SALT
FLOUR
MILK
FINE CRACKER
  CRUMBS
SHORTENING

Dip fritters into the egg-white mixture and then in fine cracker crumbs. Fry in deep, hot fat until a golden brown. Drain on absorbent paper and serve with scrambled eggs and a tossed salad.

200. American Fondue

Actually an American Fondue is a combination of a Cheese Puff and a Cheese Souffle. Scald (heat until a thin skin forms on top of the milk), but do not boil:

2 cups milk

Add:

2 cups bread cubes

½ pound cubed cheese (mild)

MILK
CHEESE
BREAD CUBES
EGGS

Separate 4 eggs. Eggs separate best when refrigerator temperature. Beat the yolks and add very slowly to the slightly cooled mixture, stirring constantly. Beat the egg whites until they form peaks. Do not overbeat. Fold into the cheese mixture. Turn into a 1½-quart greased casserole and bake at 325 degrees for 50 minutes. Makes 4 servings.

201. Swiss Fondue

A Swiss Fondue is quite another story from that of the American Fondue, and one that is fast becoming popular:

Cut cheese into small cubes. Place in a fondue or chafing dish, or a heat-proof casserole dish:

1 pound cubed Swiss cheese

¾ cup white grape juice

Cook over low heat, stirring all the time, until smooth and creamy. Serve from the chafing

SWISS CHEESE
WHITE GRAPE
    JUICE
FRENCH
    BREAD

dish over a warmer, with each person serving himself by placing chunks of Crusty French Bread onto long forks and dipping into the sauce.

Crooked River ambles along the base of the craggy walls of Smith Rock, northeast of Redmond, Oregon. If you look closely, you can see the snow-capped Cascades peeking through the canyon.

RECIPE GUIDE

Number

202. Basic Yeast Bread Dough
203. Mincemeat Roll
204. Fried Bread
205. Whole Wheat Bread
206. Orange-Raisin Bread
207. Salt-Rising Bread
208. Baking Powder Biscuits
209. Basic Plain Muffins
210. Apple Muffins
211. Blueberry Muffins
212. Bran Muffins
213. Corn-Meal Mush
214. Spoon Bread
215. Corn Bread
216. Hush Puppies

Sourdough:

217. Sourdough Starter
218. Dried Starter
219. Sourdough Biscuits
220. Sourdough Bread
221. Sourdough French Bread
222. Sourdough Muffins
223. Sourdough Hotcakes
224. Emergency Sourdough Hotcakes
225. Variations for Sourdough Hotcakes
226. Hotcake Topping

BREADS

~~~~~~

It is rather hard to make a really bad batch of bread and there are few accomplishments so satisfying. During the years that our family was growing up, I found it necessary also to be a "working gal." Being long on things to do and short on time to do them in, I came up with the following method of making bread so that our little girls could learn early to make bread without so many failures and dirtying all the dishes in the kitchen. Here's a step-by-step description of how we made our Yeast Rolls:

202. Basic Yeast Bread Dough

To make 1 loaf of bread or 1 dozen rolls, you will need:

Measuring cups	
Measuring spoons	YEAST
1 knife for level measurements	POWDERED
1 spatula to scrape the bowl	MILK
1 2-inch biscuit cutter (to make rolls uni-	FLOUR
form in size)	SHORTENING
	SUGAR
1 plastic bag large enough for bowl to fit	SALT
into easily	

Time required:

Only 35 minutes of your personal attention is required.
A total of 3 hours is needed from the time you start until

serving time. This consists of:

15 minutes to measure, mix, and knead,

1½ hours for dough to rise and double in bulk at room temperature,

20 minutes to knead and shape into dinner rolls,

40 minutes for rolls to rise or until double in bulk,

15 minutes for baking rolls

If dough is shaped into 1 loaf of bread, it takes only about 5 minutes to knead and shape into a loaf. Baking time would be increased to 40 minutes.

Baking temperature:

Dinner rolls:......................................375 degrees for 15 minutes

Bread:...............325 degrees for 40 minutes (1-pound loaf)

If you decide to double the recipe, double everything but the yeast. One yeast cake or 1 envelope of dry yeast will easily and quickly take care of 6 cups of flour. If you should more than double the recipe, after you become an old hand at the game, just keep this ratio in mind: One yeast cake for every 6 cups of flour.

Measure into a large bowl:

1⅛ cups lukewarm water . . . test with a candy thermometer to read 112 degrees, or the water should feel warm when touched to the wrist.

Add to the water:

1 package of yeast . . . let stand until yeast looks foamy, about 5 minutes.

Then add:

½ cup powdered milk granules. (By using powdered milk, you save the necessity of scalding the milk and the whole thing can be made in one bowl . . . saves time and dishwashing.)

2 tablespoons shortening or oil

1 tablespoon sugar

1½ teaspoons salt

Sift and measure onto your dough board:
    3 cups flour

Be sure these are level cups for you can always work in more
flour if needed. There is a tendency to get too much flour in
light rolls, and of course, how much flour you use depends on
your brand of flour. Some brands are more glutenous than
others. (Bargain flour isn't always the bargain you thought it
was, if you are baking much bread. Some brands will take
more flour to get the right results.) Stir and beat in the flour
. . . adding a cup at a time. When it becomes difficult to beat,
make a well with the rest of the flour on the dough board and
pour the dough into the well. Knead and work in the rest of
the flour. Use a *light* and *springy* touch when kneading dough.

When the dough begins to have an "alive feel" to it, set it
aside to rest for 10 minutes. Meanwhile, wash and grease your
mixing bowl. Knead the dough about 20 more times, slip it
into the warm bowl, and set the whole thing into a large
plastic bag. (This will prevent a crust from forming on the
dough and will keep it free from cold drafts.) Let set at room
temperature (72 to 75 degrees) until double in bulk. If you
are in a real hurry, set it in a sunny place or near a heater.
Be careful, though, that you don't overheat the dough and
kill the yeast action—which can happen if it is set too close
to a heater.

When the dough has doubled in bulk, place on a dough
board that has been dusted with flour. Do not work in any
more flour than is necessary to keep it from sticking. When
all the air bubbles have been kneaded out, pat or roll the
dough out until about ½ inch thick and cut into 2-inch rolls
with a biscuit cutter. This assures you of uniform size rolls.
Take each roll, knead and shape *lightly* with the fingers, and
place on a greased baking sheet. When all the rolls are
shaped, slip the pan back into the plastic bag and let the
dough rise until double in size (about 40 minutes). Bake for

15 minutes at 350 degrees. This temperature is for a regular baking tin. If baking in glass baking dishes, decrease the temperature called for in a recipe by 25 degrees and you will have better results.

———◆———

Variations are easy. For every 3 cups of flour used (1-pound loaf), add to the flour 1 cup of any of the following: raisins (seeded or seedless), cut-up dates, dried apricots, chopped dried peaches, prunes (cooked, seeded and chopped), or coarsely chopped nuts.

———◆———

203. Mincemeat Roll

This same Basic Yeast Bread Dough (Recipe 202) can be used in making dinner rolls, sweet rolls, cinnamon rolls . . . or, for something special, a Mincemeat Roll.

Roll the dough into an oblong or rectangular shape. Spread with butter for extra richness. Then spread with mincemeat, sprinkle with brown sugar, and roll up as you would a jelly roll. Slice into 1½-inch rolls and place side by side in a greased baking dish. Let rise until double in size and bake at 350 degrees for about 25 minutes. While they are still warm, | YEAST DOUGH
BUTTER
MINCEMEAT
BROWN SUGAR
CREAM
POWDERED
SUGAR
(ORANGE
JUICE)

brush with an icing made from mixing together a little cream and powdered sugar. A wee bit of grated orange rind with just a touch of orange juice added to the icing will enhance the mincemeat flavor; however, they are mighty tasty just plain.

For special occasions, Mincemeat Rolls can be baked in muffin tins. This gives each roll a more individual look, and they are nicer to serve to guests. For everyday fare, however, unless you have the easy-wash type of muffin tin, I can't see that it makes that much difference.

204. Fried Bread

While we're on the subject of bread dough . . . my mother-in-law taught me the following trick, and I found there's nothing quite so good on a cold winter day as "Fried Bread." I've served more Fried Bread to a succession of beaus courting our girls than I care to remember. It reached the point where the girls had me quit making it so that they would know if it was their own charm that kept the boys interested—or Mom's Fried Bread. It is really very simple to make, and it is recommended for some mighty down-to-earth eating. It is good served with butter and a light sprinkling of salt with the breakfast eggs. We like it served with Ham 'n Beans—or if it is a sweet touch the family has a yen for, mix a simple frosting and spread on the Fried Bread while it is still warm.

Cut off pieces of bread dough. Pull and stretch into round, flat, thin pieces. Poke a hole in the center if one didn't break through when you were stretching them into shape. Fry in deep fat as you would a doughnut, until a lovely golden brown on each side.

BREAD DOUGH
SHORTENING
BUTTER
SALT

The art of making good bread was a "must" to the homesteader. In days gone by, many a slice of hot, buttered bread was probably enjoyed by the warmth of this hearth.

205. Whole Wheat Bread

When making Whole Wheat Bread, you will note, it takes more yeast, sugar, and additional risings of dough to obtain the desired elastic condition of the gluten in the flour. When using white flour only, care must be taken not to let the dough rise too many times, for this breaks the glutens and the resulting bread is heavy and tough and has an acrid odor.

Beat well with an electric mixer for 2 minutes:

2 cups warm water
2 packages of yeast
⅓ cup sugar
2 cups whole wheat flour

Add:

⅓ cup melted cooled shortening
2 eggs
1 tablespoon salt

WHOLE
WHEAT
FLOUR
WHITE FLOUR
YEAST
SUGAR
EGGS
SHORTENING
SALT

Beat 1 minute and then gradually add:
4½ cups flour (white)

Knead gently but firmly until the dough is smooth and elastic. Place dough in a well-greased bowl, slip the bowl into a large plastic bag and set in a warm place to rise. When the dough has doubled in bulk, knead again, gently but firmly. Repeat this rising process three times, then shape into rolls and place on a greased baking sheet. When the rolls have doubled in size, bake in a 375-degree oven for 15 to 20 minutes. Brush the browned tops with butter or cooking oil just before taking from the oven. This gives a desirable nut-like flavor.

———◆———

When making Rye Bread, follow the directions for white bread, using a flour ratio of 2 cups of rye flour and 1 cup of white flour.

206. Orange-Raisin Bread

I don't know why we always wait for special occasions to do our fancy baking, but guess it's like everything else. We need incentive. Orange-Raisin Bread is special any old time.

Into a large bowl, put 1½ cups of warm water (112 degrees). Sprinkle 2 packages of yeast over the water and let stand until the yeast dissolves.

Add:

½ cup sugar	YEAST
1 teaspoon salt	SUGAR
¼ cup butter	SALT
	BUTTER
1 egg plus 1 egg white (you'll use the yolk later)	EGGS
	ORANGE PEEL
2 tablespoons grated orange peel	FLOUR
3 cups flour	RAISINS

Beat at a low speed until blended, then beat at a medium speed for about 2 minutes. (If you don't have a mixer, just give it the old one, two!) With a wooden spoon, stir in:

½ cup raisins
1 additional cup of flour

Set the bowl in a large plastic bag to keep out drafts and let rise in a warm place for about 1 hour. It will be light, bubbly, and more than double in bulk. Preheat oven to 375 degrees and make the topping. Combine:

¼ cup light brown sugar	BROWN SUGAR
2 tablespoons grated orange peel	ORANGE PEEL
3 tablespoons coarsely chopped pecans	PECANS

Grease a 2-quart casserole dish, stir the batter down with a wooden spoon, and pour into the greased casserole dish. Brush the batter with a mixture of 1 egg yolk and 2 teaspoons of water. Sprinkle the brown sugar mixture over the top, pressing it in with your fingertips. Let rise until double in bulk. Bake about 55 minutes, or until nicely browned. Remove from the casserole to a wire rack to cool. . . . Orange-Raisin Bread is best served while still warm, which is no problem at all. The family won't give it a chance to get cold.

207. Salt-Rising Bread

The secret of making good Salt-Rising Bread is to keep the batter as warm as possible throughout the whole process; 112 degrees is the ideal temperature but it is a little hard to come by. I find that the cupboard beside my oven is the warmest place I have that is draft free. Once you decide where to put it, the rest is easy.

———◆———

This recipe dates back to our Great Grandmother's day. She used it as a matter of necessity. Today it is fast becoming a "lost art."

Dissolve ½ teaspoon salt in 2 cups hot water. Beat in enough flour to make a very soft dough (similar to drop biscuit dough). Beat for 10 minutes; cover and set in a warm place for 8 hours. I usually prepare this in the evening and let it set overnight.

SALT
HOT WATER
MILK
FLOUR

Mix together:
1½ teaspoons salt   1 pint lukewarm milk

Add enough flour to make a stiff dough. Work this into the raised dough, mixing and kneading thoroughly. Knead in enough flour to make the batter the consistency of ordinary bread dough. Place in a lightly greased bowl, set the whole thing into a large plastic bag, and put in a warm place to rise until light and double in bulk. It is now ready to knead and shape into 2 loaves. Place the loaves in greased baking pans and set them to rise again. When light, bake in a 325-degree oven, 35 to 40 minutes. Tapped loaves have a hollow sound when done.

208. Baking Powder Biscuits

Hot biscuits can make a meal that is just a little on the "skinny side" seem extra special. . . . Biscuits are surprising, in a way—I've found that the oftener you make them, the better they get, whether you use a recipe or not. It seems to be how you handle the dough that counts, rather than exact measurements. They are much nicer if you knead the dough lightly for just a minute or two before rolling it out. A light touch does the trick.

If I don't make biscuits for a time, my first batch is never anything really to brag about, but if I turn right around and make them again the next day, by then I have my "hand" back in . . . am used to the feel of the dough, and they turn out ever so much nicer. By the time you make them several days in a row, you can tell by looking at your sifter about how full it should be for the right amount of flour. It usually takes 1 teaspoon of baking powder to a cup of flour and you soon know how much milk you need by the feel of the dough. This is how you impress your teen-age daughter by not using a recipe. It's hard for her to understand that at one time you really did start out with a recipe. If you need a starter recipe, here is a dependable one:

Sift together:
    2 cups flour
    2 teaspoons baking powder
    1 teaspoon salt
Cut in 5 tablespoons shortening and stir in
        ¾ cup milk
	FLOUR
	BAKING
	  POWDER
	SHORTENING
	SALT
	MILK

Knead lightly on a floured board. Roll ¼ inch thick and cut into biscuits. If you are in a hurry, use a paring knife and cut square ones . . . saves re-rolling the dough, which can toughen it. Place biscuits side by side on a greased baking sheet and bake at 375 degrees for 15 to 20 minutes.

209. Basic Plain Muffins

The secret to good muffins is to beat the egg, milk, and shortening together until completely blended. Sift the dry ingredients together. Hollow out the center of the dry ingredients and pour in the liquid. Stir just enough to moisten the dry ingredients. Do not continue to stir or beat. Muffin tins should be greased very lightly on the sides, with a heavier coating on the bottom. If I could have only one teflon-coated cooking utensil, I would choose a muffin tin. The fact that no greasing is required with teflon makes it possible for the batter to cling to the sides of the muffin tin as it rises. This increases the volume of muffins by almost one third. The same results can be obtained if care is taken in greasing the regular type muffin tins. Fill the tins ⅔ full and bake at once, 20 to 30 minutes in a 400-degree oven. You will need the following ingredients for Plain Muffins:

1 cup milk	MILK
1 egg	EGG
4 tablespoons shortening (melted)	SHORTENING
2 cups flour	FLOUR
1 tablespoon baking powder	BAKING
3 tablespoons sugar	POWDER
½ teaspoon salt	SUGAR
	SALT

210. Apple Muffins

Mix as directed for Plain Muffins (Recipe No. 209):

1¼ cups scalded milk	MILK
¼ cup shortening, melted	EGG
1 egg	SHORTENING
⅛ cup sugar	CORN MEAL
⅔ cup yellow corn meal	FLOUR
1 cup flour	BAKING
2 teaspoons baking powder	POWDER
1 teaspoon salt	SUGAR
	SALT
	CHOPPED

Fold into the dry ingredients before mixing with the liquid:

1½ cups chopped apples

APPLES OR
ONE OF THE
MANY
SUGGESTED
VARIATIONS

Instead of chopped apples, you may prefer to use any one of the following: raisins, chopped dates, figs or prunes, crisp bacon giblets, browned sausage crumbles . . . variations seem endless. Mixing and coating heavy ingredients with the dry ingredients before adding to the batter helps them to hold their place in the batter during the baking process. When this is not done, they sink to the bottom during baking.

———————◆———————

211. Blueberry Muffins

Made with Oregon wild mountain huckleberries, this recipe is fit for a king. . . . Mix as directed for Plain Muffins (Recipe No. 209):

⅔ cup milk	MILK
2 beaten eggs	EGGS
¼ cup shortening	SHORTENING
2 cups flour	FLOUR
5 teaspoons baking powder	BAKING POWDER
⅓ cup sugar	SUGAR
1 teaspoon salt	SALT
Fold into the dry ingredients before mixing with the liquid:	BLUEBERRIES OR HUCKLE-BERRIES
½ cup blueberries or huckleberries	

212. Bran Muffins

Mix as directed for Plain Muffins (Recipe No. 209):

⅔ cup milk	MILK
1 egg	EGG
3 tablespoons shortening	SHORTENING
1 cup sifted flour	FLOUR
1 cup bran	BRAN
4 teaspoons baking powder	BAKING POWDER
3 tablespoons brown sugar	SUGAR, BROWN
½ teaspoon salt	SALT
¼ cup raisins	RAISINS
¼ cup chopped prunes	PRUNES

There are probably as many corn-meal recipes as there are years gone by since the Indians taught us the trick of planting a fish in each hill of corn, starting us on the way to some of the best eating ever. The next time you are wondering what to cook, remember that corn meal is nourishing and satisfying.

———◆———

213. Corn-Meal Mush

I grew up in the Middle West, where winter can be long and cold. A hearty breakfast to start you on your way was an absolute necessity—such things as biscuits and gravy, ham and eggs . . . or fried corn-meal mush with lots of butter and syrup, maybe some blackberry jam . . . along with an egg or two. Now when the wind and snow start blowing, I usually find myself reaching for the corn-meal sack to make up some corn-meal mush. Because this is something you have to prepare at least a day ahead of time, I find it best to double the recipe and keep the loaves of mush in the refrigerator for slicing and frying as wanted. Here is the basic recipe and you can take it from there:

Dice a pound of salt pork and fry until crisp. Drain the salt pork and set aside. Put 4 cups of water in the top part of a double boiler and bring to a boil. Gradually stir in 2½ cups of yellow corn meal, then put the lid on and just let it cook for 50 minutes. When done, add the salt pork and 2 beaten eggs. Stir well and put in loaf pans in the refrigerator. As soon as the mush loaves are cold and set, they are ready to slice and fry.

CORN MEAL
SALT PORK
EGG

———◆———

If you are in a hurry, brush slices with melted butter and broil until golden brown, first on one side and then the other.

214. Spoon Bread

Sometimes just the pan in which something is cooked will change the whole "end results" of a recipe. Spoon Bread is such a recipe. If baked in a casserole dish, it is best served in pie-shaped wedges and eaten with a spoon. If baked in a 9 x 11 x 2-inch baking dish, it is crusty golden brown on the outside, soft inside, and best eaten with lots of butter.

Scald in a saucepan:

   2 cups sweet milk

Add:

   1 cup corn meal, stirring constantly

   3 tablespoons butter

Cool slightly and add:

   3 egg yolks, well beaten

   1 teaspoon salt

   1 teaspoon sugar

   2 teaspoons baking powder

Mix thoroughly and fold in:

   3 egg whites, stiffly beaten

MILK
CORN MEAL
BUTTER
EGGS
SALT
SUGAR
BAKING
   POWDER

Turn into a well-buttered baking dish, previously made hot. Bake in a 400-degree oven for 30 minutes.

215. Corn Bread

Some meals are just not complete without corn bread:

Combine:

   1 egg, well beaten

   1 cup milk

   3 tablespoons sugar

   4 tablespoons melted shortening

Sift and mix together:

   1 cup flour

   1 cup corn meal

3½ teaspoons baking powder

   1 teaspoon salt

EGG
MILK
SUGAR
SHORTENING
FLOUR
CORN MEAL
BAKING
   POWDER
SALT

Combine the dry ingredients with the wet ingredients, stirring just enough to moisten. Do not beat. Bake in an 8x8x2-inch baking pan at 425 degrees for 40 minutes.

216. Hush Puppies

A good hustle-bustle dish to go with fish:

Combine:

SHORTENING
EGG
CORN MEAL
FLOUR
BAKING
POWDER
SALT

2 tablespoons melted shortening
(bacon fat is best)
1 egg, well beaten
½ cup water

Sift together and add to the above:

1 cup corn meal (will be extra special if you use stone-ground corn meal)
½ cup flour
1 teaspoon baking powder
1 teaspoon salt

Heat fat in a frying pan over moderate heat. You will want about 1/16 inch of fat in the skillet. Drop the thick batter by teaspoonfuls into the skillet. Fry to a crisp, golden brown, turn, press the corn cake gently with the back of a turner to flatten and brown the cake on the other side. Drain on absorbent paper.

A sourdough pot was a miner's necessity. We found the remains of this mine deep in the Ochoco Mountains.

217. Sourdough Starter

Time was when no self-respecting homestead was without a Sourdough Starter. A goodly supply of dry yeast, or a Starter, was a "must" with the Gold Seekers or anyone who was going to be in Bush Country, cut off from people and supplies. Many humorous stories are told of the lengths to which man has gone to preserve his Sourdough Starter. Beriberi was a common, excruciating disease among men in isolated areas during the settling of this big, wide land of ours, just because they didn't always keep the Sourdough Pot going.

I find there are many misconceptions concerning the word "Sourdough." It is a term applied to anyone who lived at a time when a Sourdough Pot was a matter of necessity, whether it was the Gold Fields of Alaska or the remote areas in the settling of the West.

Sourdough Cookery can be anything that was considered Main Fare during that day and age. As an example, Trapper's Stew is considered Sourdough Cookery. Made in Dutch Ovens, it was cooked slowly over a bed of dying coals. A modern-day version of Trapper's Stew is the Oven Stew, Recipe No. 28.

A Sourdough Starter is actually a leavening agent, used before the invention of baking powder and it can be used in any recipe which requires yeast, baking powder, or soda.

The fermentation which takes place in a Sourdough Starter makes it necessary to keep it in a stone or glass jar, never in metal, thus the term "Sourdough Pots."

During the years that homemakers relied on the use of a Sourdough Pot, cooking was an art passed on from mother to daughter or from one old Sourdough to another. Successful baking was a matter of how the dough felt and looked, rather than accurate measure. This makes it especially difficult to tell a new cook how to use a Starter. For the most part, I have found that a Sourdough Starter can be used as a leavening agent in any recipe by substituting in the following manner:

First, omit the baking powder or yeast. If the recipe calls

for 2 cups of flour, substitute ½ cup of starter for ½ cup of the flour. Dissolve ½ teaspoon of baking soda in a little warm water and add to the batter at the last minute. When baking soda and an acid (in this case, the Sourdough Starter) are mixed in a wet solution, a gas is formed and this reaction is what makes batter or dough rise. Baking soda combined with sour milk will also produce this reaction.

Baking powder is a simple mixture of soda and an acid . . . which can be cream of tartar, alum, or monocalcium phosphate . . . mixed with cornstarch for dryness. Since the needed acid is a built-in part of the baking powder, it is used with sweet milk rather than sour.

When baking powder was first introduced to the public back in the 1850s, it met with a great deal of opposition. As late as 1900, commercial baking powders were not readily accepted by the general public because of the lack of understanding of the chemicals involved.

Knowing a little about the history of the various leavening agents is helpful in substituting when cooking. A quick-acting baking powder to be used immediately can be made by mixing together thoroughly, 2 teaspoons cream of tartar, 1 teaspoon baking soda, and 1 teaspoon cornstarch. Baking powder is always used with sweet milk and baking soda is always used with sour milk.

A Sourdough Pot can prove to be one of the most "fun" hobbies you've ever undertaken. Contrary to popular opinion, you don't have to get your first Starter from someone else. You can make your own. It is a simple matter of making your Starter, then replacing flour, sugar, and water with each use.

A gallon jar or crock is a "must"; never use metal. Some experts say to cover with a cloth only. An expert in this case would be an old Sourdough. I have a crock with a lid and it seems to work fine. A gallon jar does equally well by covering the lid with a plastic wrap. Just don't let the batter come in contact with the metal.

FLOUR
WATER
YEAST
SUGAR

Put all together in a jar and mix until smooth:

2 cups lukewarm water
2 packages dried yeast (dissolved in ½ cup warm water)
2 teaspoons sugar
4 cups flour

Keep in a warm place 36 to 48 hours. It will rise and fall until it wears itself out and becomes sour, and it will then have a strong acrid smell. It is now ready for use. . . . You will find that the longer you have it and keep it going, the better and more active it will become. It takes about two weeks for it really to come into its own.

When making hot cakes, biscuits, bread, etc., always hold back at least 1 cup of Starter for the next day's baking. To renew the starter, each day add:

1 cup warm water
1 cup flour
1 teaspoon sugar

When it reaches the capacity needed, you can use it again. As your Starter gets some age on it and is more active, you can immediately replace its volume. If you take out 4 cups of Starter, immediately add 4 cups of flour, 4 cups of warm water and 4 teaspoons of sugar. The sugar helps keep it working.

218. Dried Starter

I never cease to be amazed at the age of the Starters that are in existence today, some of them dating back to the late 1800s. Old-timers tell me that the easiest way to keep an "old" Starter going is to "dry" it between uses.

Add enough flour to your Starter to make a stiff dough. Roll dough as thin as possible. When the dough is perfectly dry and hard, crumble the dried Starter into a jar. Seal tightly and place in a cool, dry place until needed. It can also be stored in the freezer. It will keep for years in a dried condition and is the manner in which many Starters were brought across the plains during the Homesteader days. When ready to use again, add enough water to make it of Sourdough Starter consistency, a sprinkling of sugar to start it working, and use as you normally would.

219. Sourdough Biscuits

An all-time favorite recipe is Sourdough Biscuits. Mix together:

1 cup sourdough starter	STARTER
1 tablespoon melted shortening	FLOUR
1 tablespoon sugar	SHORTENING
	SUGAR
½ teaspoon salt	SALT
1 teaspoon baking soda	BAKING SODA

Place about 4 cups of flour on the dough board in a mound. There is no need to measure accurately. Make a well in the mound of flour and pour in the above mixture. Work in flour until you have a dough that is the texture of biscuit dough— one that is soft but easily handled. Knead lightly and roll to a thickness of about ½ inch. Cut the biscuits and place side by side on a greased cookie sheet. Set in a warm place to rise for about 30 minutes. Bake at 375 degrees for 15 to 20 minutes. Makes about 24 (2-inch) biscuits that are a delight to eat.

220. Sourdough Bread

Sourdough Bread is a good example of how to use a Starter without using any soda. You will need a good "lively" Starter for this one. If it isn't, dissolve ½ package of dry yeast in ¼ cup warm water and add to the 1⅛ cups of Starter needed in the recipe.

Use the Bread Recipe No. 202 as a basis. Substitute 1⅛ cups of Starter for the water, yeast, and powdered milk granules. To the Starter add:

2 tablespoons shortening or oil	STARTER
1 tablespoon sugar	FLOUR
1½ teaspoons salt	SHORTENING
Sift and measure onto your dough board:	SUGAR
3 cups flour	SALT

Add 2 cups of this flour to the Starter mixture. Set in a covered bowl to rise until doubled in volume. Place the dough on the floured board and knead and work in the other cup of flour. You may need additional flour, depending on the flour used. Knead the dough until it has an elasticity or a feeling of buoyancy to it. It will be smooth with a satiny finish—never sticky. Shape into a loaf (this makes a 1-pound loaf) and place in a well-greased loaf pan. Let rise until double in volume and bake at 325 degrees for 30 to 40 minutes.

221. Sourdough French Bread

Use Sourdough Bread Recipe No. 220. The only difference is in the baking. Place the kneaded loaf on a greased cookie sheet. When the dough has risen and doubled in volume, make diagonal slashes across the top of the

STARTER
FLOUR
SHORTENING
SUGAR
SALT

loaf with a sharp knife. The slashes should be about ¼-inch deep. Brush the loaf with water and bake at 375 degrees for 30 to 35 minutes. When done, the loaf will have a hollow sound when tapped with a spoon.

222. Sourdough Muffins

Mix together:

    ½ cup evaporated milk
    1 egg, beaten
    ½ cup shortening, melted

Sift together and add to the wet ingredients:

    1½ cups white flour
    ½ cup whole wheat flour
    ½ cup sugar
    1 teaspoon salt
    1 teaspoon soda
    1 cup chopped raisins (to be added to the dry ingredients)

STARTER
MILK
EGG
SHORTENING
FLOUR, WHITE
FLOUR, WHOLE WHEAT
SUGAR
SALT
SODA
RAISINS

Mix just enough to moisten all the ingredients and then fold in:

    ½ cup Sourdough Starter

Fill greased muffin tins ⅔ full and bake at 400 degrees 20 to 30 minutes.

223. Sourdough Hotcakes

Many Sourdough enthusiasts keep a Sourdough Pot going just to be able to enjoy the Hotcakes. They are extra tender and delicate with a subtle flavor all their own.

Mix together:

3 cups starter	STARTER
2 tablespoons sugar	SUGAR
¼ teaspoon salt	SALT
1 egg, well beaten	EGG
1 tablespoon butter, melted	BUTTER
(or cooking oil)	SODA

Just before baking, mix together and stir in:

1 teaspoon soda
2 tablespoon warm water

The batter should foam up almost immediately and look somewhat like meringue. If it does, you are about to have some of the best hotcakes you ever ate.

224. Emergency Sourdough Hotcakes

This is a sneaky thing to do, but if your family is clamoring for Sourdough Hotcakes, and you find that in the hustle and bustle of family living, your Sourdough Pot has gone over the hill from neglect, here's a recipe that I've worked out over the years from just such emergencies:

Into a large bowl, put:

1¼ cups warm water	YEAST
1 package of dry yeast, let dissolve, then add	POWDERED MILK
⅓ cup powdered milk granules	EGG
1 egg	COOKING OIL
1 tablespoon cooking oil	PANCAKE MIX (RICE)

Beat until well mixed, then add:

2 cups pancake mix (your favorite)

Set batter in a warm place for 30 minutes to rise. Bake on a hot griddle. When used as a "send-off" for some early-morning hunters, add 1 cup of cooked rice.

225. Variations for Sourdough Hotcakes

Hotcakes can be fun almost any time, especially when sprinkled with various tasty tidbits before frying. The easiest way to give variation is to pour the batter onto the griddle, sprinkle with any of the following, then turn and brown on the other side.

Crisp bacon crumbles
Fried sausage crumbs
Pineapple tidbits
Drained, cooked blueberries

. . . Or arrange on each unbaked hotcake, things like

Diced dates
Grated apple
Banana slices
Coarsely chopped clams
Chopped ham and grated cheese

226. Hotcake Topping

For a topping that makes a hotcake something to talk about, try this—whip together equal parts of:

Peanut butter
Butter
Spread generously on hotcakes and drizzle with honey or syrup.

PEANUT
  BUTTER
BUTTER
(MARGARINE)
SYRUP OR
  HONEY

In the matter of calories, it isn't as bad as it sounds. Protein in the peanut butter is the equivalent of several slices of bacon, and in my book, it is twice as good. Of course, I like peanut butter!

RECIPE GUIDE

Number

227. Basic Angel Food Cake
228. Sponge Cake
229. Basic Butter Cake
230. Fudge Cake
231. Applesauce Cake
232. Prune Cake
233. Basic Fruit Cake
234. Upside Down Cake
235. Basic Chiffon Cake
236. Carrot Chiffon Cake
237. Old-Fashioned Pound Cake
238. Baba Cakes
239. Lemon Sauce
240. Sourdough Applesauce Cake
241. Sourdough Chocolate Cake
242. Basic Crumb Cake
243. Lightning Cake
244. Cheese Cake
245. Chocolate Mayonnaise Cake
246. Boiled Raisin Cake

Frostings:

247. Caramel Frosting
248. Fudge Frosting
249. Whipped Cream Frosting
   (without whipped cream)
250. Basic Butter Frosting
251. Never-Fail Fluffy White Frosting
252. Cream Cheese Frosting
253. Basic Fruit Filling
254. Broiled Topping

CAKES

~~~~~~

Dessert, the Grand Finale of any meal, is determined by the size of the main course. Light desserts such as fruit and cookies and the various gelatins are used to balance a large meal, whereas cake, rich puddings, and pie are served with light meals. Individual tastes and circumstances sometimes vary this general rule, in that anyone working in the out-of-doors can often do well by beef, potatoes, gravy, salad, and hot bread . . . topped off with Apple Pie or Chocolate Fudge Cake for dessert.

Cake, rich in eggs, milk, and butter, is a highly nutritious supplement to a lighter meal. There are so many good cake mixes on the market, cooks seldom go to the trouble of preparing them "from scratch." But, even with all these wonderful cooking aids, there are still special occasions when a cake of your own is best.

There is an art to baking a really good cake—one that is tender and moist with a fine texture. It is an art that isn't difficult to master; it's just a lot of little things—little things that you, too, can learn. Without getting all involved in the "whys and wherefores," keep these simple rules in mind and you will be able to bake a cake to be proud of:

1. Always pre-heat the oven.
2. Use quality ingredients. Your cake will be only as good as the ingredients used.
   Flour: When a recipe specifically lists Cake Flour and you wish to substitute with all-purpose flour, use 2

tablespoons per cup less. When a recipe calls for 2 cups of all-purpose flour and you desire a fine-textured cake, substitute 2 tablespoons of cornstarch for ¼ cup of the flour.

Shortening: Use butter, a high-grade vegetable shortening, or a good grade of margarine (be sure it isn't the whipped variety for this would upset measurement).

Sugar: Always use granulated sugar. If a recipe specifies brown sugar, be sure it is well packed when measuring.

Eggs: Large, Grade AA eggs give best results.

3. Have all ingredients at room temperature. Eggs, milk, and shortening should be taken from the refrigerator at least 1 hour before you plan to mix the cake.
4. Measure all ingredients accurately. Use standard measuring cups and spoons with all measurements level.
5. Knowing when to beat a cake is important. (We'll talk more about this later.)
6. Understanding the type of leavening agent used is helpful. Basically, cakes fall under one of three categories: (1) Angel or Sponge Cakes depend on eggs for volume. (2) Butter cakes make use of baking powder or baking soda. (3) Baba Cakes and Sourdough Cakes are made with yeast.

From these three categories, 8 types of cake and all their many variations are derived. I'll share basic "know how" along with my favorite recipes and you can take it from there, for I realize that you, too, have favorites.

Angel and Sponge Cakes

Angel Food Cake, a delicate white cake, depends on large amounts of beaten *egg whites* for its volume.

Sponge Cake, a light sweet cake, requires a large number of *whole eggs* to achieve its volume.

The lightness of these delicate cakes is dependent on a gentle motion in combining ingredients, well-sifted flour and sugar to incorporate air into the dry ingredients, and proper beating of the egg whites. The manner of beating isn't so important as it is to stop beating when the egg whites are very stiff but still shiny in appearance.

The choice of pan is important and a tube pan works best for this type of cake. These cakes do not require any shortening and the pans in which they are baked are left *ungreased.* This allows the batter to adhere to the sides of the pan as the cake rises, thus creating greater volume.

The texture of an Angel Food Cake or a Sponge Cake is so delicate when it first comes from the oven that it cannot hold its own weight. Careful handling at this time is necessary. Turn the pan over gently and stand on a rack to cool . . . takes about an hour. Carefully loosen the cake from the edges of the pan with a spatula. If you find it necessary to bake a Sponge or Angel Cake in a loaf pan, after the cake is done (springs back when touched lightly), invert the pan and place a wood block or something similar under each corner of the pan so there is a space of about 1 inch between the cake and the table, to allow room for air to circulate.

227. Basic Angel Food Cake

Sift and measure:

EGG WHITES
FLOUR
SUGAR
CREAM OF
TARTAR
SALT
VANILLA

1 cup all-purpose flour (if cake flour is used, add 2 tablespoons)

To the measured flour, add:

¾ cup sugar

Sift the flour and sugar together 5 times. Incorporate as much air as possible. Into a large bowl put:

12 egg whites (room temperature)
½ teaspoon salt

Beat egg whites until foamy and add:

1½ teaspoons cream of tartar

Continue beating egg whites until they are firm enough to stand alone. Do not continue to beat, for over-beaten egg whites collapse during baking. Gradually add to the beaten egg whites:

    1 cup sifted sugar

Beat with a gentle motion while adding the sugar so that the egg whites retain their moist, shiny appearance. Carefully fold in:

    1 teaspoon vanilla

Sprinkle 1 tablespoon of the sifted flour and sugar mixture over the egg whites and fold in, using a gentle folding motion; cut down through the center of the egg whites, up the sides, and down through the center in the other direction. Continue to do this until all the flour and sugar have been added to the egg whites.

The art of folding batter sometimes takes a little practice because, if over-mixed, the cake will be heavy and, if under-mixed, the texture of the cake will be coarse. Pour into a 10-inch *ungreased* tube pan and bake in a pre-heated 350-degree oven for about 1 hour.

Variations are easy:

Chocolate Angel Food Cake: Substitute ¼ cup cocoa for ¼ cup of the flour and sift with the sugar.

Maraschino Cherry: Sprinkle bits of well-drained cherries into the batter as you place the batter into the tube pan. You can do the same thing with well-drained pineapple tidbits and shredded coconut.

228. Sponge Cake

Sift together 3 times:

    1 cup sifted cake flour

    ½ teaspoon salt

Put into a small bowl:

    5 egg yolks

    1 tablespoon lemon juice

    1 teaspoon vanilla

CAKE FLOUR
EGGS
SUGAR
LEMON JUICE
VANILLA
SALT

Beat until the consistency of batter. Takes about 2 minutes at high speed with your electric mixer. Put the egg whites into another bowl. Beat until firm enough to stand in peaks and gradually add:

1 cup sugar

Fold the egg-yolk mixture into the egg whites. Sprinkle the flour into the mixture, a little at a time, folding it into the batter with that gentle up and over motion. This is best accomplished with a spatula, using quick, light movements. Bake in an *ungreased* 10-inch tube pan for about an hour in a 325-degree oven.

A Jelly Roll is actually a variation of Sponge Cake. Use Sponge Cake Recipe and add 2 more tablespoons of water to the egg yolks. All other ingredients and methods of mixing remain the same. Bake in a shallow, oblong pan about 8 by 15 inches. Completely line the pan with wax paper. Bake at 350 degrees 15 to 20 minutes. Loosen the cake from the sides of the pan and invert on a cloth. Working quickly, remove the wax paper from the cake and trim the crisp edges away. Roll the cake in the cloth gently but firmly. Place on a rack to cool. When the cake roll is cooled, unroll carefully, removing the cloth as you unroll. Spread the cake with your favorite filling and carefully re-roll. Jam, jelly, or canned cherry-pie filling can be used; creamed puddings are good; whipped cream or softened ice cream can be used.

Butter Cakes

Butter Cakes depend on baking powder or baking soda for a leavening agent—baking powder being used with sweet milk and soda with sour milk. There are two methods of mixing Butter Cakes:

Conventional Method: Butter and sugar are mixed and blended together until the sugar is dissolved and the mixture has the creamy texture of whipped butter. This is what is meant by the term "cream together." The eggs are added next. A recipe usually says "beat well after the addition of each egg." This is the one place in mixing a Butter Cake where you can't over-beat. The batter will look smooth and creamy when it is "just right." Now comes the crucial point. Do not over-beat during the alternate addition of the dry ingredients and the liquid. Stir rather than beat—just enough to blend the ingredients. Use a slow to medium speed in mixing cakes. High speed hardens the gluten in the flour, causing the cake to have a bread-like texture.

When mixing a cake by hand, a total of 600 strokes is needed to blend the dry ingredients with the wet. It is all right to rest while beating a cake by hand, but do keep track of the strokes. You will note specific beating directions on commercial cake mixes. These directions are tested and should be followed to the letter. It does make a difference.

Muffin Method: The wet ingredients are all beaten together until foamy and added to the dry ingredients which have been sifted together. Not all Butter Cakes adapt themselves to this method of mixing and the texture of the cake is always of a coarser nature. This method of mixing is usually used in making Coffee Cakes.

When pouring batter into the cake pans, put slightly less batter in the center of the pan. Bake at temperature given without opening the oven door until the minimum time is up. If the cake is beginning to pull away from the sides of the pan . . . bounces back when touched lightly . . . insert a tooth-pick in the center. If it comes out clean, remove the cake immediately.

It is so easy to over-bake a cake, causing it to be dry and tasteless. When the cake is done, remove from the oven and let stand in the pans for a moment or two. Loosen the sides of the cake from the pan with a knife and turn out on a rack to cool. If the cake doesn't want to leave the bottom of the pan, place a damp cloth on the bottom of the pan for a minute.

229. Basic Butter Cake

Cream together:

  ⅔ cup sugar

  ¼ cup shortening

Add:

  1 egg

Beat until thick and creamy. Sift together:

  1½ cups all-purpose flour

  ¼ teaspoon salt

  2 teaspoons baking powder

Add the dry ingredients to the batter alternately with:

  ¾ cup milk

  1 teaspoon vanilla

Pour into 2 well-greased 8-inch cake pans. Bake at 350 degrees, 25 to 30 minutes.

Variations are simple. Chocolate chips can be folded into the batter. Chopped dates and nuts make a tasty change. You can melt one square of baking chocolate and add to ½ the batter. Fill the baking pans by spoonfuls, alternating the chocolate batter with the plain for a marble cake. Various frostings and fillings can further whet the appetite.

MILK
SUGAR
SHORTENING
EGG
FLOUR
BAKING POWDER
SALT

230. Fudge Cake

Important occasions at our house are usually observed with the baking of this specialty:

Mix together and set to cool:

  ½ cup cocoa

  1½ teaspoons soda

  2 teaspoons cinnamon.

  ½ cup boiling water

Cream together:

  ½ cup butter

  2 cups sugar

Add and mix well:

  2 eggs

Sift together:

  1⅞ cups flour (2 cups less 2 tablespoons)

  1 teaspoon salt

COCOA
BUTTER
SUGAR
EGGS
FLOUR
BUTTERMILK
SODA
VANILLA
CINNAMON
SALT

Mix together and add alternately with the dry ingredients to the butter, sugar and egg mixture:

1 cup buttermilk

1 teaspoon vanilla

Blend in the cooled chocolate mixture, being careful not to over-beat. Bake in 3 (9-inch) cake pans at 375 degrees for 25 to 30 minutes.

231. Applesauce Cake

Substituting fruit sauce for the liquid in a Butter Cake creates an entirely new taste and texture. I've used the same old Applesauce Cake recipe for years. It is moist and tasty and such a good cake to take camping that I usually double the recipe and make two because one of them always disappears the same day they are baked. Moral of the story: maybe you had better double the recipe too!

Cream together:

1 cup granulated sugar

1 cup brown sugar

1 cup shortening

Beat in:

2 eggs

1 cup raisins

1 teaspoon salt

1 teaspoon cinnamon

1 teaspoon nutmeg

1 teaspoon cloves

When mixture is nice and fluffy, add:

2 teaspoons soda

2 cups flour

2 cups applesauce

SUGAR
BROWN SUGAR
BUTTER
EGGS
RAISINS
SALT
CINNAMON
NUTMEG
CLOVES
SODA
FLOUR
APPLESAUCE

Beat 3 minutes at medium speed and turn into a 9 x 11 x 2-inch baking dish. Bake in a 350-degree oven for about 40 minutes, or until a toothpick if inserted in the center comes out clean.

You really don't need any frosting. Applesauce Cake is just right for that "little something" with a cup of coffee.

232. Prune Cake

You have to have eaten a Prune Cake just once to truly appreciate what a wonderful cake it can be. Here's your chance:

Cream together:

  ¾ cup shortening

  1 cup sugar

Add:

  3 eggs, beating well after the addition of each egg

In another bowl, mix:

  1 cup prune pulp

  ¼ cup sour cream

  ¾ cup prune juice

Sift together:

  2¼ cups all-purpose flour

  3 teaspoons baking powder

  1 teaspoon soda

  ½ teaspoon allspice

  ½ teaspoon cinnamon

  ½ teaspoon nutmeg

  ½ teaspoon salt

SHORTENING
SUGAR
EGGS
PRUNE PULP
SOUR CREAM
PRUNE JUICE
FLOUR
BAKING POWDER
SODA
ALLSPICE
SALT
CINNAMON
NUTMEG

Add dry ingredients alternately with the sour cream and prune-juice mixture. Stir only enough after each addition to blend thoroughly. Be careful not to over-beat. The trick in making this cake is to get the shortening and sugar the fluffiest ever. Then use a bit of discretion when mixing in the dry ingredients and the "prune-and-sour-cream" mixture. Pour into 2 greased 9-inch layer-cake pans, 1½ inches deep. Bake at 350 degrees for 30 minutes. When the cake is cool, put the layers together with a Honey Almond Filling made by combining in a heavy saucepan:

  ⅓ cup butter

  ⅔ cup honey

  ⅓ cup sugar

  ½ teaspoon salt

  ¼ teaspoon cinnamon

BUTTER
HONEY
SUGAR
CINNAMON
SALT
ALMONDS

Boil for 2 minutes *exactly* and remove from the heat. Beat about 10 minutes, or until very thick and taffy like. Fold in ½ cup of almonds (grated or slivered). Put the layers together with the Honey Almond Filling.

Serve the Prune Cake with whipped cream for topping. We won't even talk about calories . . . but it's worth not counting them just to have a piece of this cake.

Fruit Cake, a member of the Butter Cake family, requires special baking to be successful. Butter Cake batter is used to bind large amounts of nuts and fruit together. Long, slow steaming and baking is necessary. Small loaf pans and flat 1-pound coffee cans make ideal baking containers. Line the pans with wax paper and fill about ⅔ full with batter. Cover the pans with wax paper and tie securely. Place on a rack in a kettle with a tight-fitting lid. Pour water to a depth of 1 inch in the kettle. Bring to a gentle boil and let the cakes cook in the steam. A 1-pound cake will take 2 hours. Add ½ hour steaming time for every additional pound of cake. When the cakes are steamed, take from the steam kettle and remove the wax paper from the top of the pans. Place the cakes in a 250-degree oven and continue to bake for 1½ hours for cakes weighing between 1 and 4 pounds. Here, too, for every additional pound, add ½ hour baking time. The cakes are done when a toothpick inserted in the center of the cake comes out clean. Spread all 4 sides of the cakes with marmalade while they are still warm. Wrap in wax paper and store in an air-tight container.

The following Fruit Cake recipe is the result of much experimenting and "substituting this for that." I find I have trouble keeping enough made during the Holiday Season, but that is one of its nice features. It is a Fruit Cake that doesn't have to be made ahead of time to be good, yet it is so moist it will keep for several weeks.

233. Basic Fruit Cake

Cream together:
  2 cups sugar
  ¾ cup shortening
Add:
  1 cup applesauce
  1 cup mincemeat
Beat in:
  3 cups flour
  3 teaspoons soda
  ½ teaspoon cinnamon
  ½ teaspoon allspice
Fold in:
  1 cup raisins
  1 cup nutmeats
  1 cup candied fruit
  1 cup maraschino cherries

SUGAR
SHORTENING
APPLESAUCE
MINCEMEAT
FLOUR
SODA
CINNAMON
ALLSPICE
RAISINS
NUTMEATS
CANDIED
   FRUIT
MARASCHINO
   CHERRIES

In fact, you can add as little or as much of this sort of thing as you want to. If you don't care for candied fruit, leave it out and add a cup of dates instead. You have probably noticed there is no egg in this recipe. This is half the secret of the moistness of this cake. The other half of the secret is in the baking. . . .

To bake: Use small loaf pans or an Angel Food Cake pan, pouring batter to a depth of 1½ inches. Baked in the Angel Food Cake pan, the Fruit Cake becomes the shape of a Christmas wreath and can be decorated with hardsauce applied with a pastry tube.

Now for a shortcut in baking: Place a cake pan with about 1 inch of water in it in the bottom of the oven. Place the cakes about the third rack up from the bottom of the oven and bake at 275 degrees for 2 hours. During the last 20 minutes or so of baking, you will want to test with a toothpick for doneness because some ovens vary. Don't over-bake, but you do want the testing toothpick to come out clean when inserted in the middle of the cake.

234. Upside Down Cake

Upside Down Cakes — those delightful affairs enriched with sliced apples, apricots, prunes, peaches, cherries, or pineapple — are all made with a simple Butter Cake as the basis. Before pouring the batter into the cake pan, spread the bottom of the pan well with butter. Sprinkle generously with sugar and arrange the fruit of your choice over the sugar. Pour the batter over the fruit and bake in a 350-degree oven 40 to 50 minutes. When the cake is done, turn onto a cake plate. Allow the pan to remain on the cake only long enough for the syrup to drip onto the cake.

FRUIT OF YOUR CHOICE
BUTTER CAKE BATTER
BUTTER
SUGAR (WHITE OR BROWN)

235. Basic Chiffon Cake

Chiffon cakes have the delicate texture of a Sponge Cake with all the richness of a Butter Cake. Quick and easy to make, liquid shortening and lots of eggs are used.

Measure and sift together:
    2 cups all-purpose flour
    3 teaspoons baking powder
 1½ cups sugar
    1 teaspoon salt
Make a well in the dry ingredients and add the following, in the order given:
    ½ cup oil
    6 unbeaten egg yolks
    ¾ cup water or unsweetened fruit juice

FLOUR
SUGAR
OIL
EGGS
BAKING POWDER
CREAM OF TARTAR
SALT
(UNSWEETENED FRUIT JUICE)

Mix together on low speed until all ingredients are blended. Do not over-blend. In another bowl, beat together until frothy:
    6 egg whites
Add:
    ½ teaspoon cream of tartar
Continue beating until the egg whites are very stiff but still retain a glossy look. Gradually fold the egg-yolk mixture into

the beaten egg whites. Do not stir. Place in an *ungreased* 10-inch tube pan and bake 50 minutes at 325 degrees. Increase the oven temperature to 350 degrees and continue baking the cake for 10 more minutes, or until a delicate golden brown. Cool the cake in the same manner that you would an Angel Food Cake.

Variations:

Orange Chiffon: Substitute ¼ cup of orange juice for ¼ cup of the water specified and fold in 3 tablespoons grated orange rind.

Chocolate Chiffon: Fold into the batter 2 squares of coarsely grated semi-sweet chocolate.

236. Carrot Chiffon Cake

The more I cook with carrots the more I become convinced they are the nicest vegetable ever. They are certainly the most versatile. They can be baked, creamed, buttered, pickled, or used to make a Chiffon Cake like this one:

Sift together:

- 2 cups flour
- 2 teaspoons soda
- ½ teaspoon salt
- 2 teaspoons cinnamon
- 2 teaspoons baking powder

Beat together:

- 1½ cups oil
- 2 cups sugar

Add:

- 4 eggs . . . one at a time, beating well after each addition

FLOUR
SUGAR
OIL
EGGS
CARROTS
PINEAPPLE
NUTS
SODA
BAKING POWDER
SALT
CINNAMON

Blend in the dry ingredients at low speed. Last of all, fold in:

- 2 cups carrots, grated very fine
- 1 cup crushed pineapple, well drained
- 1 cup nuts

Bake in an ungreased long loaf pan or a 10-inch tube pan for 50 minutes at 350 degrees.

237. Old-Fashioned Pound Cake

*This is an old favorite with us—it can be served in so many
ways: frosted, with fruit, ice cream, or just "as is." Besides, it's
nourishing; look at those ingredients!*

Cream until fluffy:
    2 cups butter
    2 cups sugar (adding gradually)
Beat in gradually:
    10 egg yolks (which have been beaten until
        thick and lemony)
Beat alternately into butter-sugar-yolk mixture:
    10 egg whites (which have been beaten until stiff) . . . and
    4 cups sifted flour . . . Beat 5 minutes more and
Stir in:
    ¼ cup brandy
    ½ teaspoon mace (or 1 teaspoon lemon extract)

BUTTER
SUGAR
EGGS
FLOUR
MACE
BRANDY

Grease 2 loaf pans and line with heavy paper. Bake at 325
degrees for 1½ hours. If cakes seem a little too brown during
the last part of baking, place piece of heavy brown paper over
tops of pans for a while.

238. Baba Cakes

*Sometimes yeast is used as a leavening agent in the art of
cake making. Baba Cakes dipped in Lemon Sauce are enough
to make one's mouth water:*

Mix together:
    ½ cup lukewarm water
    1 yeast cake
    ½ cup flour
    ¼ teaspoon salt
Cover and let rise until double in bulk.

YEAST
FLOUR
EGGS
BUTTER
SUGAR
SALT

Cream together:
   ¾ cup butter
   ½ cup sugar
Add:
   4 eggs
   ¼ teaspoon salt
Beat until thick and lemony in appearance and add:
   1 cup flour

Beat again until smooth. When the yeast sponge has doubled in bulk, combine the 2 batters and beat thoroughly. Fill well-greased muffin tins half full. Let rise until ⅔ full and bake in a pre-heated 350-degree oven.

239. Lemon Sauce

Mix together in the top of a double boiler:
   1½ tablespoons corn starch   LEMON JUICE
   ½ cup sugar   SUGAR
   1½ cups hot water (stir constantly while   CORN STARCH
     adding)   BUTTER
Cook, stirring constantly, until the mixture thickens. Add:
   2 tablespoons lemon juice
   1½ tablespoons butter
More or less of sugar and lemon juice can be used to adjust the flavor to your family's liking. Served hot or cold, it's simple and good. If you prefer orange flavor, just substitute orange juice for the lemon.

———◆———

240. Sourdough Applesauce Cake

If you never use a Sourdough Pot for anything else, it is worth having just to be able to make these two cakes. Directions for making your own Sourdough Pot are given earlier.

Mix the following ingredients together, cover the bowl and

let stand in a warm place while you mix the rest of the cake:

1 cup sourdough starter
¾ cup non-fat dry milk granules
1 cup sifted white flour
1½ cups applesauce
½ cup raisins

Cream together:
½ cup white sugar
½ cup brown sugar
½ cup shortening

Add the following, and beat well:
1 egg
½ teaspoon salt
1 teaspoon cinnamon
½ teaspoon nutmeg
½ teaspoon allspice
½ teaspoon cloves
2 teaspoons soda
½ cup chopped nuts

SOURDOUGH STARTER
DRY MILK GRANULES
FLOUR
APPLESAUCE
RAISINS
WHITE SUGAR
BROWN SUGAR
SHORTENING
EGGS
SALT
CINNAMON
NUTMEG
ALLSPICE
CLOVES
SODA
NUT MEATS

Combine with the sourdough mixture and beat by hand, 100 strokes. Bake at 325 degrees for 35 to 45 minutes.

241. Sourdough Chocolate Cake

Mix the following ingredients together and let them stand for at least 3 hours in a warm place:

½ cup sourdough starter
1 cup warm water
1½ cups flour
¾ cup dry milk granules
6 tablespoons cocoa

Cream together:
1 cup sugar
¾ cup shortening
½ teaspoon salt
1 teaspoon vanilla

SOURDOUGH STARTER
FLOUR
DRY MILK GRANULES
COCOA
SUGAR
SHORTENING
EGGS
SALT
VANILLA
SODA

Add:

2 eggs; beat well after the addition of each egg

1½ teaspoons soda dissolved in 2 tablespoons warm water
Combine with the sourdough mixture and beat by hand, 100 strokes. This will make three 9-inch layers. Bake at 325 degrees for 25 to 30 minutes.

242. Basic Crumb Cake

Some of our most delightful cakes are made by combining two or more proven methods of mixing, and some are the results of defying all the known rules. Coffee Cakes are sometimes made with a Butter Cake batter, but usually they are made this way:

Mix together the following ingredients by flaking between your thumb and first three fingers:

2 cups brown sugar

1 teaspoon cinnamon

2 cups flour

½ cup shortening

BROWN SUGAR
SHORTENING
FLOUR
BUTTERMILK
EGGS
CINNAMON
SODA
VANILLA

Measure and reserve 1 cup of this mix for the top of the cake. To the remaining crumb mixture add:

2 eggs, well beaten

1 cup buttermilk or sour milk

1 teaspoon soda

1 teaspoon vanilla

Grease a 9 x 13 x 2-inch baking pan. Dust with flour (this makes for easy removal of the cake) and pour in the batter. Sprinkle the reserved cup of crumb mix over the top of the batter and bake at 350 degrees for 25 to 30 minutes.

———◆———

These cakes are easy to make for that little bit of "some-

thing sweet" with a cup of coffee or glass of milk—and variations are endless.

Spicy Crumb Cake: Add ½ teaspoon nutmeg and ¼ teaspoon allspice to the dry ingredients. Chopped nutmeats are good too. Allow ½ cup nutmeats per recipe.

Jelly Topping: Spoon your favorite jelly over the top of the batter. Cut the jelly into the batter with a knife. Bake as directed and drizzle a powdered-sugar glaze over the top of the cake while it is still warm. To make the glaze, blend together until mixture drips thickly from a spoon:
 1 cup powdered sugar
 1 teaspoon lemon juice
 Add water until of desired consistency.

Fruit-filled Crumb Cakes: Dust lightly with flour, 1 cup of dried fruit such as raisins, cut-up dates, chopped apples, or cut-up dried apricots, and fold into the batter just before baking.

243. Lightning Cake

Lightning Cake is an old standby. We have it with pudding . . . sometimes with fruit sauce; but never with icing. It is always good and you can make it as fast as lightning . . . well, almost.

Put all together in one bowl and beat:
 1 egg
 ½ cup sugar
 1 cup flour
 1 teaspoon baking powder
 ¼ teaspoon salt
 ¼ cup milk
 3 tablespoons melted butter
 ¼ teaspoon lemon extract or 1 teaspoon vanilla extract

EGG
SUGAR
FLOUR
BUTTER
MILK
BAKING POWDER
SALT
LEMON EXTRACT
(VANILLA EXTRACT)

Grease pans well, dust with flour and pour batter into pans

1¼ inches deep. This will make 1 sheet cake 7 x 11 inches or 2 (8-inch) layers. Bake 25 minutes in a 350-degree oven.

244. Cheese Cake

Delightful, airy Cheese Cakes are as easy as pie to make, in fact easier. Perfect with a heavy meal, they can be prepared a day ahead of time, giving you lots of time for last-minute main-course preparation.

Mix thoroughly together:
  2 cups graham cracker or cookie crumbs
  ⅔ cup melted butter
  ¼ cup sugar
  1 teaspoon cinnamon
Pat into the bottom and around the sides of a 10-inch tube pan. Cream together and mix until very fluffy in texture:
  1 pound cream cheese
  ½ cup sugar
  ¼ cup flour
  ¼ teaspoon salt
Beat together and gradually add:
  4 egg yolks
  juice and grated rind of 1 lemon

GRAHAM CRACKERS OR COOKIE CRUMBS
BUTTER
SUGAR
CINNAMON
CREAM CHEESE
EGGS
WHIPPING CREAM
LEMON
VANILLA
FLOUR
SALT

Whip until stiff and fold into the well-beaten yolk mixture:
  1 cup whipping cream
  1 teaspoon vanilla
Beat until frothy:
  4 egg whites
Continue beating and add:
  4 tablespoons sugar

When the whites form stiff peaks, fold into the batter and pour into the crumb shell. Bake at 300 degrees for 1 hour.

245. Chocolate Mayonnaise Cake

The following cake recipe has all sorts of things going for it. It is rich, moist, velvety, deep in chocolate flavor . . . and it doesn't require any eggs, milk, or shortening! It's such a hit in our family, I watch for mayonnaise "specials" so that I will always have a good supply of the main ingredient. You'll never appreciate it until you try it, so here 'tis:

Sift together:
- 2 cups flour
- 1 cup sugar
- 4 tablespoons cocoa
- 1 teaspoon baking powder
- 1 teaspoon soda

Add:
- 1 cup mayonnaise
- 1 cup cold water
- 1 teaspoon vanilla

FLOUR
SUGAR
COCOA
BAKING
  POWDER
SODA
MAYONNAISE
VANILLA

Beat 3 to 5 minutes. Bake in an 11 x 7-inch well-greased cake pan or 2 (9-inch) layers. Temperature: 350 degrees. Time: 30 to 35 minutes.

246. Boiled Raisin Cake

Now for an old homesteader recipe: Boiled Raisin Cake. In homesteader days, a woman knew how to make the most of what she had on hand. At the same time, she did it in such a way that "her man" felt the satisfaction of "doing well" by his family. This was her gift of love to him. If ingredients were lacking in her humble kitchen, she assured him that she didn't need them anyway, and proceeded to prove it with recipes like the following—which requires no milk, very little shortening, no eggs, yet is delicious.

Simmer together for 10 minutes:

   1 pound of seeded raisins
   3 tablespoons shortening
   3 cups hot water
   2 cups sugar
   1 teaspoon cinnamon
   ¾ teaspoon ginger
   ½ teaspoon cloves

| RAISINS |
| SHORTENING |
| SUGAR |
| CINNAMON |
| GINGER |
| CLOVES |
| NUT MEATS |
| FLOUR |
| SODA |
| SALT |

Mix 1 cup chopped nut meats with 3½ cups sifted flour. Stir into cooled raisin mixture and beat until well blended. Dissolve together:

   2 teaspoons soda
   ½ teaspoon salt
   ¼ cup warm water

Add to the batter and beat well. Pour into 2 well-greased loaf pans, or 1 large 9 x 11-inch cake pan and bake in a 375-degree oven for 45 minutes, or until the cake leaves the edges of the cake pan and the cake springs back when touched lightly in the middle.

Boiled Raisin Cake is especially good with Lemon Sauce . . . and, if by some chance your spouse doesn't like raisins—and mine doesn't—drain the raisin mixture and stir flour and nut meats into the cooled liquid. Use only the liquid in making the cake. When you make the Lemon Sauce, divide the sauce in half. Serve half of it plain and mix the drained raisins with the other half. The rest of our family happens to like raisins! This way, everyone is happy.

Cake Frostings

A cake and its frosting should be compatible. The crowning touch . . . flavor, texture, and eye appeal are all important. The following frostings meet all the necessary requirements. In addition, they need only basic ingredients and are simple to make.

The extra time needed to make a cooked frosting is time

well spent, for the resulting flavor and texture are superior to those of uncooked frostings. Generally, a cooked frosting is used to glorify a Butter Cake.

———◆———

247. Caramel Frosting

Use a saucepan with a heavy bottom for this one. Melt ½ cup sugar over low heat. As the sugar melts, stir to prevent sticking and burning. Continue stirring until the syrup is caramel in color. (This is what is meant by the term "caramelized sugar.") Add ¼ cup boiling water and continue stirring until all the crystals are dissolved. Add:

1½ cups sugar
 2 tablespoons butter
½ cup milk
 pinch of salt

SUGAR,
  GRANULATED
BUTTER
MILK
SALT
VANILLA

Boil to the soft-ball stage (238 degrees on a candy thermometer—or when a drop is placed in cold water, a soft ball forms that can be picked up between the fingers). When the mixture reaches the soft-ball stage, set to cool. Do not stir while cooling for this causes a grainy texture. When the mixture reaches room temperature, add 1 teaspoon vanilla and beat until thick and creamy. Spread on the cake. For variation, sprinkle with chopped nuts.

248. Fudge Frosting

Boil together:
   2 cups sugar
 ½ cup cocoa
   1 cup cream or undiluted evaporated milk
When mixture reaches the soft-ball stage (see preceding recipe), remove from heat, add 2 tablespoons butter, and 1 teaspoon vanilla.

SUGAR,
  GRANULATED
COCOA
CREAM OR
  EVAPORATED
  MILK
BUTTER
VANILLA

Set to cool without stirring. When the mixture has cooled to room temperature, beat until it loses its glossy look and spread on the cake.

249. Whipped Cream Frosting
(without whipped cream)

Mix together until smooth:
  2 tablespoons flour
  ½ cup milk
Cook over low heat until a thick paste is
formed. You will need to stir constantly. When
thick and smooth, pour in a saucer to cool. In
the meantime, cream together:
  ¼ cup butter
  ¼ cup shortening (for a true-white frosting, use a white
    vegetable shortening)
  ½ cup sugar, granulated

MILK
FLOUR
BUTTER OR
  WHITE
  VEGETABLE
  SHORTENING
SUGAR, GRAN-
  ULATED
VANILLA

When this is creamy, light, and fluffy . . . and be sure it is . . .
it should have the appearance of whipped butter . . . gradually add the flour-and-milk paste and continue beating with
an electric mixer for about 5 minutes. Add 1 teaspoon vanilla
and continue beating for 1 minute. This will frost 2 (8-inch)
cake layers. If you are wondering where the frosting got such
a name as Whipped Cream Frosting . . . try it!

250. Basic Butter Frosting

*Uncooked, rich Butter Frostings keep well for several days
and are easy to make.*

Combine together and beat until thick, creamy, and of
spreading consistency:

  3 cups powdered sugar
    pinch of salt
  ½ cup melted butter
  2 to 4 tablespoons milk

POWDERED
  SUGAR
BUTTER
MILK
SALT

Variations:
  Chocolate: Melt 2 squares of chocolate and blend into the

mixture. In this case, you will probably need only 2 tablespoons of milk.

Orange: Substitute orange juice for the milk and add 1 teaspoon finely grated peel.

Lemon: Substitute 2 tablespoons of lemon juice and 2 tablespoons of orange juice for the milk and add 1 teaspoon of finely grated lemon peel.

Coffee Butter: Use strong coffee in place of the milk.

251. Never-Fail Fluffy White Frosting

Frostings that are light and delicate in both texture and flavor are best with Chiffon, Angel, and Sponge Cakes. This Fluffy White Frosting meets all the requirements and the following method of making never fails:

Into a medium-sized mixing bowl, put:

- 1 egg white
- 1 cup sugar (granulated)
- ¼ teaspoon cream of tartar
- ½ cup boiling water

Begin to beat at once with rotary beater or electric mixer. Beat until thick and fluffy. Add ½ teaspoon vanilla or you can omit the vanilla and add ½ teaspoon of lemon extract with a little grated lemon rind.

EGG WHITE
SUGAR
CREAM OF TARTAR
VANILLA
(LEMON EXTRACT)
(GRATED LEMON RIND)

252. Cream Cheese Frosting

Cream Cheese Frosting and Carrot Chiffon Cake (Recipe No. 236) were just meant for each other:

Cream together:

- 1 (8-ounce) package cream cheese
- ½ cup butter
- 1 box of powdered sugar (1 pound)
- 1 cup coconut
- 1 teaspoon vanilla
- ½ teaspoon rum flavoring

CREAM CHEESE
BUTTER
POWDERED SUGAR
COCONUT
VANILLA
RUM FLAVORING

253. Basic Fruit Filling

A fruit filling can be used between cake layers, adding flavor as well as being practical, for a filling helps to keep a cake moist. The following recipe is very basic, for white sugar can be substituted for brown sugar, a teaspoon of lemon juice can be added when using citrus fruit, and a teaspoon of cinnamon can be added when using dried fruits:

Mix together:
- ½ cup sugar
- 1 tablespoon flour (be sure it is level)
- 1 teaspoon of cinnamon or lemon juice, depending on your choice of fruit

Add:
- 1 cup water
- 1 cup chopped dried fruit, such as raisins, dates, figs or prunes . . . or . . . if using crushed pineapple, cooked pureed apricots, or peaches . . . use 2 cups crushed fruit

FRUIT OF YOUR CHOICE
SUGAR
FLOUR
CINNAMON OR LEMON JUICE

Cook slowly, stirring constantly, until thick and clear. When the filling is completely cooled, spread between cake layers.

254. Broiled Topping

Broiled toppings are quick, easy, and a delight to eat. Perfect for sheet cakes and coffee cakes, they are made like this:

Combine together:
- 6 tablespoons melted butter
- 2 tablespoons flour

Stir in:
- 1⅓ cups flaked coconut
- ½ cup coarsely chopped pecans
- ½ cup brown sugar
- ¼ cup cream or evaporated milk

BUTTER
FLOUR
BROWN SUGAR
FLAKED COCONUT
PECANS OR NUT MEATS
CREAM

Spread on the warm cake. Place under a pre-heated broiler for 3 minutes, or until lightly browned.

RECIPE GUIDE

COOKIES

There are almost as many cookie recipes as there is Sagebrush in Eastern Oregon. Since a full cookie jar is a "must" in a home with children, the following wide choice of recipes —plus the fact that it is just as easy to double the recipe as it is to make a single batch—makes cookie-baking practical as well as fun. Nutritious and good eating, cookies and milk easily supply the extra nourishment that is sometimes needed between meals . . . or when served with fresh or stewed fruit, they provide that "something sweet" to end a heavy meal.

Generally, cookies are mixed in the same manner that you would a Butter Cake . . . just a matter of creaming the shortening and sugar together, beating in eggs and adding the dry ingredients alternately with the liquid. Cookies should be baked on a shelf near the top of the oven. Be sure there is room for circulation of heat between the edge of the cookie sheet and the sides of the oven. Cookies should be removed from the baking sheet and placed on a wire rack to cool as soon as they are taken from the oven. There is a tendency to over-bake cookies. They will continue to cook in their own heat after they are taken from the oven. I have found that, as a rule, one-third less baking time than that specified will produce a better product. Test the first sheet of cookies carefully to determine the time needed. They are done when browned delicately and the center of the cookie does not dent when touched very lightly.

When the cookies have cooled, they can be stored in airtight jars or tins, or they can be stored in the freezer for as long as needed. Frozen bakery goods has a way of being fresher from the freezer! Do not mix types of cookies when storing, for the crisp cookies will absorb moisture from the soft cookies and neither one will be good.

On Rolled Cookies...

Basically there are two types of cookie dough—"soft dough" for Drop Cookies and "stiff dough" for Rolled Cookies. There is a special "knack" for making good Rolled Cookies. It helps to chill the dough and then handle it as little as possible. The fewer times you roll the dough out, the better the texture will be. Because it is necessary to roll and re-roll the dough for round cookies, a great deal of care is needed to see that additional flour is not worked in, just from rolling the dough. In making square cookies, however, you don't have to worry— one cutting and they are done. Sometimes the lazy way of doing things turns out to be the better way!

255. Basic Rolled Cookies

Following is a good Basic Rolled Cookie Recipe that can be used any number of ways:

Cream together:
    2 cups sugar
    2 cups butter
Add:
    4 eggs
    1 teaspoon vanilla
Blend in:
    5 cups sifted flour
    1 teaspoon salt
    1 tablespoon baking powder

SUGAR
BUTTER
EGGS
VANILLA
FLOUR
BAKING
  POWDER
SALT

If the dough should be stiff, add a tablespoon of milk. The size of the eggs has a great deal to do with the texture of the dough. Divide the dough into 4 equal portions. Roll dough out to about ¼ inch thick. Cut cookies, sprinkle with sugar, and bake at 350 degrees for 8 to 10 minutes . . . or, this same dough can be prepared in a number of other tasty ways, such as with chocolate chips or coconut or raisins or nuts or dates. Makes about 5 dozen cookies.

256. Date Bars

Roll a portion of the Basic Cookie dough out to about ¼ inch thick. Spread with a date mixture and then crumble cookie dough over the dates. Bake about 35 minutes in a 350-degree oven. Cut in bars while still warm and roll in powdered sugar. Use the Fruit Filling Recipe No. 258.

BASIC DOUGH
FRUIT
    FILLING
    (RECIPE
    258)

257. Spice Thins

Roll dough into 1-inch balls. Then roll each ball in a mixture of:

BASIC DOUGH
SUGAR
GINGER
NUTMEG
CINNAMON

1½	cups sugar
1½	teaspoons ginger
¼	teaspoon nutmeg
¼	teaspoon cinnamon

Place on a lightly greased cookie sheet. Flatten each ball to a ⅛-inch thickness with a drinking glass that has been dipped in the sugar mixture. Use a glass that has a pretty design cut in the bottom. Makes for pretty cookies. Bake 10 to 12 minutes at 350 degrees.

258. Fruit Filling

This filling is good with any basic cookie dough. Combine together:

SUGAR
DATES
RAISINS
FLOUR
LEMON RIND
LEMON JUICE
SALT

½	cup sugar
½	cup chopped dates
½	cup chopped raisins
1	tablespoon flour
½	teaspoon grated lemon rind
½	teaspoon lemon juice
½	teaspoon salt
¼	cup water

Simmer together for 5 minutes. Cool completely before using.

259. Gingerbread Men

For the "busy" young ones in your family, making Gingerbread Men can be a good way to keep them occupied:

Cream together:

  ⅓ cup shortening

  ¾ cup sugar

When this begins to have the appearance and texture of whipped cream, add:

  1 well-beaten egg

(A hint for the new cook: These two steps, the creaming of the shortening and sugar, and blending in of the egg really determine the texture of your cookies or cake. It pays to take extra time at this point in mixing.)

Beat in:

  ½ cup molasses

  2 teaspoons soda which have been dissolved in 2 teaspoons hot water. (Do not use boiling water, just extremely hot)

Sift together:

  2¼ cups flour

  ½ teaspoon cinnamon

  1 teaspoon ginger

| SHORTENING |
| SUGAR |
| EGG |
| MOLASSES |
| SODA |
| FLOUR |
| CINNAMON |
| GINGER |

Combine the dry ingredients with the creamed mixture. Chill the dough at least 2 hours for easier handling; otherwise it will be quite sticky. Roll to ⅛-inch thickness and cut, either into round cookies or Gingerbread Men. Place on a greased baking sheet and bake at 350 degrees for about 10 minutes. Makes about 6 dozen, 1½-inch cookies.

If you are making little round Ginger Snaps and want them to have the crackled surface commercial ones have, simply brush each cookie with water before baking.

260. Egg-Yolk Paint

Egg-Yolk Paint can be used to decorate all sorts of cookies.

Beat together:

  2 egg yolks

  ½ teaspoon water

| EGG YOLKS |
| FOOD |
| COLORING |

Divide among several small custard cups. With liquid food coloring, tint each portion the desired color.

You will need a small, inexpensive paint brush for each color. The paint is used on the unbaked cookie and then baked on. This project is more fun than finger painting for youngsters, and if done in the evening, the whole family often wants to help.

For further cookie trims, mix together:

2 cups powdered sugar

2 tablespoons hot water

1 teaspoon vanilla

POWDERED
SUGAR
VANILLA

This is the type that can be garnished with candied cherries, colored sugars, cinnamon candies, silver shot . . . all the things that are available to make your cookies pretty. This particular icing is ideal for Santa's beard, for it does dry hard.

Nature's paintbrush has dripped shades of red, green, and gold with splashes of black on the Painted Hills near Mitchell, Oregon, in the John Day country.

On Raisins...

Before we go on to Drop Cookie Recipes, I'd like to share this trick with raisins because it is one that is well worth the extra few minutes it takes to do. About a week before you plan to start your Christmas baking, place 2 pounds of raisins in a large jar. Cover with hot water and add a slice of lemon. Cover and store in the refrigerator until needed. When you are ready to bake fancy yeast breads or cookies, drain the raisins well and don't throw away the liquid; it can be used instead of water in cookies or breads for a tantalizing taste treat in many recipes. . . .

Back to the drained raisins: Use in any recipe calling for raisins just as you would raisins direct from the box. They will be extra moist, and the soaking seems to give the raisin a fullness of flavor that the dried raisin just doesn't have.

The first time I soaked raisins was entirely by accident. I had a quantity of raisins that were just plain hard and I couldn't bring myself to throw them away, even to the birds, so I added some water and set them on the shelf to see if they would plump up. Meanwhile, we were called back to the Middle West. It was two months before we returned and I discovered the long-forgotten raisins. I used them all in what my family claimed were the best sweet rolls and cookies they had ever eaten. With that sort of encouragement I have been soaking raisins for baking ever since. I don't always take time to prepare them throughout the year, but at Christmas time, I see to it that only pre-soaked raisins go into the Christmas goodies.

On Drop Cookies...

Drop cookies are mixed in the same manner as Rolled Cookies. The dough is softer and is placed on the cookie sheet by dipping into the dough with a teaspoon and pushing the dough from the end of the spoon onto the cookie sheet with your fingertip or another spoon. Allow 2 inches around each cookie for the dough will spread as it bakes.

261. Carrot Cookies

Carrot Cookies are good to feed to small fry during that phase most of them go through when you have trouble getting them to eat foods they should have. Extra vitamins are a bonus of Carrot Cookies. They are simple to make—but be sure to make plenty, because they are usually a hit with the whole family.

Mix them as you would a Butter Cake. You know . . . cream shortening and sugar, add egg, then dry ingredients alternately with the mashed carrots. Now for the recipe:

¾ cup shortening
¾ cup sugar
1 egg
1 teaspoon vanilla
1 cup mashed cooked carrots. (to save time, use baby food carrots)
2 cups flour
2 teaspoons baking powder
1 teaspoon salt
1 cup chopped nuts   (optional)

SHORTENING
SUGAR
EGG
VANILLA
COOKED
  CARROTS
FLOUR
BAKING
  POWDER
SALT
(NUTS) –
(RAISINS)

Mix as usual and drop by teaspoon on a cookie sheet. Bake at 350 degrees, 10 to 12 minutes. These cookies should be iced while still warm. For the icing: Mix juice and grated rind of 1 small orange. Blend with powdered sugar to make a stiff frosting. Spread on the warm cookies. For extra goodness and nutrition, add a cup of raisins at the same time that you add the nuts. Makes about 5 dozen cookies.

262. Mincemeat Cookies

Blend together:

½ cup soft shortening

1 cup sugar

Cream until fluffy. Then add:

2 eggs (beat until thick and lemony in appearance)

Sift together:

2½ cups sifted flour

¼ teaspoon soda

½ teaspoon salt

1 teaspoon vanilla

SHORTENING
SUGAR
EGGS
FLOUR
SODA
SALT
VANILLA
MINCEMEAT
CREAM

Add dry ingredients alternately with 2 tablespoons of thick cream to the shortening mixture. Mix lightly, gather into a round ball, and place the dough in the refrigerator for about 1 hour to chill. Remove and roll very thin, about 1/16-inch thick.

You can cut this dough into rounds if you like, but I have found it better to cut it into squares. On each square, place a rounded teaspoon of mincemeat. Fold over like a turnover, then press the edges together, either with your fingertips or with a fork that has been dipped in flour. Puncture the top of each cookie with a fork so that steam will escape in baking. Place the filled cookies on a cookie sheet and bake at 375 degrees for 8 to 10 minutes, or until a golden brown. Makes about 3 dozen.

263. Peanut Butter Cookies

Beat together until thick, smooth and creamy:

1 cup butter

1 cup peanut butter

1¼ cups sugar

¾ cup firmly packed brown sugar

2 eggs

1 teaspoon vanilla

Sift together and add:

2½ cups sifted flour

BUTTER
PEANUT
  BUTTER
SUGAR
BROWN SUGAR
EGGS
VANILLA
FLOUR
BAKING SODA
SALT

2 teaspoons baking soda
½ teaspoon salt

Drop by rounded teaspoons onto a baking sheet. Press with the back of a sugared fork to make criss-crosses. Bake at 350 degrees, 8 to 10 minutes. Cool immediately on a wire rack. Makes about 6 dozen.

———◆———

264. Sour-Cream Cookies

There is something about sour cream that makes final baking results always just a little bit extra . . . extra tender . . . extra moist . . . and extra tasty.

Cream together:
  ½ cup shortening
  1 cup sugar
Add and beat in:
  1 egg
  ½ teaspoon lemon extract
Sift together:
  2 cups flour
  1 teaspoon baking powder
  ½ teaspoon salt
  ¼ teaspoon baking soda
  ½ teaspoon nutmeg
  ½ teaspoon cinnamon
Add:
  ½ cup sour cream (alternately with the dry ingredients) to the creamed mixture.

SHORTENING
SUGAR
EGG
LEMON
  EXTRACT
FLOUR
BAKING
  POWDER
SALT
BAKING SODA
NUTMEG
CINNAMON
SOUR CREAM

Drop by teaspoonfuls, 2 inches apart on a well-greased baking sheet. Bake at 375 degrees, 12 to 15 minutes. Makes about 3½ dozen 2-inch cookies.

If you prefer a blander cookie, leave out the spices and lemon and add a teaspoon of vanilla extract instead. These cookies are welcome during the Christmas Season as a pleasant change from the usual over-rich holiday fare.

265. Spice Drop Cookies

This cookie is a favorite with children. Cream together:

½ cup shortening	SHORTENING
1 cup sugar	SUGAR
Add and beat until fluffy:	EGGS
2 eggs	CONDENSED
½ cup condensed tomato soup, undiluted	TOMATO
1 cup chopped nuts	SOUP
Sift together and add:	NUTS
1½ cups sifted flour	FLOUR
2 teaspoons baking powder	BAKING
½ teaspoon salt	POWDER
½ teaspoon ground cinnamon	SALT
½ teaspoon all spice	CINNAMON
½ teaspoon ground cloves	ALL SPICE
½ teaspoon ground nutmeg	GROUND

Drop by teaspoonfuls onto a well-greased cookie sheet. Bake at 350 degrees, 12 to 15 minutes. Will make about 5 dozen cookies.

266. Apple Bars

The ease and quickness of baking Bar Cookies makes them the popular answer for a quick dessert.

Cream together:	BROWN SUGAR
2 cups brown sugar	SHORTENING
⅔ cup shortening	EGGS
Add and beat until fluffy:	SALT
2 eggs	VANILLA
¼ teaspoon salt	FLOUR
1 teaspoon vanilla	BAKING
Sift together and add:	POWDER
2 cups sifted flour	RAW APPLE
2 teaspoons baking powder	NUT MEATS
Stir into the batter:	(APRICOTS, DRIED) (RAISINS)

1½ cups chopped raw apple
½ cup chopped nut meats

Bake in a 9 x 12 x 2-inch baking dish for 35 to 40 minutes. Don't forget to grease the pan and use a 350-degree oven. Cookies are done when the top is touched lightly and no dent remains. Serve warm with whipped cream. Makes about 24 squares.

Variations: Substitute chopped, dried apricots for raw apple, or cook 2 cups of raisins in 1¾ cups of water until all the water is absorbed. Stir in ½ teaspoon of baking soda and add at once to the cookie batter.

———◆———

267. Fudge Brownies

The important thing in making Brownies is not to over-bake.

Melt together over hot water:
    4 squares unsweetened chocolate
    ½ cup butter
When the chocolate and butter have cooled slightly, beat in:
    4 eggs, one at a time
    2 cups sugar
    1 teaspoon vanilla
When fluffy and well mixed add:
    1 cup sifted flour
    1 cup coarsely chopped walnuts

UNSWEET-ENED CHOCOLATE SQUARES
BUTTER
EGGS
SUGAR
VANILLA
FLOUR
WALNUTS

Mix well and spread in a greased 9-inch square pan. Bake at 325 degrees, 35 to 40 minutes. Cool thoroughly in pan, then cut in squares or bars. Makes about 2 dozen delicious Brownies.

RECIPE GUIDE

PIES

~~~~~~

Ask almost anyone to name a favorite dessert and the answer is usually "pie." Though there are many quick methods of making piecrust on the market today—in the form of ready-made crust, mixes, and dough sticks—both economy and flavor-wise, nothing really quite equals a good all homemade pie straight from the oven.

In making pie, it isn't the filling that's a problem, it's the crust! Here, too, there are many methods of mixing. The art of flaking the shortening with the flour and adding just the right amount of icewater seems to be one that is difficult for most people. The method of flaking the flour and shortening together is a matter of personal preference. Pastry blenders are available on the market, or the shortening can be cut into the flour with the use of two knives, cutting and tossing the ingredients together until the shortening pieces are the size of small peas. I prefer to flake with my fingers. Place your thumb on your third finger and then let it slip lightly over the second and first finger in that order. Now do it with flour and shortening, flaking the ingredients together until the shortening flakes are about ½ inch in diameter. Add liquid. Shape dough into a ball and roll thin. Fold carefully in half and place on one half of the pie tin. Unfold the dough to the other side of the tin.

Do not stretch the dough. Let it drape and fit itself to the sides of the pie tin. Repeat the same process with the other section of dough when making 2-crust pies. When the rolled dough is folded in half and ready to place in position on the pie, take a sharp knife and cut pretty designs, such as daisy patterns. This not only makes the pie more attractive, it allows the steam to escape while the pie is baking.

When the top crust is in position, trim off the excess crust from around the edge of the pie, then flute the edges of the pie, using a fork or your fingertips to press the two edges together. I personally like to use my fingertips to create a pretty fluted edge.

When making single-crust pies—such as cream pies where the crust is first baked and then put together with the filling—prick the unbaked pie shell with a fork all around the inside edges as well as across the bottom.

268. "Never-Fail" Pie Crust

The following pie crust recipe has so many advantages, I rarely work with others. Ingredients need not be refrigerated prior to using, the dough is easily handled, and the recipe can be doubled or tripled—something that is not usually recommended with other methods. Since the recipe can be made successfully in quantity, I usually make up 6 cups of flour at once. This way, there is enough for several pies and some extra dough to keep in the refrigerator for emergency desserts. This "extra" dough can be kept in an air-tight plastic container in the refrigerator 10 to 14 days. When ready to use, let dough stand at room temperature for at least 1 hour before rolling. Of all the recipes I have shared with radio listeners over the years, I really believe this one has proved to be the most requested:

Flake together:

   2 cups flour

   1 cup shortening

This next step is the "magic touch." Stir in:

   ½ cup evaporated milk, undiluted

   1 teaspoon salt

FLOUR
SHORTENING
EVAPORATED MILK
SALT

Stir together just until the mixture begins to cling together and can be formed into a ball of dough. Cut dough in half and place one section on a lightly floured board. With a rolling pin, roll the dough lightly. Roll the dough from the center out. Turn the circle of dough over, lightly flouring the board between turns. This keeps the pie shell from puffing up and then shrinking. Bake near the top of the oven in a 425-degree oven, 12 to 15 minutes. After the first 5 minutes of baking, if the crust shows signs of becoming brown too quickly on the edges, place in a lower position in the oven.

269. Baking Berry & Fruit Pies

Pie fillings are many and varied, yet methods of making are quite basic:

With damp fingers, flute the top and bottom edges of the crust together, to prevent the filling from seeping out the edges of the pie during baking. Bake in a 425-degree oven on the next to the lowest rack (5 to 6 inches from the bottom element) for 10 minutes. Turn the oven down to 350 degrees and continue baking the pie 30 to 40 minutes more. If thick, lovely juice bubbles up through a golden brown crust, you can be sure it's done.

270. Thickening for Fruit Pies

For every 3 cups of fruit, mix together with the sugar:

2½ tablespoons of tapioca or 2 level tablespoons of flour

FRUIT
SUGAR
TAPIOCA OR FLOUR
LEMON JUICE
SALT

Mix with fruit (fresh or canned) and place in an unbaked pie shell. In making fruit pies, I always use ⅛ teaspoon of salt and 1 tablespoon lemon juice to bring out the flavor of the fruit. Add nothing else! No "off" flavors! Top with another crust in which you have cut a pretty design.

Fruit varies in tartness and sugar amounts can only be sug-

gested. The following suggestions are meant to be a guideline only. They are based on 3 cups of fruit per pie:

Blackberry Pie	½ to ¾ cup sugar
Blueberry Pie	1 to 1½ cups sugar
Cherry Pie	¾ to 1 cup sugar
Gooseberry Pie	¾ to 1 cup sugar
Loganberry Pie	½ to ¾ cup sugar
Peach Pie	½ to ¾ cup sugar
Rhubarb Pie	¾ to 1 cup sugar

———◆———

271. Apple Pie

Apple Pies require very little thickening. This Apple Pie is very simple but very delicious:

Peel and slice 8 apples. Sprinkle with:
- ¾ cup sugar
- 1 teaspoon cinnamon
- 1 tablespoon flour

Drizzle the apples with the juice of:
- ½ lemon

APPLES
SUGAR
CINNAMON
FLOUR
LEMON
BUTTER

Dot with butter. Top with crust. It's fun to make the design of an apple with a leaf or two on the top crust. Bake at 375 degrees for 50 to 60 minutes. During the last 5 minutes of baking, brush the crust with "half and half" milk. (Canned milk makes a lovely glaze with no "off" flavor.)

272. Mincemeat Pie

Mincemeat Pie is baked just as you would any fruit pie. The secret is in the filling used. The following recipe makes 9 pints—filling for 9 pies—and is well worth the time and effort required to prepare.

Into a large kettle put:

2 quarts of coarsely ground cooked meat (venison, beef, or pork, or a combination thereof)	MEAT (COOKED VENISON BEEF OR PORK)
3 cups ground suet	SUET
6 cups chopped apples	APPLES
4 cups seedless raisins	SEEDLESS RAISINS
1 (15-ounce) box of seeded raisins	SEEDED RAISINS
1 (15-ounce) box of currants	CURRANTS
1 tablespoon salt	SALT
1 tablespoon ground cinnamon	CINNAMON
1 tablespoon ground ginger	GINGER
1 tablespoon ground cloves	CLOVES
1 tablespoon nutmeg	NUTMEG
1 teaspoon allspice	ALLSPICE
1 teaspoon mace	MACE
8 cups apple cider	APPLE CIDER
2 cups brown sugar	BROWN SUGAR

Simmer for about 2 hours, stirring often to keep it from sticking. It can be stored in pint-size containers in the freezer, or processed with a pressure cooker. Pint jars take 60 minutes at 10 pounds pressure.

273. French Prune Pie

Dried Prunes can be glamorous, and "cooked in the refrigerator" they take no more than 2 minutes of your time. Fill a glass fruit jar with dried prunes. Add boiling liquid to cover. This liquid can be water or left-over syrup from canned fruits. Cool to room temperature, put the lid on the jar and place in the refrigerator for at least 2 days (3 or 4 days are even better). You'll have tender, luscious fruit in a deep-flavored, full-bodied juice. Now, try this French Prune Pie:

Lay 2¾ cups of pitted "refrigerator-cooked" prunes in the

bottom of a pie shell. Make a mixture of:

1 egg	PRUNES
⅓ cup sugar	EGG
dash of salt	SUGAR
	SALT
½ cup prune juice liquid	PRUNE JUICE
1 tablespoon lemon juice	LEMON JUICE

Pour this over the prunes. Make a crumb topping by mixing together:

	FLOUR
	BROWN SUGAR
¼ cup flour	ALLSPICE
½ cup brown sugar	BUTTER
½ teaspoon allspice	WALNUTS
¼ cup butter	
½ cup chopped walnuts	

Sprinkle over the pie and bake at 450 degrees for 15 minutes. Reduce heat to 350 degrees and bake 25 minutes longer. Believe me, after a bite of French Prune Pie you will no longer think of prunes as everyday fare.

274. Pumpkin Pie

Pumpkin Pie is my personal favorite. For each pie, whip together:

1½ cups cooked pumpkin	PUMPKIN, CANNED
2 eggs	EGGS
1 cup evaporated milk	MILK
1 cup sugar (½ white and ½ brown)	WHITE SUGAR
	BROWN SUGAR
¼ teaspoon salt	SALT
¼ teaspoon nutmeg	NUTMEG
¼ teaspoon cinnamon	CINNAMON
¼ teaspoon allspice	ALLSPICE
½ teaspoon vanilla	VANILLA

Pour into a pastry-lined pie pan and bake 10 minutes at 400 degrees and 25 minutes at 375 degrees. Be very careful not to over-bake. Bake just until a knife inserted in the center comes out clean. A pumpkin pie will continue to bake in its own heat for a short time after being removed from the oven.

275. Raisin Pie

My spouse keeps telling me raisins were meant to be used in pies only—nowhere else. This is his favorite pie.

Soak together for 2 hours:
    1 cup raisins
    2¼ cups water
Mix together:
    1¼ cups sugar
    2 tablespoons flour

RAISINS
EGG
SUGAR
FLOUR
LEMON
SALT

Add the following to the flour and sugar. Beat together until smooth:
    1 egg, well beaten
    3 tablespoons lemon juice
    2 teaspoons finely grated lemon rind (optional)
    ⅛ teaspoon salt

Combine with the plumped raisins and cook in the top part of a double boiler until thickened. Takes about 15 minutes and you will need to stir occasionally. Set to cool. This type of filling must be completely cooled before placing in the pastry shell. Interlace ½-inch strips of pastry dough in a lattice-work design to top the pie.

276. Rhubarb Pie

Rhubarb is always a welcome treat, come early spring. We like it in pie. Mix together and let stand while making the pie crust:

    1 cup sugar
    2 tablespoons flour
    2 eggs, well beaten
    ⅛ teaspoon salt

RHUBARB
SUGAR
EGG
FLOUR
SALT

Dice 3 cups of rhubarb into the unbaked pie shell. Pour the sugar-and-egg mixture over the rhubarb. Interlace cut strips of pastry dough in a lattice-work design for a topping—or for variation, use the topping mixture given for French Prune Pie.

277. Meringue

With cream pies, it is important that both the baked crust and filling be cool. Adding a warm filling to a warm crust causes soggy bottom crusts, and adding a meringue to a warm filling causes watery meringues. The trick to producing good cream pies is to make up the various parts well ahead of time, combining just before serving. Browning the meringue takes mere minutes. The following recipe makes enough meringue for one 9-inch pie:

Beat the whites of 2 eggs until stiff but not dry. Add a dash of salt. Gradually beat in 4 tablespoons of sugar. Sprinkle over the top as you beat. Continue beating until smooth and glossy. Pile lightly on top of the pie, being careful to seal the edges of the pastry because there will be some shrinkage as it browns and you don't want the filling to show when it's done. Brown in a 325-degree oven 15 to 20 minutes.

EGG WHITES
SUGAR

278. Cream Pie Filling
(or Pudding)

In the top of a double boiler, put:
   2 egg yolks (beaten until thick)
Add to the egg yolks, beating until thick and smooth:
   ¾ cup sugar
   2 tablespoons flour
   ½ teaspoon salt
   2 cups milk   (add last)

EGG YOLK
SUGAR
FLOUR
SALT
MILK
VANILLA

Cook in the top of a double boiler until the mixture drops from a spoon like cold honey. Stir constantly for about 10 minutes. When it is nice and thick, remove from the fire and add 1 teaspoon vanilla. Cover with a lid to prevent scum from forming on the top and set aside to cool.

For variation, grate semi-sweet chocolate into the cooled filling—or stir ½ cup cocoa into the sugar when mixing. Instead of topping with meringue, top with whipped cream and grate chocolate over the cream. The same thing works with coconut. Creamed Fruit Fillings are a matter of stirring in bananas or oranges or well-drained cherries; it depends on you and your kitchen cupboard.

◆

279. Lemon Cream Pie

If you want to please the family and yourself, bake this Lemon Cream Pie. Its flavor is as refreshing as the smell of juniper and sage after a rain:

Prepare pastry (½ of recipe for "Never-fail Pie Crust) and make an unbaked 9-inch pastry shell. Chill in the refrigerator while you prepare the filling.

Cream together:

  1 cup sugar
  2 tablespoons butter

Add:

  4 egg yolks, one at a time. Beat until fluffy after the addition of each yolk.
  2 tablespoons flour
  1 cup milk
  1 teaspoon grated lemon rind
  ⅓ cup lemon juice

Beat until stiff but not dry:

  4 egg whites
  ¼ teaspoon salt

PASTRY SHELL
SUGAR
BUTTER
EGG YOLKS
FLOUR
MILK
LEMON RIND
LEMON JUICE
EGG WHITES
SALT

Fold the beaten egg whites into the yolk mixture and pour into the pastry shell. Bake on lower shelf in a 425-degree oven about 30 minutes, or until a knife inserted in the center comes out clean.

280. Affinity Pie

This is an old recipe, straight from Grandma's kitchen. Maybe she had an "affinity" for bananas, hence the name. . . .

Mix together until well blended:

¾ cup sugar	BANANAS
¼ teaspoon salt (just enough to bring out flavors)	SUGAR
	EGGS
	MILK
2 tablespoons flour	FLOUR
1 tablespoon cornstarch	CORNSTARCH
Add:	SALT
	GRATED
2 egg yolks, well beaten	LEMON
2 cups hot milk	RIND

Cook in a double boiler, stirring constantly until very thick and smooth. Stir in the grated rind of ½ lemon. Cover a baked pie shell with sliced bananas (usually takes 2). Pour in the cooled cream filling and top with meringue.

Meringue for Affinity Pie

Beat 2 egg whites until stiff, but not dry. Add 4 tablespoons sugar, one at a time, beating well after the addition of each spoon of sugar. Last of all, beat in ½ teaspoon lemon juice. Top the pie and bake in a slow oven, about 300 degrees, until a golden brown.

281. Fried Pies

Fried pies can be made with either baking-powder biscuit dough or doughnut dough . . . texture of dough is a matter of personal preference. And, in today's kitchens, fillings are quick and easy. Well-flavored applesauce can be used; canned cherry-pie filling is quick and tasty; canned apricots or peaches sprinkled with a bit of sugar and cinnamon are delicious; in fact, variations of fillings are half the fun of making and eating Fried Pies.

BISCUIT DOUGH OR DOUGHNUT DOUGH (RECIPE 282) FRUIT FILLING POWDERED SUGAR DEEP FAT

Roll dough to a thickness of ¼ inch and cut into 6-inch rounds. (A 2-pound coffee can makes a good "cutter.") Place 2 tablespoons of filling on each round. Fold the dough over, making a half circle. Moisture your fingertips and press the edges together. Fry the pies in deep fat (370 degrees) until puffed and brown. Drain on absorbent paper. Fried pies can be dusted with powdered sugar if you like the additional sweetness, or served plain with wedges of cheese.

There is serenity in cattle country.

282. Potato Doughboys

This recipe is a good basis for Fried Pies as well as for tender, tasty Doughboys — or doughnuts. Mashed potatoes make the difference!

Mix together while hot:
- 1 cup mashed potatoes
- 1 cup sugar
- 1 tablespoon butter

Let cool, then add:
- 2 eggs
- 3 cups sifted flour
- 1 tablespoon baking powder
- ½ teaspoon salt
- ⅓ cup milk plus 1 tablespoon milk
- 1 teaspoon vanilla

MASHED POTATOES
SUGAR
BUTTER
EGGS
FLOUR
BAKING POWDER
SALT
MILK
VANILLA
SHORTENING
POWDERED SUGAR
MILK

Mix together to form a soft dough. Roll out ½ inch thick on a lightly floured board. Cut with a biscuit or doughnut cutter and fry in deep fat (370 degrees) about 1 minute on each side. Turn only once while frying. Drain on paper towels, or split a clean brown paper sack and use in place of paper towels. Sprinkle with powdered sugar while warm.

◆

When using a skillet as a deep-fat fryer, have the melted shortening about 1½ inches deep. Adjust the burner to medium heat (this happens to be No. 3 on my stove). Try a test Doughboy first. If it browns on each side to the desired doneness and still cooks in the middle, you are in business.

283. Pan Dowdy

This recipe is another very old one, and always in demand. Pan Dowdy can be made with apples, blackberries, cherries, fresh peaches, rhubarb—in fact, fresh fruit of all kinds.

Wash and prepare the fruit just as you would in making pie. Arrange 3 cups of fruit in a well-buttered 8-inch square baking pan that is 2 inches deep. Mix the following ingredients together and sprinkle over the fruit:

1 cup of sugar, more or less, depending on the tartness of the fruit. (Brown sugar is good with apples and peaches)
1 teaspoon lemon juice to bring out the flavor
A dash of salt
½ teaspoon cinnamon or other spices, if desired

FRUIT OR BERRIES
SUGAR
LEMON JUICE
SALT
(SPICES)
BISCUIT DOUGH
EGG WHITE

Dot with butter and add:
½ cup water

Make a baking-powder biscuit dough. Roll ¼ inch thick, cut several slashes for steam escapes, and place over the top of the fruit. Flute the edges of dough around the baking pan just as you would the top crust of a pie.

Mix together:
1 egg white
¼ cup water

Brush the Pan Dowdy with the egg-white mixture and bake in a 325-degree oven 25 to 30 minutes. Brush once again during the baking period with the egg-white mixture. The Pan Dowdy is done when syrup bubbles up through the steam escapes and the topping is a delicate golden brown. Delicious served while still warm with cream. Makes 6 generous servings.

RECIPE GUIDE

PUDDINGS

〰〰〰〰〰〰〰〰〰〰〰〰〰〰〰〰〰〰〰〰〰

284. Old-Fashioned Rice Pudding

Old-fashioned rice pudding made in the oven of a wood range is a taste treat most of our youngsters have never had. This used to be an economical as well as delicious dessert, for it baked slowly in the oven all afternoon and came out all "caramely" at supper time. It is still a good dessert—if you plan it when you have a roast or something in the oven that takes low heat.

Mix together:
- ½ cup raw rice
- 4 cups milk
- ½ cup sugar
- ½ teaspoon salt
- dash of nutmeg
- ½ cup raisins

RICE
MILK
SUGAR
SALT
NUTMEG
RAISINS

Bake in a well-buttered 1½-quart casserole, uncovered, for about 3 hours. It is important that you maintain an oven temperature of 275 degrees, for the slow baking caramelizes the milk and sugar and gives the rice a flavor you can never get with quick cooking. When a brown film forms over the top of the pudding, stir it well and then let it bake gently on. You will need to stir about every 45 minutes. The pudding is done when the rice is tender and has absorbed the milk.

285. Carrot and Potato Steamed Pudding

Cream together:
    ¼ cup shortening
    1 cup brown sugar
Add:
    2 eggs (beating well after the addition of each egg)
    1 cup grated raw carrots
    1 cup grated raw potatoes
Sift together:
    1¼ cups sifted flour
    1 teaspoon soda
    ¼ teaspoon salt
    1 teaspoon cinnamon
    ½ teaspoon cloves

SHORTENING
BROWN SUGAR
EGGS
CARROTS
POTATOES
FLOUR
SODA
SALT
CINNAMON
CLOVES
(CITRON)
LEMON PEEL
RAISINS
(WALNUT MEATS)

Take ½ of the flour mixture and dredge the following fruits and nuts:
    ⅓ cup finely chopped citron
    ⅓ cup finely chopped candied lemon peel
    1 cup seedless raisins
    1 cup finely chopped walnut meats

Add the flour and spices to the shortening and egg mixture gradually, beating well after each addition. Last of all, combine with the fruit and flour mixture, stirring until well blended.

Fill a well-greased 1½ quart mold ⅔ full. Cover tightly and set on a rack in a kettle. Fill the kettle with boiling water to a depth of 2 inches. Cover the kettle and steam pudding for 3 hours, or until a toothpick inserted comes out clean. Add more water if needed.

A good way to do all this is to use a covered casserole dish for the pudding. Place inside a roaster on a rack. Pour 2 inches of boiling water in the roaster. Cover and set the whole thing in a 350-degree oven for 3 hours. This makes a delicious holiday pudding and is best served with Lemon Sauce or Hard Sauce.

286. Lemon Sauce

Mix together and bring to a boil while stirring constantly:

½ cup sugar	SUGAR
3 tablespoons flour	FLOUR
	SALT
¼ teaspoon salt	LEMON OR
1 cup water	ORANGE

When the mixture boils, remove from the heat and add the juice of 1 lemon or orange . . . whichever you prefer. The important thing is not to boil after the fresh flavor has been added, for boiling kills it.

287. Peach Crunch

Most families object if you do too much experimenting with the main course. For some reason they prefer the "tried and true." Dessert, however, is something they often like to have a little different. Meals usually need to be rounded off with just a simple dessert. Peach Crunch is such a dessert:

Arrange 2 cups of sliced peaches in a shallow baking dish. Mix together:

½ cup crushed corn flakes	
½ cup brown sugar	PEACHES
½ teaspoon cinnamon	CORN FLAKES
	BROWN SUGAR
⅛ teaspoon ground cardamom (can be	CINNAMON
omitted but it seems to give more punch	(CARDAMOM)
to the cinnamon)	

Sprinkle this mixture over the peaches. Dot with butter and bake in a 350-degree oven for about 25 minutes, or until bubbly and hot.

If you don't happen to have corn flakes on hand, you can substitute with ½ cup of buttered bread crumbs. The results, of course, are entirely different but then they are also entirely tasty. Peach Crunch is good served warm "as is," but is even better topped with either cream or ice cream.

288. Old-Fashioned Plum Pudding

Mix all together:

1½ cups flour	FLOUR
1½ cups stale bread crumbs	BREAD
¾ pound raisins	CRUMBS
¾ pound currants	RAISINS
¾ pound suet	CURRANTS
1 cup molasses	SUET
3 ounces candied orange peel	SUGAR
1 teaspoon nutmeg	MOLASSES
1 teaspoon mace	CANDIED
1½ cups sugar	ORANGE
Beat together until fluffy:	PEEL
6 eggs	NUTMEG
	MACE
	EGGS

Pour beaten eggs into the above ingredients and mix until well blended; takes about 10 minutes.

Place a large square of unbleached muslin or clean white material on the counter. Sprinkle and coat with flour. Place the pudding in the center of the cloth. Bring all the sides of the cloth together and secure with a strong string. Allow room for expansion of the dough. Plunge the whole thing into a kettle of boiling water and simmer for 5 hours. Then, as soon as it is cool enough to handle, remove the cloth, slice and serve with a Hard Sauce.

289. Hard Sauce

Hard sauce is an uncooked dessert sauce with many variations. Basically, there is nothing to it.

Just cream together:

1 cup sugar	SUGAR
½ cup butter	BUTTER
flavoring	FLAVORING

Tricks to perfection:

The longer you beat it, the creamier it will be. Make well ahead of time to allow time for thorough chilling.

Variations:

Date Hard Sauce:
Use brown sugar instead of white and add finely chopped dates.

BUTTER
BROWN SUGAR
DATES

Egg Hard Sauce:
Use powdered sugar and add one un-cooked egg yolk.

POWDERED
SUGAR
BUTTER
EGG YOLK

Orange Hard Sauce:
Add 1 tablespoon orange juice and a bit of grated rind.

BUTTER
ORANGE JUICE
GRATED RIND
SUGAR

Lemon Hard Sauce: Add 1 tablespoon lemon juice and a bit of grated rind . . . or just let your personal preferences be your guide and add whatever appeals.

BUTTER
LEMON JUICE
GRATED RIND
SUGAR

290. New-Fashioned Frozen Plum Pudding

Marinate the following in ½ cup of Maraschino Cordial for 5 hours:

¼ cup shredded citron
¼ cup chopped dates
¼ cup chopped figs
¼ cup chopped nuts
12 to 14 chopped maraschino cherries

CHERRY
CORDIAL
CITRON
DATES
FIGS
NUTS
MARASCHINO
CHERRIES

Simmer the following in a small amount of water for 5 minutes to make them plump:

¼ cup currants
¼ cup seeded raisins

CURRANTS
RAISINS
ICE CREAM

Mix everything together with ½ gallon vanilla ice cream. Refreeze in either individual molds or 1 large mold to be sliced later. Cover molds with plastic wrap or foil to prevent ice crystals from forming. Takes about 4 hours in the freezer to bring out the best in all the flavors.

291. Old-Fashioned Bread Pudding

I think most of us end up with an accumulation of dry bread about twice a month. Aside from bread crumbs used in coating meats, etc., about the best good family eating for dry bread is Bread Pudding:

For every 2 cups of bread cubes (can be torn or cut), you will need:

2 cups milk	DRY BREAD
3 tablespoons butter	MILK
½ cup sugar	SUGAR
2 eggs	EGGS
dash of salt	BUTTER
1 tablespoon vanilla	VANILLA
	SALT

Mix all together—except the bread—and beat well. Grease a baking dish. Place the bread cubes in the baking dish. Cover with the milk-and-egg mix. Set the baking dish in a pan of water in the oven and bake at 350 degrees for about 1 hour or until a knife inserted in the center comes out clean.

Old-Fashioned Bread Pudding is good served plain but is still better with a little cream, or it can be served with a hot pudding sauce such as caramel, lemon, orange, or chocolate. For a party touch it can be spread with jelly, topped with meringue, and returned to the oven until a golden brown. Before baking, it is good sometimes to add raisins or dates. This is such a down-to-earth type of dessert, with so many possible variations, you can serve it frequently.

Apricots in Season . . .

It pays to make the most of Apricots in season. They can be the basis for some special desserts. Frozen, either with or without the skins, they can be processed in a matter of minutes. The skins tend to give the frozen ones an "off flavor" but they are easy to skin. It's all in knowing how:

Put a large kettle of water on to boil. When the water has reached a full rolling boil, place the Apricots in a large strainer and immerse them in the boiling water for 15 to 30 seconds. Take from the boiling water and run cold water over them. The peels will slip right off. All you have to do now is split them, remove the seeds, pack in rigid containers, and cover with a heavy syrup (equal amounts of sugar and water simmered together for 5 minutes) leaving ½-inch head space.

Why not save back some of those skinned apricots and have Apricot Dumplings for the evening meal. . . .

292. Apricot Dumplings

In a saucepan, put:
   3 tablespoons butter
   1 cup milk
Keep the heat low and bring to a simmer. Add just a pinch of salt to bring out the flavor.

APRICOTS
BUTTER
MILK
SALT
FLOUR

Mix together:
   1 cup milk
   1 cup flour

Add to the heated milk and butter, stirring constantly. Cook until it no longer sticks to the spoon. Spread this paste on a floured board, working in just enough flour so that you can roll it very thin. Cut into squares.

In the center of each square, place 2 or 3 Apricot halves, skinned. (See directions for skinning preceding this recipe.) Wrap in the thin paste, rolling into smooth balls. Drop the little dumplings into slightly salted boiling water. Cook just until they rise to the top of the water. Drain in a sieve carefully to avoid breaking. Sprinkle with powdered sugar and cinnamon. Serve with hot butter . . . different and delightful!

293. Apple Crisp

Apple Crisp is quick and simple to make. Cheddar Cheese does special things for this recipe.

Combine together and place in a baking dish:

4 cups peeled, sliced, tart apples
2 tablespoons lemon juice
½ cup sugar

Mix together in another bowl:

¾ cup flour
½ teaspoon cinnamon
¼ teaspoon salt
½ cup sugar
1 cup shredded cheddar cheese

APPLES
CHEDDAR
  CHEESE
SUGAR
FLOUR
BUTTER
LEMON JUICE
CINNAMON
SALT

Cut in 6 tablespoons butter until the mixture resembles coarse corn meal. Spread this over the apples and bake in a 375-degree oven for 30 minutes, or until the apples are tender. Cool slightly and garnish with whipped cream.

294. Hot Fudge Sundae Topping

This ice-cream topping can be used on Snow Ice Cream, or better still, on real ice cream. By putting in a dab of this and a dab of that, I quite by accident discovered a Hot Fudge Sundae Topping that is unusually good:

Mix together:

¾ cup instant cocoa mix . . . the kind you make chocolate milk for the youngsters with . . .
1 cup brown sugar . . . be sure it's brown
½ cup canned milk
2 tablespoons butter

INSTANT
  COCOA
BROWN SUGAR
CANNED MILK
BUTTER

Cook until the sauce is thick, stirring it all the time with a wire whisk. It is important that you use a whisk because stirring in this manner makes it creamy and smooth. Takes about 2 minutes to thicken. Serve hot over vanilla ice cream.

———◆———

295. Cream on Fruit

That old food budget can be a real demon, especially when you are young and just learning how to cook and manage. I think those were the years when I really started putting my training in food to good use. I saved all the eggless cake recipes and economy recipes I could find, and we still use them.

Cream on fruit is something we would all like to indulge in if we had the money and could afford the calories. With a large family, cream on fruit can prove to be a downright luxury. There are many economical substitutes on the market today, but here is a tasty substitute and it is inexpensive to make:

1. Heat 1 cup sweet milk until it is boiling.
2. Add ½ teaspoon butter.
3. Beat together the whites of 2 eggs and 1 tablespoon sugar.
4. Mix together ½ cup cold milk and 1 teaspoon cornstarch.
5. Add this to the egg whites and sugar (#3) and stir until light and smooth.
6. Now, add #4 and 5 to the boiling milk and cook until it thickens. *It must not boil.*
7. Set to cool.

MILK
EGG WHITES
BUTTER
SUGAR
CORNSTARCH

It should be the consistency of thick, fresh cream and all you have to do is use it as though it were!

296. Gingerbread Dessert

Rare is the family that does not like Gingerbread. There are many good mixes on the market, but it is really more fun to make your own . . . and it seems to taste better too.

For hot Gingerbread Squares, cream together:

½ cup butter
½ cup brown sugar
Beat in:
1 cup dark molasses
2 eggs
Sift together:
2½ cups sifted flour
¼ cup cocoa
2 teaspoons baking powder
1 teaspoon cinnamon
½ teaspoon ground ginger
½ teaspoon ground nutmeg
½ teaspoon cloves
½ teaspoon soda
½ teaspoon salt

BUTTER
BROWN SUGAR
DARK
    MOLASSES
EGGS
FLOUR
COCOA
BAKING
    POWDER
GINGER
CINNAMON
NUTMEG
CLOVES
SODA
SALT
COFFEE

Add dry ingredients alternately with ¾ cup strong coffee or water. This will be a rather thin batter. Pour into a well-greased shallow baking pan and bake in a 350-degree oven for 30 minutes.

Serve plain or with one of the following: whipped cream; cream cheese softened with a little cream; lemon sauce; or a slice of ice cream and a bit of chocolate sauce.

297. Snow Ice Cream

When the snow starts to fall, a clamor goes up at our house for Snow Ice Cream. While this isn't exactly a "company dish," it is fun to make. The kids love it and have found that any time I make it, the grown-ups eat their share too.

Beat until thick and lemony:

Sugar
Eggs
Milk
Vanilla
Snow

    1 cup sugar

    2 eggs

Beat in 2 cups of milk (canned milk may be used). Add a good portion of vanilla—and send someone after a large pan of clean snow. Fold the snow into the egg and milk mixture. Add snow until ice cream is thick and bulky. Eat at once. We usually prepare vanilla, but it is fun to experiment with other flavors such as banana and orange—or to use brown sugar instead of white and add a caramel flavor. Any way you do it, it's fun!

Even the Cascades have a sense of togetherness.

RECIPE GUIDE

DESPERATION MEALS

〜〜〜〜〜〜〜〜〜〜〜〜〜〜〜〜〜〜〜〜〜〜〜〜〜

Desperation meals—you know the kind I mean: there's a little of this and a little of that, but what to do with it? Sometimes, however, desperation meals turn out to be family favorites and you find yourself preparing them over again on purpose. Part of the fun of these meals, aside from the smugness of feeling "I didn't waste a thing," is being able to name your own creation. As for your author, she has created a few things that weren't worth naming, but you can't win them all . . . and when you stop to think about it, I'm sure that not all the dishes tried in test kitchens are worth naming either . . . so let's have our own test kitchen.

You'll note I haven't given any measurements. That's because I haven't any. These recipes are the results of some desperate times of my own and I just put in what I had.

298. Hot Dog Meat Loaf

If it's "blue Monday," with too many wieners thawed out from a week-end camping trip, the very thought of hot dogs can leave a good deal to be desired. Out of desperation I suggest:

Grind 7 or 8 wieners, add a couple of eggs, a cup of bread crumbs, and enough milk to moisten. Better add chopped onion too. Leave out any seasoning, for the wieners have quite a bit of their own. Shape it all into a meat loaf, surround with potato halves, and bake at 400 degrees or just until the potatoes are tender. Baste the potatoes occasionally. The meat loaf will be just right when the potatoes are done.

HOT DOGS
EGGS
BREAD
   CRUMBS
ONION
MILK

299. Kidney Bean Salad

For a vegetable dish that is "just right," I suggest Kidney Bean Salad:

Drain a can of red kidney beans, add some chopped onion and celery, then instead of coating with a salad dressing, use some smoked barbecue sauce very sparingly.

KIDNEY BEANS
ONION
CELERY
SMOKED
   BARBECUE
   SAUCE

300. 7-Layer Casserole

If your family likes casseroles and you find yourself with too many other things to do, here is one of those fine recipes that can really be thrown together in a hurry—and no one but you will be the wiser.

Use a large 2-quart casserole dish with a tight-fitting lid. Grease well, then make layers of the following:

RICE
WHOLE-
   KERNEL
   CORN
SALT
PEPPER
TOMATO
   SAUCE
ONION
GREEN
   PEPPER
GROUND BEEF
BACON

1st layer: 1 cup uncooked rice.

2nd layer: 1 can drained whole-kernel corn with salt and pepper sprinkled sparingly.

3rd layer: 1 (8-ounce) can of tomato sauce mixed with ½ can of water. Pour this over the mixture.

4th layer: ½ cup chopped onion and ½ cup chopped green pepper mixed together.

5th layer: 1 pound of ground beef crumbled over all.

6th layer: 1 (8-ounce) can of tomato sauce mixed with ¼ cup of water. Season with salt and pepper again.

7th layer: Cover with 4 strips of bacon which have been cut in half.

Cover and bake for 1 hour at 350 degrees. Uncover and bake 30 minutes longer, or until the bacon is crisp.

There is lots of sagebrush in Eastern Oregon . . . . Black Butte and Mt. Jefferson are in the background. All that remains of this homestead is the round brick cistern.

301. Open-Face Bologna Sandwiches

Grind 1 pound of bologna, using the coarse blade in the meat grinder. Mix the ground bologna with:

BOLOGNA
RELISH
MAYONNAISE
MUSTARD
(PINEAPPLE SLICES)

⅓ cup relish
⅓ cup mayonnaise
1 tablespoon mustard

This can be used as a sandwich filling; or if company's coming, toast slices of bread, butter well, and spread with the bologna mixture. Top each open-face sandwich with a slice of pineapple. Place under the broiler until piping hot.

302. Bologna Cups

On a baking sheet, arrange 4 thick slices of bologna (⅛-inch thick). On each piece of bologna place a generous helping of dressing. Take 4 slices of bologna and slash the edges in at least 4 places to keep them from curling. Lay the slashed pieces on top of the dressing. Bake in a 350-degree oven 30 to 40 minutes. The bottom slice of bologna will curl up, forming a cup to hold the dressing and the top slice will droop down. The juice drips down through the dressing, and all in all, makes some pretty good eating. Served with baked potatoes and a green salad, with fruit for dessert, it does very nicely. . . .

BOLOGNA
DRESSING

303. Special Sauerkraut and Wieners

It's the little things that make this recipe tasty.

Melt ¼ cup butter and add:
  1 cup chopped onions
  1 teaspoon caraway seeds
Cook until the onions are tender. Then add:
  2 cups kraut
  2 tablespoons brown sugar

BUTTER
ONIONS
CARAWAY
  SEEDS
KRAUT
BROWN SUGAR
WIENERS

Cover and cook over low heat for 30 minutes. Make slashes across the wieners (1 pound) and spread the surfaces lightly with mustard. Place on top of the kraut . . . cover and cook for 10 minutes more. Serves 4.

———◆———

The next time you make Potato Salad, add 1¾ cups of drained cold kraut and 1 pound of cooked frankfurters which have been cut into 1-inch pieces. It's good!

304. What's It

The following dish can be fixed in just the length of time it takes to cook rice. Simmer together:

¾ cup sliced onions	ONIONS
½ teaspoon salt	SALT
¼ teaspoon pepper	PEPPER
⅛ cup Worcestershire sauce	WORCESTER-
1 or 2 tablespoons vinegar, depending on how tangy you like things	SHIRE SAUCE VINEGAR
¼ cup sugar	SUGAR
1 cup catsup	CATSUP
1 12-ounce can of pork lunch meat, cut into cubes	CANNED LUNCH MEAT (PORK)

Serve over individual mounds of cooked rice. Lime and pineapple gelatin salad are good served with this and will give your meal "color appeal," which is almost as important as "taste appeal."

305. Cottage Cheese Omelet

This recipe is really easy . . . but it's good. Serve with toast and a green salad and fresh fruit for dessert.

Beat together:

6 tablespoons cottage cheese	
6 eggs	COTTAGE CHEESE
a pinch of pepper	EGGS
1 teaspoon flour	PEPPER
(no salt is needed, for seasoning in cottage cheese is usually sufficient)	FLOUR

Butter and heat a heavy skillet. Add the omelet and cook over low heat until firm but tender. Serves 4.

306. Cheese and Bacon Specials

I don't know about you, but Sunday night supper is the hardest meal of the week for me to cook. We've usually been outdoors most of the weekend, and when I come back into the house where it is warm and cozy, I'm so lazy that I would rather go hungry than summon up the energy to cook. . . . But my family has different ideas—they're starved. So, I'm always on the prowl for recipes that are easy, inexpensive, and at the same time satisfying, to get me through that Sunday-night cooking slump. We like this one:

Mix together:

	EGGS
2 well-beaten eggs	CHEDDAR CHEESE
2 cups shredded cheddar cheese (8 ounces)	SALT
½ teaspoon salt	PEPPER
⅛ teaspoon pepper	PAPRIKA
½ teaspoon paprika	WORCESTERSHIRE SAUCE
½ teaspoon Worcestershire sauce	LEMON JUICE
1 teaspoon lemon juice	GARLIC SALT
½ teaspoon garlic salt	CELERY SALT
dash of celery salt	BACON
	BUNS
	TOMATOES

Cut 4 strips of bacon in half and fry slowly until lightly browned. Split 4 sandwich buns and brown under the broiler until golden. Now you are all set to build your "Specials." Spread the cheese mixture on the lower half of each bun. Spread the top half of each bun with butter. Then place a slice of tomato and 2 strips of bacon on each of the "tops." Arrange on a cookie sheet and place under the broiler until the cheese is melted and the bacon is crisp. Serve immediately. Results? Very few dishes, everyone is well satisfied, and as my mother used to say, "The cooking didn't amount to a hill of beans!"

307. Creamed Dried Beef on Toast

Saute' in ¼ cup butter:
    4 ounces of dried beef

When the edges of the beef curl, blend in:
    ¼ cup flour
    ⅛ teaspoon pepper

DRIED BEEF
BUTTER
FLOUR
MILK
PEPPER

(no salt is needed, for the dried beef is salty enough)
Cook, stirring constantly until the flour is lightly browned.

Add, all at once:
    2 cups milk

Continue to stir until the gravy bubbles. Continue to cook for 1 more minute. Serve on buttered toast squares to 4 hungry people. Carrot curls and celery sticks can add that something "crunchy" to the meal.

Remains of an old windmill for pumping water in desert country recall a fast-disappearing age. Fort Rock shows in background.

RECIPE GUIDE

Number

308. Camp Spaghetti
309. Barbecued Lima Beans
310. Meal in a Packet
311. "Sweet" Sweet Potatoes
312. Baked Beans
313. Potato Salad
314. Macaroni Salad
315. Pan Bread
316. Indian Bread
317. Camp Biscuits
318. Pear Honey
319. Fried Apples
320. Apple Butter
321. Raw Cranberry Relish
322. Cranberry Jell
323. Cranberry Cherry Relish
324. Pickled Pears
325. Watermelon Preserves
326. Wild Plum Preserves

COOKIN' IN THE BOONDOCKS

Whether camping with a bale of straw for a bed and a tarp for weather protection—or with a camper and all the conveniences—any woman who tags along as "chief cook and bottle washer" will tell you it's quite a trick to get the job done and still have time for all the things you want to do. Sometimes, though, shortcuts on the spot do the trick. Here is a good "on-the-spot" example:

308. Camp Spaghetti

Mix together a size 303 can of spaghetti sauce (approximately 2 cups) and 3 cups of water for every cup of uncooked spaghetti you plan to use. Bring this to a boil. Break the

SPAGHETTI
SAUCE
(CANNED)
SPAGHETTI

uncooked spaghetti into short lengths and add to the boiling sauce. Cook until tender right in the sauce. Results . . . only 1 pan to wash. It is quick and easy, is a taste change from the "usual," and the family loves it.

◆

If freezer space warrants, freeze water in quart plastic bottles to have on hand for camping trips. Tuck the frozen bottles of water in the cooler along with the crisp, crunchy things and meats. Food will keep well for two or three days this way, depending of course on how warm the weather is. I like this method of keeping things cool; the water stays in the bottles as the ice melts, to be used in cooking or drinking, and the cooler stays dry and cold.

309. Barbecued Lima Beans

The following recipe is a good one to fix ahead of time for sixteen hungry campers:

Boil 2 quarts of lima beans until tender. Brown:

1½ pounds chopped bacon	LIMA BEANS
1 cup chopped onions	BACON
1¼ teaspoons minced garlic	ONIONS
Add:	GARLIC
3 tablespoons prepared mustard	MUSTARD
½ teaspoon salt	SALT
2 teaspoons Worcestershire sauce	WORCESTER-
2 teaspoons mild chili powder	SHIRE SAUCE
2½ cups condensed tomato soup	CHILI POWDER
¼ cup vinegar	TOMATO SOUP
4 teaspoons brown sugar	VINEGAR
2 cups of the bean liquid	BROWN SUGAR

Place the drained, cooked beans in a large baking dish. Cover with the sauce and bake for 30 minutes in a moderate oven. Re-heat in an open kettle when ready to serve at camp.

310. Meal in a Packet

Try this one for a tasty, filling meal "on the spot":

Prepare a packet in the following manner for each camper to be served: Place a large hamburger in the center of a large piece of aluminum foil. Top with:

a slice of onion	HAMBURGER
4 or 5 slices of potato	ONION
3 or 4 strips of carrot	POTATO
2 pieces of celery	CARROT
(any other vegetable you like)	CELERY

Pull the foil up to form a cup. Into each packet, pour a tablespoon of sauce made like this:

½ cup tomato catsup	TOMATO CATSUP
2 tablespoons Worcestershire sauce	WORCESTER-SHIRE SAUCE
1 teaspoon prepared mustard	MUSTARD
(juice of 1 lemon)	LEMON

Seal the foil edges tightly. Place along the edges of the hot coals of the campfire. Turn from time to time to prevent burning. The whole process takes about 45 minutes.

———◆———

If the man in your life plans to go hunting without you, prepare the Oven Stew given earlier. Freeze the main portion in a 2-pound coffee can. Secure the lid with tape for extra security. When your hunter picks up his gun and heads for the woods, hand him the frozen stew. At lunch time, when he's famished, it's a simple matter for him to heat the stew in the coffee can over an open fire—then bury the empty can after the meal and be on his merry way.

———◆———

311. "Sweet" Sweet Potatoes

Sweet potatoes are often overlooked when planning meals for camp-outs but they are worth remembering:

Drain a can or two of sweet potatoes. Add some butter and 2 or 3 spoons of jelly such as apple or orange marmalade. Cook and heat all together right over the fire.

CANNED SWEET POTATOES
JELLY

Another easy way: Divide the contents of 2 cans of sweet potatoes among 4 to 6 squares of heavy-duty aluminum foil. Spoon crushed pineapple over each one. Dust with a bit of cinnamon. Seal the foil and place the packets on the grill for 15 to 20 minutes.

CANNED SWEET POTATOES
PINEAPPLE
CINNAMON
FOIL

Still another easy way: You can always fall back on the old favorite method of slicing and browning in the skillet in which you have just fried bacon or ham. Season with a little salt and pepper and be prepared "for seconds."

CANNED SWEET POTATOES
BACON FAT
SALT
PEPPER

312. Baked Beans

Baked Beans are always welcome at camp or on a picnic. For the quick and easy kind, heat the oven to 350 degrees and mix together:

a large can of pork and beans
½ cup catsup
2 tablespoons vinegar
½ cup brown sugar
(1 package of dehydrated onion soup mix)

PORK & BEANS
CATSUP
VINEGAR
BROWN SUGAR
(ONION SOUP MIX)
BACON

While the soup mix is optional, it does make a tasty difference. Crumble in cooked bacon giblets and bake at 350 degrees for at least 30 minutes. Stir once or twice during the baking.

Beans cooked this way are good served hot for the meal in the making, or they are just as good cold on a picnic. You could double the recipe and have them both ways.

313. Potato Salad

A picnic is hardly a picnic without Potato Salad. . . .

Marinate 4 cups of cooked, cubed potatoes while still warm in a mixture of:
¼ cup salad oil
2 tablespoons vinegar
Allow at least 2 hours for marinating, then add:
2 hard-cooked eggs
1 cup diced celery
3 tablespoons chopped onion
½ cup salad dressing, mayonnaise or sour cream dressing
1 teaspoon salt
¼ teaspoon pepper

POTATOES
SALAD OIL
VINEGAR
EGGS
CELERY
ONION
SALAD DRESSING
(SOUR CREAM DRESSING)

For a quick sour-cream dressing, mix:
  ½ cup sour cream
  1 cup mayonnaise

| | Sour Cream
Mayonnaise |

For variations in flavor, add:
  chopped green pepper
  pimento
  sweet pickle

| | (Green
    Pepper)
(Pimento)
(Sweet
    Pickle) |

You could leave them out and instead add:
  grated carrots
  sliced radishes
  cucumber

| | or
(Carrots)
(Radishes)
(Cucumber) |

You can always add:
  diced ham or luncheon meat

| | (Ham or
    Lunch
    Meat) |

314. Macaroni Salad

It is too easy for Macaroni Salad to have a flat, uninteresting flavor. Give it a tangy taste by adding a cheese sauce. It's quick and easy with the help of a dehydrated cheese sauce. (Macaroni salad with a "cheese flair" is a good way to use leftover Macaroni and Cheese.)

Combine cheese sauce and cooked macaroni.
Add:
  ⅔ cup diced celery
  2 hard-cooked eggs, sliced or chopped
  ¼ cup chopped sweet pickle
  1 teaspoon salt
  ½ cup commercial sour cream (optional)
  ½ cup mayonnaise

| | Macaroni
Cheese Sauce
Celery
Eggs
Sweet Pickle
Sour Cream
Salt
Mayonnaise |

These measurements are just about right for 4 cups of cooked macaroni.

315. Pan Bread

Eastern Oregon is a land of Rodeos, Buckaroo Breakfasts, and Pan Bread. In the event that you have never attended a Buckaroo Breakfast, I will tell you a bit about them. . . . They usually start serving at dawn. We've waited as long as 45 minutes, in spite of the fact that we usually manage to arrive just as day breaks. You'd be surprised how early people can get up when the air is heavy with the aroma of hot coffee, steaks, bacon and eggs, pancakes, fried potatoes, and that delicious Pan Bread. It is usually pretty frosty that time of morning in Sage Brush country, even in summer. This whets the appetite all the more.

Everything is cooked and served out in the open to the rhythm of some good old country western music. The beat that sets your toes to tapping is usually supplied by a Tub Thumper. This unique instrument is made by inverting an old wash tub. A hole is drilled in the middle of the bottom of the tub and a heavy cord about 4 feet long is run through the hole and secured on the inside with a piece of wood or rubber to keep the cord from slipping on through. The other end of the cord is fastened to the end of a broom handle. The opposite end of the broom handle is grooved and fits on the rim of the tub. The ingenious player—holding the broom handle in such a way that the string is taut—proceeds to slap and thump the string much as you would a bass fiddle. The music they get out of those contraptions is amazing. . . .

Now for the best part of all, the Pan Bread. *Not having a recipe of my own, we set out bright and early one sunny Saturday morning, headed for the Big Desert Country and the home of Reub Long, the well-known rancher and horseman. I*

*felt that if anyone knew how to make just plain old Pan Bread,
Reub would. Pan Bread is never Pan Bread unless it is made,
cooked, and eaten outdoors. A man on the trail or range
didn't burden himself with unnecessary clutter.*

*He stuck to the essentials—like a 50-pound sack of flour,
some baking powder, salt, a little shortening, and a frying pan.
Modern man has gussied his Pan Bread up with an egg or two,
but eggs and horses don't "gee it off" too well. Our man on the
trail gets his fire started, shortening heating in his fry pan, and
he's ready to begin. (He doesn't carry a mixing bowl—he pre-
pares his dough right in the sack of flour!)*

———◆———

Reub Long says there isn't any regular recipe for Pan
Bread. . . . "Just open up the 50-pound sack of flour, make a
hollowed-out spot in the flour, pour in a little water, probably
a cup, add a teaspoon or so of baking powder, a little salt,
and some melted shortening . . . a tablespoon or two . . . then
start mixing in what flour will mix into the liquid and that's it.
Make into a doughy blob that will fit the skillet. Have the
skillet hot and well greased. Take your fist and punch the
bread down well. Poke a hole in the middle—makes it cook
better in the center. Brown over a hot bed of coals on one
side . . . flip . . . and brown the other side. Stand the bread on
end on a hot rock near the fire while you make the next 'blob.'
This way each cowboy has hot Pan Bread." Reub says Cow-
boys usually refer to them as "Pones." Pones are made as large
as the skillet will allow—with at least one Pone for each Cowboy.

A man prided himself on being able to turn the Pan Bread
by tossing it into the air and catching it in the skillet. With
scarce rations and tired bodies yearning for the comfort of
food, the cook couldn't afford a "miss of the flip."

Pack Trip to the High Cascades

Food planning and preparation for a pack trip is still another story, as you will soon see. From our home on the edge of the Oregon Desert, the majestic snow-capped Cascade Mountains greet us each morning. Their beauty is as changeable as the seasons. There are times when they have a hard, cold, formidable look. As if in compensation, there are frosty winter mornings when the world is white and the mountains reflect the glow of the sunrise, radiating a soft pink offset by Oregon's blue, blue sky . . . but no matter what garment the mountains wear, they lure us to them.

We're an outdoor-loving family and during winter we plan all the trips we will make to the mountains—come spring and the roads thaw enough to be at all passable. Many times ours have been the first tracks into the high country. One spring we decided that as soon as the snow was gone we would hike into the Green Lakes. These lakes are nestled in the Cascades between old Broken Top Crater and the South Sister Mountain, about a 20-mile drive from Bend, Oregon, by the beautiful Century Drive route.

Being blessed (?) with a pet burro . . . we felt that with the help of Dynamite (the burro's name for obvious reasons), we could take enough food and supplies to last our family of five for three days. This would require considerable food, no matter how well you figured, and no greenhorns ever planned more carefully and scientifically. Half the fun of the trip was the discovery of all the available dehydrated products. We decided it was all a matter of menu planning and then exploring the supermarkets for dehydrated products, to obtain the desired results. We purchased dehydrated soups and mashed potatoes, dried fruit, powdered milk, canned meat, dried meat and bacon—then managed to get each pack to weigh only 40 pounds. This included cooking utensils, axe, and tent.

We found that a package of paper plates weighed less than our tin plates (saved on dishwashing too). We used gallon cans for cooking utensils, aluminum foil plates to fry bacon in . . . just place them on a bed of hot coals and you are in business. When we were finally ready to return home, we buried the kitchen, so to speak, and that was that! No blackened pots and pans to clean.

We each planned to carry our own sleeping bag and decided against taking air mattresses because of their weight; anyway, "spouse" promised me a pine-bough bed. (If yours does, I suggest you check the size of the boughs!)

Our only doubts were whether old Dynamite would pack. After all, he was practically the baby of the family and had

"Dynamite"—practically the baby of the family.

never had to do anything harder than stand at the back door and mooch for pancakes and popcorn. Getting that burro into the truck for the trip to the high country was the challenge of the weekend.

If you have never loaded a burro on a truck, you haven't lived. Whether he gets into the truck is all a matter of mood. If he wants to, he'll knock you down getting in. If he doesn't want to, you're tempted to knock him down before it's over— that is, if you could think of a way to do it. Spouse Harry finally achieved the desired results by tying a towel around the burro's head, then going in circles with Dynamite until they were both so dizzy they could hardly stand up . . . finally staggering into the back of the truck. My job was to slap the tail gate shut the minute they were both in, but I was laughing so hard I almost forgot my part of the job. I won't go into details about the next few minutes, but believe me, with Dynamite loaded, we were practically there.

In no time at all, we were at our destination and busy with all the details of packing Dynamite for the trail trip, with everything we could short of overloading him. After a good deal of arranging and re-arranging, we were ready to hit the trail. At this point, a forest ranger came along and kindly advised us that there was no point in making pack mules of ourselves . . . that Dynamite could easily carry our five sleeping bags . . . that if he were overloaded, he had sense enough to know it and would just lie down and refuse to go.

The ranger took everything off the burro and reloaded him, sleeping bags and all. He tied the pack on with what he called a Squaw Hitch, explaining that when a pack is put on this way it rides free without rubbing the burro and making him sore. He told of seeing burros after a day on the trail rubbed so raw they were bleeding. After seeing what a blessing this bit of knowledge was, I strongly recommend that anyone contemplating such a journey find someone to explain how to tie a Squaw Hitch. Dynamite didn't mind the extra weight and seemed anxious to get moving. He was so loaded it was hard to tell which end was which. We thanked the ranger . . . and we thanked him double when we returned, for by then we truly realized what a favor he had done us. Harry took the lead rope, we gathered up our exploring "offspring," and were on our way.

At first Dynamite was as eager as the rest of us to get started. He put his nose in the small of Harry's back and practically pushed him up the trail, that is, until we were about a third of the way up. Then, by the side of the trail, we came on an unusually large tree for this altitude . . . its great gnarled roots had spread out over the path, forming basins to hold water. Actually, the puddle in front of Dynamite couldn't have been more than two to three feet wide, but do you think that burro would get his feet wet? Not on your life! Furthermore, the denseness of the forest meant we must stick to the trail. We decided to sit down, rest, and think the situation over.

If you've ever owned a burro, you well know they aren't dumb or even stubborn; it's just that they have a mind of their own. They are a highly intelligent animal and refuse to do something until they are sure it is going to be all right. In other words, they won't leap just because you tell them to and then suffer for your misjudgment afterwards. They think it over, look it over, and then act. After having a burro as a member of the family for several years (we got him when he was just a baby), we've come to the conclusion that they really are not as stubborn as people generally believe. If you respect their intelligence, you get much more cooperation out of them. I say this in retrospect. At the time, I was so exasperated I felt our burro was just plain ornery . . . we wanted him to cross the muddy spot so we could be on our way.

We then decided on a new approach. Dynamite had a weakness for fig bars, and apparently this was the time to pamper him a little. After all, he had been packing beautifully. I took up a position on the far side of the puddle, holding the fig bars just out of reach. Then Harry got behind Dynamite and pushed, hoping to help things along. I coaxed and relinquished fig bars one by one while Harry pushed and shoved. As the final fig bar went "down the hatch," our last bit of patience went with it. At that very moment that so-and-so burro stepped gingerly across the puddle, gently took the box from my hand, ate it too, and went steadily on up the trail as if nothing had happened. We had to hurry to catch up with him.

The trail itself is beautiful, following Fall Creek all the way to the meadow. Fall Creek is very aptly named, for it does just that. It is one continuous fall after another. Every ten to twenty feet there is another waterfall of two to three feet in height. The water is sparkling clear. As you trudge upward, with the stately firs on your left and the rushing waters on your right, the beauty is awesome. The cares and frustrations of daily living fade into nothingness and things seem to fall into proper perspective.

As we gained altitude, the trees became smaller and sparser. The creek grew quieter with fewer falls. About two-thirds of the way up is the lovely meadow we would cross. Here is the beginning of the wild flowers. Indian Paint Brush and Dark-Eyed Susans intermingle with lush green grass, and the South Sister Mountain looms grandly in the distance. But there was one obstacle between us and that inviting meadow: a stream about six feet wide.

Not very optimistic about being able to coax Dynamite across, we decided the best tactics in this case would be force. Hope of getting him to walk the stepping stones would have been ridiculous. He could walk the cattle guard at home without batting an eye, but that was to get something he wanted!

We decided this was the proper time to unpack the marshmallows, his second great weakness. Popcorn is his first one. I took off my shoes and threw them across to the other side, picked up Dynamite's lead rope, and waded out into the middle of that icy, icy water. There I stood, coaxing that critter with a marshmallow and pulling for all I was worth, while Harry stood on the bank and pushed for all he was worth. Just as I was pulling my hardest and Harry was pushing his hardest, Dynamite decided to go. He leaped across the stream as though it wasn't there. He caught me off balance and I did the fanciest "didoes" you ever saw, to stay on my feet . . . I wasn't about to sit down in that ice water! I felt as if I had thrown every bone in my body out of place, but I did manage to stay right side up. It was Harry's turn to laugh now.

After we reached the meadow, sooner than we had hoped, it was again necessary to cross Fall Creek on the right, to stay on the trail to the Green Lakes. The creek is deep here, probably three to four feet, and quite swift. A sturdy foot bridge of small fir poles spans it. Dynamite refused even to look at the bridge, and because the water was more than belly deep for him, we decided to pitch camp, leave him tied to a tree, and hike on into the lakes and back before evening. Since this wasn't really a fishing trip, where we camped was not important.

While Harry put up the tent and got a fire going for me to do the "cooking bit," the children made out the bed rolls. We soon sat down to a dinner of creamed dried beef, mashed potatoes, and carrot sticks. To top the meal off, we had hot biscuits, dried apricots, and a candy bar. We don't always eat that well at home!

With dinner out of the way, we gave Dynamite a well-earned carrot. On second thought, I was not so sure he had earned it, but then I guess we all have our moments. We tied him to a tree and took off up the trail. The climb went quickly without encumbrance of burro or packs. We were soon at an altitude where the trees were so sparse that they seemed to have grown there by mistake; the soil was of a pumice nature. Then we came on the Green Lakes nestled among the splendor of an all-blue sky and snow-capped mountains. The quiet was unbroken even by a bird's call. The lakes shimmered quietly like three great, green emeralds in the sun. We sat on a knoll under a straggly tree and rested. . . . We were reluctant to leave, but it was getting late in the day and we wanted to be back in camp before nightfall. With a mutual promise to return there soon, we headed back down the trail.

From the Green Lakes down to the meadow, Fall Creek ripples along beside the trail on a bed of lava flow and rocks. The sun was hot and penetrating in spite of the lateness of the day. Cumulus clouds hovered over the South Sister Mountain on our right. On our left was a bank of wild flowers of every variety imaginable—a sheer mountainside of solid color, ranging from the palest pink to brilliant flamingo red, intermingled with dainty blues and sunny yellows. From time to time we caught a glimpse of snow-tipped Broken Top Crater. The air was heavy with silence, broken only by the sound of the rippling water. It was like being in another world, one you hated to leave.

But never fear, there are always things to bring you down to earth again, like a burro braying in the distance. Hearing the pathetic braying of Dynamite, we quickened our lagging steps and soon arrived back at camp. We were anxious to get our evening meal started because we were all hungry—but first things first. In this case it was Dynamite. We all tried to get him in a good mood, but he absolutely ignored us. He actually pouted: he stomped his front feet in the dirt and looked off in the opposite direction instead of nuzzling us as he usually did. He not only ignored us that evening, but the entire three days we camped there. He didn't make up until we slapped a pack on him to go home. Then he started following the youngsters around wanting attention. Now that is what I call just plain cussedness.

Though we hated to leave, Dynamite was eager to go. The minute he was loaded he started off. He stepped gingerly across the stream without any coaxing whatsoever and took off down the trail. We practically had to trot to keep up with him. He didn't falter once. When he reached the bottom of the trail and we relieved him of his pack, he hopped into the truck as nice as you please. He was headed home where life consisted only of mooching pancakes and popcorn, so he was all cooperation.

You see, burros really are an intelligent animal . . . I think!

316. Indian Bread

Bread is always a problem on a camping trip. Hungry appetites clamor for twice as much as they would ordinarily have, and you certainly can't take that much with you. Biscuits and Chapati (Indian Bread) are two tasty ways of coping with the situation. To make the Indian Bread:

Place a couple of cups of wholewheat flour into a bowl. Make an indentation in the center. Add just enough water to form a *very dry* dough. Sprinkle dough with salt as though you were seasoning unsalted food for taste. Knead the dough well with the fingers and divide into lumps the size of an egg. Roll and shape each piece into the size and shape of a very thin pancake. Brown on both sides in a lightly greased skillet (grease as you would a cookie sheet). Press with a cloth before removing from the skillet to expel the air. Eat while still hot.

WHOLE WHEAT FLOUR SALT SHORTENING

If you are reading this with tongue in cheek, try it sometime when you are fifty miles from the nearest loaf of bread and you will find it is delicious. Our own family thinks it is delicious even with bread just around the corner.

317. Camp Biscuits

For hot biscuits, here is the economical and efficient way for campers to make them (you prepare the basic mix before the trip):

Sift together:
- 12 cups flour
- 4 tablespoons baking powder
- 2 tablespoons salt

FLOUR BAKING POWDER SALT SHORTENING POWDERED MILK

Cut in 2 cups shortening. Store in a heavy plastic bag when trail packing, or in a covered tin for more conventional-type camping. When ready to use, measure out two cups of the mix, stir in ¾ cup of milk made from combining water and powdered milk. Shape into biscuits with your fingers, place in a well-greased skillet . . . or use pie tins as we did. Scrape some of the coals from the fire to one side so that they won't be too hot. This is where you have to use good old common sense. Set the tins on the coals and let the biscuits slowly brown for about 10 minutes on each side. . . . This goes to show what you can do without an oven.

318. Pear Honey

Years ago, when we lived in the Middle West, one of our favorite outings was to get up before dawn, arm ourselves with our rifles, a jar of Pear Honey, a loaf of freshly baked bread, and head for the timber. This was in the years before any "little testers" came along. We'd sit quietly under a big old oak tree, watch the sun come up and keep our eyes open for red squirrels.

We've eaten fried squirrel, baked squirrel, stewed squirrel, squirrel and dumplings, and barbecued squirrel. . . . I think we've tried squirrel every conceivable way there is to prepare it.

There aren't any squirrels to speak of in Eastern Oregon, none that you would want to eat at any rate. In the event that your home is where they are in abundance, no special recipe is needed. Just use your favorite chicken recipes. The meat is dark, lean, tender and juicy. What more could you ask? But what I really want to tell you about here is the Pear Honey we took along on trips—and still often do! It is delicious and makes the jaunt more fun, especially if you don't get what you were hunting.

Mix together and simmer until thick:

PEARS
SUGAR
LEMON
GINGER
(ORANGE)
(CINNAMON)

- 6 cups chopped pears, (wash, core, and pare)
- 4 cups sugar
- 1 lemon, sliced very, very thin
- ½ teaspoon ginger

For variation, substitute cinnamon and an orange for the lemon and ginger. When it has reached a thick honey-like consistency, pour while boiling hot into pint jars and seal at once.

Water in Desert Country

Eastern Oregon, being "desert country," has a unique and most interesting water system. The history of its canals and subsidiary ditches makes fascinating reading. I have always felt that historical signs posted in strategic places, telling the history of Eastern Oregon's water systems, would be of great interest to the tourist, and at the same time, be a constructive means of combating the pollution problem.

I will tell you a little bit about this water system for, need-

This is a wooden flume used to carry the water across a rugged terrain. When it reaches leveler ground, the water will run in open canals.

less to say, no kitchen can operate without water, and consequently no area is ever developed unless water can be made available. People who live in the populated areas of Eastern Oregon enjoy an abundance of the purest water in the world. It is virtually free of mineral. This may be bad for teeth, but it is certainly satisfying to the palate and it brews the most delicious cup of coffee you ever loitered over.

Here in Central Eastern Oregon, seven months of the year, the water runs from the swift Deschutes River into the canals and from there into subsidiary ditches where each rancher takes his share from a Head Gate. It is stored in ranch cisterns and then pumped into the home with a pressure pump. The other five (winter) months of the year, the water is turned into the ditches only once a month, weather permitting, at which time everyone gleefully fills his cistern and hopes the supply will last till the next month.

Those with large cisterns usually have filter systems and purify their own. Those with smaller cisterns often jokingly say theirs is "pasteurized" (it runs through many pastures). Because of this, they use it everywhere but in the kitchens. Water for cooking and drinking is hauled from town in five-gallon cans or what you have.

There are many who have 1,000-gallon tanks buried and haul all their water from town, using a smaller 300-gallon tank to haul with. Then there are those who haul in barrels; in fact, you see water being hauled in barrels, tubs, horse tanks . . . every contrivance that will hold water. I guess this just goes to show to what lengths people who prefer living in the Boondocks will go to keep from seeing the neighbors' "smoke." It isn't a case of being anti-social . . . but of loving those wide-open spaces.

"A Good Cup of Coffee"

East of the Cascades, people probably drink more coffee over a campfire than they do over the dinner table. You will get the clearest Camp Coffee by placing the ground coffee in the coffee pot and boiling the precious water in a separate container. When it reaches a full rolling boil, pour it over the ground coffee and let it stand 5 to 10 minutes, or until the grounds have settled. The pot should be placed on a hot rock near the fire so that it will stay hot and at the same time not boil. Boiling coffee breaks down the oil modulus and imparts a strong, rancid taste.

Whether camping or at home, keep the "extra" coffee in a thermos bottle. This saves reheating. If you are a "working gal," when you dash home at noon for the shortest hour of the day, the coffee is hot and ready.

Brewing a cup of coffee that will satisfy the palate of everyone concerned is somewhat like frying an egg to suit everyone. I will give you only a few basics and then you are on your own to develop the art of making a good cup of coffee—for that is truly what it is, an art. . . .

1. The first rule of good coffee is to have an absolutely clean pot.
2. Select the grind that goes with the particular pot. This eliminates any muddiness in the coffee. Good coffee should be absolutely clear. For a perfect cup of coffee, use a coffee filter. You'll find filters on display near the coffee section in the supermarket. There is one for every type of coffee maker.
3. Use fresh, cold water. Hot-water pipes often have mineral deposits which will affect the flavor of the coffee.

Authorities tell you to use 2 tablespoons of coffee per cup and percolate 6 to 8 minutes. If this ratio makes the hair rise on your head, cut the amount in half—one tablespoon of coffee per cup of water and percolate 3 minutes only. Glass coffee-makers have an advantage in that you can see the color of the coffee and cease perking when it suits your own individual taste.

319. Fried Apples

Fruits, jams, jellies, and relishes served as side dishes tempt and tantalize the taste buds. Side dishes made from apples have always been favorites. Many years ago, when the homesteaders began to develop this great Cattle Country, the first step in settling down was to plant an apple orchard and build a barn and a cabin. It was usually done in that order too! All that remains today of many of these old homesteads is the apple orchard.

Our favorite abandoned apple orchard is between Prineville and Madras on a side road, if you could call it that, way back off in the Boondocks. In case you are wondering what Boondocks are, it is an expression used in Cattle Country to denote "the end of nowhere." There are fourteen varieties of apples in that old orchard—and I'll wager the homesteaders had a special recipe for every variety. . . . Some apples are just better "keepers" and some make better pies. . . . It takes a hard, tart, crisp apple to make good Fried Apples—an excellent side dish to serve with venison steaks or fried chukar:

No measurements are needed for making good Fried Apples. In the bottom of a skillet, place a small amount of butter. Add the sliced apples(leave the peel on) and fry over medium heat until they begin to brown. Sprinkle with brown sugar and just a dash of cinnamon and continue frying and turning occasionally. When the sugar begins to crystallize they are done.

APPLES
BUTTER
BROWN SUGAR
CINNAMON

320. Apple Butter

The easiest way to make apple butter is in the oven. Just put all the ingredients together in a roaster:

4 cups sweet cider or mild vinegar
8 cups apple sauce
4 cups brown sugar or white
2 teaspoons cinnamon
2 whole cloves

Stir frequently, cooking in a 325-degree oven until the mixture is smooth, dark, and thick.

APPLE SAUCE
SWEET CIDER
  OR VINEGAR
BROWN SUGAR
  OR WHITE
  SUGAR
CINNAMON
CLOVES
  (WHOLE)

This amount will take about an hour. When of the desired texture, pour boiling hot into sterilized jars and seal at once. Do not over-cook, for remember, it will thicken still more as it cools.

321. Raw Cranberry Relish

Grind equal amounts of cranberries and oranges, peel and all. Mix together and sweeten to taste.

CRANBERRIES
ORANGES
SUGAR

322. Cranberry Jell

I prefer Raw Cranberry Relish, but the head of the household doesn't care for it, so we make Cranberry Jell for him:

Remove stems and blossom ends from one pound of cranberries. Wash thoroughly. Add 2 cups of water and 2½ cups sugar. Simmer until the cranberries pop open and are tender. Just takes a few minutes. Stir in 1 package of strawberry or cherry gelatin and chill in a pretty mold. That's all there is to it.

CRANBERRIES
SUGAR
GELATIN

323. Cranberry Cherry Relish

We all like this—even the head of the household:

Cut into small pieces or run through a food chopper, using a coarse blade:

    1 orange
    1 lemon

Add:

    1 cup canned pie cherries
  1½ cups raw cranberries, washed and stemmed
    1 cup brown sugar
    1 cup white sugar
    1 cup raisins
   ½ teaspoon cinnamon
   ¼ teaspoon nutmeg
   ¼ teaspoon cloves
   ½ cup vinegar

CRANBERRIES
ORANGE
LEMON
PIE CHERRIES
  (CANNED)
BROWN SUGAR
WHITE SUGAR
RAISINS
CINNAMON
NUTMEG
CLOVES
VINEGAR

Simmer over low heat until thick. Stir from time to time to prevent sticking. Serve as a side dish.

324. Pickled Pears

Drain 2 large cans (size 2½) of pear halves. To the syrup, add:

PEARS (CANNED)
SUGAR
VINEGAR
CINNAMON STICKS
CLOVES

1 cup sugar
¾ cup vinegar
2 cinnamon sticks
6 whole cloves

Simmer together for 5 minutes. Add the pears to the pickling syrup and reheat to the boiling point. Chill and serve as a side dish. Additional vinegar may be added if a tarter flavor is desired.

325. Watermelon Preserves

Watermelon seems to thrive with little or no effort in Northeastern Oregon. Their abundance on the market makes it possible to enjoy them all summer long. The Chief Tester at our house considers Watermelon Preserves a "must." It's a "sweet and spicy" side dish that adds zest to any meal.

Trim the green skin and red flesh from the thick rind. Leave about ⅛ inch of the pink flesh because it makes the preserves so much prettier. Don't leave any more than that, however, or your preserves will be mushy. Cut

WATERMELON RIND
GINGER
SUGAR
LEMON

the rind into pieces and place in a large bowl. Cover with water to which you have added 2 tablespoons of salt for every 8 cups of water. Let this stand 5 to 6 hours. This is to make the rinds crisp. Rinse and let stand in fresh water for half an hour. Now you are ready to start your preserves.

For every 2 pounds of prepared rind, sprinkle 1 tablespoon of ground ginger over the rind. Cover with water and boil until fork-tender. Drain again.

While the rind is draining, make a syrup of:

4 cups sugar
juice of 2 lemons
7 cups water

Boil for 5 minutes only. Add the drained rind to the syrup and simmer for 15 minutes. Pack in pint jars and seal at once.

326. Wild Plum Preserves

Southeastern Oregon is the type of country where you have to "sit a spell and get acquainted" to truly appreciate it. In passing through, you would never know it was a bird hunter's paradise and that those innocent-looking streams were laden with trout. It is the one place you can go deer hunting and become so busy finding Indian arrowheads and other artifacts that you forget to look for the deer. . . . You will find other good eating there, also. Those bitter, puckery wild plums that grow in the canyons make delicious preserves that is especially fine with meat. This preserves can be made by using a commercial pectin, but "old-timers" prefer the boiling method, using a ratio of 5 parts of plums and 5 parts of sugar. Some like to make it runny and serve spooned over wild game. It is almost a "must" with roast venison or roast goose.

Pit and cut the plums in quarters if they are large and in halves if they are small. *Do not, under any circumstances, cook the pits* be- | WILD RED PLUMS SUGAR

cause if you do, the resulting preserves will be so puckery and bitter you will be unable to eat it.

For every 5 cups of plum pulp, add 5 cups of sugar. Slowly bring to a boil in its own juice. Boil just exactly 5 minutes. Pour into sterilized pint jars and seal at once.

Never double the recipe when making jellies and jams of any kind. For perfect results every time, in both flavor and texture, they should be made in small amounts.

Tips on Making Jelly...

In managing on a "broken shoestring," it's easy to become bogged down and forget to "look up" at all the abundance at hand. Berries in season can be a real bonanza. On our berry-picking jaunts as we fill our buckets, we take time out tò wash the berries, package them in plastic bags, and secure the bags with a rubber band. (Berries have a tendency to juice in traveling and the plastic bag catches the juice.) We then put them in as cool a place as possible. Back home again all we have to do is put our bags of berries in the freezer. This is a big advantage, for by this time everyone's enthusiasm has quietly gone down the drain. Another advantage is that, come using time, if we want to make jelly or jam, our berries are unsweetened so there is no danger in upsetting the sugar ratio in the recipe.

I have found this method works well with raspberries, blackberries, huckleberries, and blueberries. The berry that isn't satisfactory is strawberries. They definitely need sugar when freezing. Strawberries do travel well though, if you are careful to pick them with good long stems. If you are ever fortunate enough to find a wild strawberry patch that yields more than the usual amount of berries, pick enough for a few glasses of strawberry jam. You'll be glad you did.

Salmonberries which grow along the coast are often overlooked, but these bitter-tasting salmon-colored berries make up into some of the most delicious jelly you ever spread on a slice of toast. We use the guideline in the pectin package for making Loganberry Jelly whenever we make Salmonberry Jelly. Our family is so fond of this jelly that we try to arrange a trip to the coast each year when the berries are ripe. We take the needed pectin, sugar, jelly glasses, and paraffin with us and make jelly at camp, using the camp stove. This has proved to be such fun that we try to make a second trip to the High Cascades when the Oregon Grape are ripe—and proceed to make Wild Grape Jelly the same way. In making Grape Jelly from the grapes of Oregon's state flower, you do need to dilute the grape juice, using 2 cups of water for every 3 cups of juice.

Strange as it may sound, I have found it pays to buy pectin by the case, along with a supply of reconstituted lemon juice. Then whenever the "jelly mood" hits me, I have everything I need to make it. It is ever so much more fun to make jelly and jam in the winter time, using frozen berries and fruit. It's a wonderful rainy or snowy day project; the sparkling glasses of jelly will perk up the gloomiest of days.

I always use a commercial pectin in making jelly because it takes the trial and error out of the procedure. Besides, it eliminates the long boiling process. You have a finished product with a fresh-fruit flavor; and in the long run, more jelly per cup of juice.

Basic Juice Preparation for Jelly...

Wash the berries and place in a large kettle. Add just enough water to keep the berries from sticking before they start forming their own juice. Use a masher to force the juices out. Bring the berries to the boiling point. *Do not let boil or even simmer.* Heat through just enough to be able to mash the juice free of the pulp and seeds. Boiling makes the juice bitter tasting, and this is the difference between gourmet jelly and just plain jelly.

Next, place a double thickness of cheesecloth over a large kettle. Pour the fruit into the cloth. Fold the corners to make a bag, and twist . . . it helps to press the bag with a masher. For jelly that sparkles, pour the juice through a second clean cloth to remove any pulp that may have escaped into the juice the first time. In making jams and jellies from wild fruits and berries, use the guideline in the pectin package for the fruit that is nearest in tartness to the one you have on hand.

RECIPE GUIDE

SHORTCUTS WITH PRESSURE COOKING

Sometimes we just don't have time for conventional cooking. The following fourteen meals designed for the "hurries" are especially good and are made possible with a pressure cooker. They should see you through any hectic two weeks. If you haven't come up with some additional recipes of your own by then, just start over. They're worth repeating soon.

In adapting your own recipes for use in a pressure cooker, just remember it takes only a third as much time as ordinary cooking. In other words, if a recipe ordinarily takes an hour and a half, it will take only 30 minutes with a pressure cooker. Cut down the liquid called for in the non-pressure recipe to just one-half, for the speed of pressure cooking eliminates much evaporation.

Altitude does affect pressure cooking. For every additional 1,000 feet over the first basic 2,000 feet, add 5 minutes' additional cooking time.

A 4-quart pressure cooker is a practical choice for family cooking. It is small enough to be handled easily and large enough to be practical. Different brands of pressure cookers have different types of pressure controls. It is important to read the manual that comes with your cooker to become completely familiar with its workings.

When using a pressure cooker, there are really only two basic rules to keep in mind. If these are followed, a pressure cooker can be a carefree joy to cook with:

1. Always wait until the gauge indicator is at zero before

removing the pressure control weight. If the pressure cooker does not have a gauge, be sure it has cooled sufficiently before you remove the "control weight."

2. Some recipes specify, "let pressure drop of its own accord." Set the pressure cooker on a cooling rack and let it do just that. Other recipes suggest "cooling immediately." This can be accomplished by placing the cooker in a large pan of cold water or by holding under running water. However, do not let the water run on the steam gauge. It is at this point only, that you remove the "pressure control weight."

One major advantage of the pressure cooker is its way with economy cuts of meat. These cuts have a great deal of connective tissue which requires long periods of patient cooking to bring out the best in them when using regular cooking methods. Such extended cooking is virtually impossible for the working wife; but with the help of a pressure cooker, anyone can prepare these tasty budget-stretchers—and the results are delicious.

A pressure cooker can give you more time for exploring. Dead juniper such as this makes up into lovely wooden bowls and lamps.

327. Stew Meat

Stew meat is a real friend to a pressure cooker as well as your budget. With the help of your cooker it will take only 30 minutes to have tender, juicy meat cubes.

Sprinkle 1½ pounds of beef cubes with salt and pepper. Roll them in flour and brown well on all sides in a small amount of fat. Drain off the excess fat, add 1 cup of water, and cook at 10 pounds of pressure for 30 minutes. Reduce pressure at once. Serves 4.

STEW MEAT
SALT
PEPPER
FLOUR

If time is short, serve "as is" with mashed potatoes. A yellow vegetable, a green salad, and a bit of ice-cream sherbet— all add up to a gourmet meal designed for the "hurries." If time permits, go one step further and make a . . .

328. Beefsteak Pie

Prepare stew meat according to the directions in the preceding recipe. Before removing from the pressure cooker add:

1 teaspoon onion flakes
  or dice a small onion
2 cups canned tomatoes
  or if your family doesn't care for tomatoes, add 2 cups water
1 cup canned peas
  or 1 cup canned green beans

STEW MEAT
ONION
  FLAKES
TOMATOES,
  CANNED
PEAS, CANNED
FLOUR

Make a paste with 4 tablespoons flour and ½ cup of water. Bring the above mixture to a boil and thicken by adding the flour-and-water paste slowly, stirring constantly until it is thick and creamy. Pour in a long baking dish. (We prefer the "or" alternatives of this recipe.)

— Or —

Prepare biscuit dough. Roll dough to a thickness of ¼ inch, making it the size of the baking dish. Place on top of the meat filling. Cut gashes in the dough to allow steam to escape. Bake in a pre-heated oven (425 degrees) until the crust is well browned. Serve at once to 4 hungry people.

329. Chicken Gizzards with Milk Gravy

Chicken Gizzards served with hot biscuits, milk gravy, and tossed salad make inexpensive good family eating. They can also be a "quickie" meal.

Season 2 pounds of chicken gizzards with salt and pepper, roll in flour, and brown in a small amount of fat until crusty and brown on each side. Drain off the fat and save to be used later in making the gravy. Add ½ cup of water to the gizzards. Cook under 10 pounds of pressure for 15 minutes. Remove the gizzards to a platter and make the gravy. Serves 4.

CHICKEN
    GIZZARDS
FLOUR
SALT
PEPPER
SHORTENING

Milk Gravy

To the chicken crumbs in the kettle add:

3 tablespoons fat (use the fat in which the gizzards were browned)

3 tablespoons flour

CHICKEN FAT
FLOUR
MILK
SALT
PEPPER

Stir together over low heat until the flour starts to brown. Add all at once:

2 cups milk

Turn the heat up and stir the mixture constantly until it thickens. Let it bubble for just a minute. If you prefer a thinner gravy, add a little more milk, continue stirring, and bring to the boiling point again. Season with salt and pepper to taste.

The whole meal is on in just a little more than a half hour, all depending on how fast you are at stirring up biscuits!

When I first started to housekeep, I had to strain more than one dish of gravy through a sieve in order to have smooth gravy. My mother finally came to the rescue and gave me two simple rules and I've never had any trouble since:

When making Milk Gravy, cook the flour and fat together just until the flour starts to brown. Be careful not to burn the flour. Then add the milk all at once. Stir to keep from sticking until it is thick and creamy and starts to bubble. This is contrary to what the "books" tell you but I've found it was one of those times when Mama knew best.

To make **Brown Gravy,** strain off the excess fat. Add a quart of water to the pan in which the roast or "what have you" has been cooked. Stir and work loose all the valuable and delicious extractives that have settled in the bottom of the pan. (I say valuable because they are packed with nutrition.) Bring to a boil. Meantime, make a flour-and-water paste by mixing together until smooth, ½ cup flour and ½ cup water. Add gradually to the boiling liquid, stirring constantly. When it is the desired thickness, let simmer just a bit to thoroughly cook the flour. Here again, you may want to add more thickening. It's all a matter of individual preference.

330. Barbecued Spareribs

It usually takes 1½ to 2 hours to prepare Barbecued Spareribs. Here's how you can do it in 30 minutes with your pressure cooker:

Cut 3 pounds of spareribs into serving pieces. Roll and coat in a mixture of:

½ cup flour
1 tablespoon paprika
1 teaspoon salt

SPARERIBS
FLOUR
PAPRIKA
SALT
SHORTENING
GARLIC
ONION
BROWN SUGAR
CHILI POWDER
BLACK PEPPER
CATSUP
TOMATO SAUCE
VINEGAR

Brown in ½ cup shortening in the pressure cooker, using it as you would a skillet. Drain off the excess fat. Mix together and add:

1 clove garlic, mashed
½ cup chopped onion
¼ cup brown sugar
½ teaspoon chili powder
¼ teaspoon black pepper
½ cup catsup
¾ cup tomato sauce
2 tablespoons vinegar

Cook with 15 pounds of pressure for 30 minutes. Reduce pressure at once. Arrange the ribs on a platter. Let the sauce simmer to thicken (will only take a minute or two), then pour it over the ribs. If you haven't watched your P's and Q's, the main dish is ready and you aren't.

331. Hawaiian Chicken

*This next recipe does take longer to prepare, but the fixings
are easy and it requires very little watching. It is inexpensive
and hearty. There is only one requirement. For the ultimate
in flavor, be sure to use olive oil.*

Dredge cut-up pieces of stewer chicken in flour seasoned
with salt and pepper. Brown in a small amount of olive oil.

Meanwhile, heat the pressure cooker for a minute or two.

Add and brown all together:

3 tablespoons olive oil
2 teaspoons sugar
1 small onion, chopped fine
1 tomato, peeled and cut in very small
   pieces

STEWER
   CHICKEN
OLIVE OIL
SUGAR
ONION
TOMATO

Add:

browned chicken pieces
2 cups water

FRESH
RICE

Cook at 10 pounds pressure for 30 minutes. Reduce temperature immediately by running cold water over the pressure
cooker. Remove the chicken to a platter and keep in a warm
place. Add 1 cup of rice to the liquid and simmer until the
rice absorbs the liquid. Takes 10 to 15 minutes. Heap the
rice in a bowl and top with a large pat of butter.

332. Burger Babes

*This unusual and tasty way to prepare hamburgers will
speak for itself. Mix together:*

1½ pounds hamburger
   1 egg
1½ slices of fresh bread, broken into crumbs

HAMBURGER
EGG
BREAD
BACON
TOMATO
ONION
MUSHROOM
   SOUP
MUSHROOM
   SLICES

Divide and shape into 8 hamburger patties.
Make patties about ¼-inch thick. Take 8
slices of bacon and form 4 crosses. (A cutting
board is a good place to put these together.)
On top of each cross, place a hamburger patty,

a slice of tomato, a slice of onion, and a second hamburger patty. Pinch the edges of the patties together, sealing the tomatoes and onions in. Bring the bacon ends up and over the hamburger stack. Secure with toothpicks. Carefully brown the bundle on the top and on the bottom. Place in the pressure cooker side by side. Cover with:

    1 can of mushroom soup
    1 can of mushroom slices

Cook under 10 pounds of pressure for 8 minutes. Cool pressure cooker immediately by running cold water over the top. Serves 4.

———◆———

333. Chili Con Carne

Chili Con Carne can be made in almost no time at all . . . and here's how. Heat the pressure cooker. Then add:

    1 pound of ground beef
    2 tablespoons fat

GROUND BEEF
SHORTENING
KIDNEY BEANS
  (CANNED)
TOMATOES
  (CANNED)
GARLIC
ONION
CHILI POWDER

Brown the beef, breaking it apart with 2 forks as it browns. Add:

  2½ cups cooked kidney beans (canned)
    2 cups cooked tomatoes
    1 clove of garlic, minced very fine
  ¼ cup chopped onion
    3 teaspoons chili powder

Close cover securely and cook for 15 minutes at 15 pounds of pressure. Let pressure drop of its own accord. Serves 4 generously.

334. Lima Beans & Beef

Bean dishes, well known as high-protein budget-stretchers, are almost impossible for the working girl to prepare on a working day without the help of a pressure cooker. This recipe can be prepared in half an hour and needs only fruit for dessert.

Soak 2 cups of dried lima beans overnight.
Brown in 2 tablespoons of fat:

    1 pound of ground beef
    1 cup onions, sliced

Add the following ingredients:

    soaked beans
    ½ cup water
    2 teaspoons salt
    1 No. 2 can tomatoes
    2 teaspoons sugar
    2 teaspoons Worcestershire sauce

LIMA BEANS
GROUND BEEF
ONIONS
SALT
TOMATOES
SUGAR
WORCESTER-
  SHIRE
  SAUCE

Cook under 15 pounds of pressure for 30 minutes. Let stand for 5 minutes, then reduce pressure instantly. Serves 4.

335. Sweet 'n Sour Lamb Chops

Heat the cooker. Add a small amount of shortening to the bottom of the cooker and brown 4 lamb chops to a delicate brown on both sides. If you prefer, substitute pork chops or ham slices.

While meat is cooking, make a sauce by combining:

    ¼ cup vinegar
    ¼ cup brown sugar
    1 teaspoon salt
    ⅛ teaspoon pepper
    ¼ teaspoon ginger

LAMB CHOPS
VINEGAR
BROWN SUGAR
SALT
PEPPER
GINGER
LEMON
ORANGE

Pour over the chops. Add slices made from

    1 lemon
    1 orange

Cook under 15 pounds of pressure for 10 minutes. Cool at once by running cold water over the pressure cooker . . . if directions for your cooker permit this.

336. Sloppy Joes

Sloppy Joes are ready as quickly as if you had ordered them over the counter, if you do them this way:

Brown 2 pounds of hamburger. Then add:

1 onion, chopped fine	HAMBURGER
4 stalks celery, chopped fine	ONION
1 tablespoon mustard	CELERY
1 tablespoon Worcestershire sauce	MUSTARD
1 cup catsup	WORCESTER-
1 can tomato soup	SHIRE
1 can water	SAUCE
1 teaspoon salt	CATSUP
¼ teaspoon pepper	TOMATO SOUP
	SALT
	PEPPER

Cook under 10 pounds of pressure for 20 minutes. Reduce pressure at once. They are done in the length of time it takes to butter the buns and prepare a tray of carrot and celery sticks.

337. Stuffed Bell Peppers

Cut the tops off 6 green peppers, about ¾ inch down. For the filling, brown 1 pound of hamburger. Then add:

1 chopped onion	GREEN BELL
2 cups tomato (canned)	PEPPERS
1 teaspoon celery salt	HAMBURGER
1 cup bread crumbs	TOMATO
1 teaspoon salt	(CANNED)
¼ teaspoon pepper	CELERY SALT

Simmer together until thick. Fill the peppers. Put the tops back on the peppers and place on the rack in your pressure cooker. Cook under 10 pounds of pressure for 15 minutes. Reduce pressure at once.

ONION
BREAD
CRUMBS
SALT
PEPPER

338. Short Ribs, "Plain and Simple"

Roll 2 pounds of short ribs in flour. Season with salt and pepper and brown in fat, being careful to brown well on all four sides. Drain off all excess fat. Add:

1 cup water
1 onion, chopped fine
1 tablespoon Worcestershire sauce
2 tablespoons vinegar

Cook under 15 pounds of pressure for 30 minutes. Place cooker under cold, running water to cool at once, and serve to 4 hungry people.

SHORT RIBS
ONION
WORCESTER-
  SHIRE
  SAUCE
VINEGAR
FLOUR
SALT
PEPPER

339. Stuffed Round Steak

Make a dressing by mixing together:

1½ cups soft bread crumbs
2 tablespoons grated onion
1 teaspoon salt
¼ teaspoon pepper
1 teaspoon poultry seasoning

BREAD
  CRUMBS
ONION
SALT
PEPPER
POULTRY
  SEASONING
ROUND STEAK

Spread over the surface of one thick round steak. Roll up as you would a jelly roll. Tie with a heavy string. Brown carefully in a small amount of fat in the bottom of the pressure cooker. When browned, remove the roll, place the rack in the bottom of the cooker, and return the steak roll to the cooker. Add ½ cup water. Cook under 15 pounds of pressure for 30 minutes. Make a brown gravy with the drippings. Slice and serve. It is extra-special eating, regardless of what you serve with it.

340. Sausage Balls

Combine and make into 1-inch balls:

1 pound pork sausage	SAUSAGE
½ pound fresh ground pork	FRESH GROUND PORK
½ cup uncooked rice	RICE
1 teaspoon cinnamon	CINNAMON (CLOVES)

Brown slowly on all sides. Add ½ cup water and cook under 15 pounds pressure for 20 minutes. Reduce pressure at once by running cold water over the cooker. Remove sausage balls from the juices and make a milk gravy. For a special taste appeal, add ⅛ teaspoon cloves.

This recipe is similar to Porcupines, which also can be made in a pressure cooker.

The great outdoors forever beckons.

FROZEN FOODS

In homesteader days, a homemaker spent many hours each day preserving food for her family. Meat was canned and smoked, fruit and vegetables were canned and sometimes dried, and many foods were enjoyed only in season. Today it is different. Women really have come a "long, long way," for foods of every description and season are available right in their own kitchens in the freezer. A minimum amount of time is spent in the "freezer to stove to table routine." Thanks to freezers, careful planning and buying makes it possible to enjoy substantial savings in the year's food budget. Pastries can be purchased in quantity (usually at a lower price) to have on hand for quick meals.

With a freezer you can really make the most of the food at hand because you rarely have left-overs. In fact, you will find yourself cooking with an eye to "planned-overs"; those extra meals tucked away in the freezer for busy times will give you more time to enjoy your family and shared hobbies.

In cooking for a family and trying to make the most of your grocery budget, it is easy to be "penny wise and pound foolish." If you have a perfectly good casserole dish in the making, don't spoil it by adding that dab of corn or peas that was left over, unless it will really do something for the casserole. It is better to have two (2-pound) coffee cans in the freezer—one for vegetable left-overs and one for meat scraps. These can be combined for a hearty vegetable and meat soup, or the meat scraps can be used in casseroles. If it is something that really doesn't have any future potential, it is better just to throw it away than to ruin a main dish.

A welcome visitor at camp, picnic, or in your own backyard.

If it bothers your frugal soul to throw away food, feed it to the birds. This has become such a family joke that from the time our children were able to talk, they knew that some things were "for the birds." I realize this isn't a practical answer for everyone, but the moral of the story is—it really isn't wise to load your freezer or refrigerator up with all sorts of odds and ends that you know you will never use.

Freezers can be upright, chest, dual-temperature freezer-refrigerator combinations—or the freezer unit in the standard single-control refrigerator, designed primarily for one to two weeks' supply of food. However, I have kept well-packaged breads, pastries, beef, lean pork, fruits, and vegetables much longer in these units. Meats, though, tend to become dry, and fruits and vegetables to lose some of their flavor. . . . But limited though their use is, they're better than no freezer at all!

In a chest freezer, packages to be frozen must be placed against the walls or in a special "quick freeze" section and then moved to the baskets or center of the freezer for long-term storage. An upright freezer takes less space and makes food more accessible, and the freezing coils are normally located in each shelf. This means food freezes faster and can be placed directly on the shelves for "quick freezing." A dual-temperature refrigerator-freezer combination is used in the same manner as an upright freezer.

Owning and using a home freezer just naturally means having a large quantity of frozen food on hand—which of course brings up the question, "What would I do if there is a power failure or the unit in my freezer ceases to work?"

Freezer Failure:

A unit failure in your freezer can throw you into a regular panic . . . and there is always a tendency to peek and see how things are doing, but please don't. In a good freezer, if you keep the door shut during the power failure, food will stay frozen at least two days. Should the freezer be located in a warm place, or if the supply in the freezer is low, check at the end of 24 hours. The more food there is, the longer it will stay frozen. If the power is to remain off longer than is safe, add dry ice to the freezer.

According to current authorities, food which has begun to thaw may be refrozen if the food still contains some ice crystals, or if the temperature of the food has not gone beyond 30 degrees above zero. Partially thawed food does not need repackaging except in cases where leakage or soaking of the wrapping has occurred. *Cooked food may be heated and refrozen as many times as you like, but never, never, refreeze fish or seafood.*

If uncooked food thaws, you can cook and then refreeze. This can become a huge task . . . I know . . . I had to do it one time . . . but later on all those pre-cooked meals were wonderful, just waiting in the freezer to be used. So, even with freezer failure, there can be that proverbial silver lining to the cloud.

Cleaning a Freezer:

Cleaning a freezer always looks like such a monstrous job but it really isn't. There is only one rule to remember: *Do not chip and poke at the ice with a knife or anything else.* You just cannot pry the ice off. In a chest freezer, you risk scratching the surface of the walls, and in an upright freezer you risk puncturing lines which would allow the gas to escape. It is almost impossible to repair these tiny leaks—and be sure you have found all of them.

There are electric defrosters available on the market, but great care must be taken to place the defroster in such a way that it will not melt the plastic liners in the freezer.

To Defrost:

Here is an easy way to defrost: Unplug the freezer and remove the food. Place the food in cardboard boxes and cover with a blanket. Frozen food will keep this way 5 to 6 hours even in the summertime. Next, take beach towels, or what have you, and lay them on the shelves of an upright freezer or in the bottom of a chest freezer. If you are in a great hurry, place pans of steaming hot water on the towels in the freezer, shut the door, and go on about your other work.

In about half an hour, replace the water with more hot water. Again, just shut the door and be on about your business. (Do not use a heat lamp to hasten the thawing. It can melt the plastic liners of the freezer.) In a short time you will hear the ice start to fall. Take another pan and put in it the chunks that have fallen and pour them into the sink. This will keep the towels from getting too soaked. The towels will catch the drips and can easily be rung out. When your freezer is completely defrosted, wash the shelves with a solution of soda water and dry. Plug the freezer back in and put your food away. As you put the packages away, I suggest you check them for breaks in the wrap. If there are any breaks, now is the time to rewrap. A proper wrap and care of frozen food is probably the most important factor there is in determining whether your finished meal is delicious or mediocre.

To keep the quality of frozen food purchased over the counter in your local food store at top quality, it should be slipped into a plastic bag and secured tightly with a rubber band before storing in your freezer. Generally a good freezer wrap is used by the producers on these products, but sometimes it is of inferior grade and not meant for long-term storage. Occasionally the seal becomes broken in handling. After a week or two in the freezer, these products will show signs of freezer burn or rancidness unless they are rewrapped.

It is almost too easy to hurry home from the market and pop chickens, hamburger, fish, and frozen vegetables into the freezer in their present wrap. This is all right if you are absolutely sure you will be using the product within a week's time, but if you are buying with an eye to freezer-banking the products and plan to keep them for a longer period of time, be sure to rewrap. Freezer bags of various sizes kept for this purpose are inexpensive and can be used over and over.

Freezer Packaging Tips:

Eighty-five per cent of inferior frozen food is due to improper wrapping. It is important to get a tight seal. In meat, this is sometimes a little difficult because of the odd-shaped packages. Quite by accident, I discovered that by first wrapping the meat with a plastic wrap (tucking all around the meat, sealing out every bit of air), then wrapping in a regular good grade of freezer wrap paper (heavily waxed on one side and plain on the other)—a near perfect seal was obtained.

Never, never use butcher paper for freezer wrap, no matter what the package label claims; it just isn't suitable for freezing. Meat wrapped first in plastic wrap and then in freezer paper will keep indefinitely in the freezer.

In packaging meat patties, tear off a strip of plastic wrap about 36 inches long. Place the patties in a row the length of the paper, leaving about 1½ inches between patties. Fold the sides of the plastic in and over the tops of the patties. This completely seals them in. Now, fold the covered meat patties back and forth over each other, accordion style. Place the stack of patties into a large freezer bag, sealing out as much air as possible and securing the end of the bag with a rubber band, or better still, a pipe cleaner . . . for you will be opening and closing the bag whenever patties are needed. (The pipe cleaner is easier to work with than a rubber band.) Whenever patties are needed, just count out the number you will need, snip them off with the scissors, and put the rest back in the freezer. The patties will thaw quickly because the row of them can be laid out flat.

When freezing meat of any kind, be sure to lay the packages flat on the freezer shelves of an upright freezer or in the "quick freeze" compartment of a chest freezer, for fast freezing. Wait until the packages are frozen to stack them. If care is taken in freezing and packaging meat, it will keep more than a year without loss of flavor or quality—except in the case of poultry and pork (and, of course, fish) which should be used within a 6-months' period.

Using Freezer Food:

Food in your freezer will do much more for you if you give a little thought to the amount of each food frozen, as well as to the use of it. Food frozen and not used is just as wasteful as money earned and not used wisely. Its value becomes zero. In freezing any food in quantity, keep in mind which season of the year it is the most plentiful, then watch your local markets for the best buy. For example, plan on certain fruits and vegetables to run you through the winter months, or until this type of food is in season and can be purchased more economically at the local market. Keep in mind that it is better to understock than to overstock. Stock your freezer in such a way that you have ample room left for breads and pastries purchased on "special" as well as room for home-baked favorites and casseroles.

Freezer Tips...

Freeze extra gravy and chicken broth in ice-cube trays. Store the frozen cubes in a plastic freezer bag. Adds a delectable flavor to many a casserole dish.

Extra chicken and turkey can be used in many ways. It is probably best just to store the meat in family-size packages in the freezer and use as the mood hits you. It's good in sandwiches, casseroles, meat pies topped with biscuits, creamed turkey on toast, and in popovers.

Store extra dressing in a casserole dish. Cover with a freezer wrap and freeze. When ready to serve at a later date, top with some of the frozen gravy cubes and pop into a hot oven until serving time. It's just as moist and tasty as the first time served.

Save and freeze bits of meat until you have enough to make a good meat pie.

TV dinners from left-overs: For one combination, on each foil plate place a serving of frozen carrot cubes and a nice large helping of mashed potatoes, along with a generous serving of the scrappy beef you froze when you cooked the last roast. Place a butter cubelet on top of the potatoes and carrots. Sprinkle the meat lightly with salt and pepper; or if you have some frozen gravy cubes on hand in the freezer, place a gravy cube on top of the meat. Cover the plates with foil and freeze. When ready to use, just remove them from the freezer and pop them into a hot oven (400 degrees) for 30 to 40 minutes. Remove the foil and serve piping hot.

Package left-over hamburger patties with 2 tablespoons

of barbecue sauce. Wrap in foil and freeze. When ready to use, heat in their foil wrappings. For outdoor cooking, heat the packaged hamburgers right in the coals for a few minutes.

To freeze mashed-potato left-overs "as is," instead of making into potato cakes, add one level teaspoon of baking powder to about 10 potatoes when mashing. You won't be able to taste the baking powder and it will help retain the fluffiness after freezing.

To freeze lima beans: Blanch them in the pods in boiling water from 3 to 4 minutes, depending on the size of the beans. Cool in icewater and then squeeze the beans out of the pods. They pop right out! Discard the imperfect or over-mature beans. Wash the beans in cold, running water; drain, package, and freeze.

Next time you clean celery, cut the tops off, wash well, and pop into a plastic bag and freeze. After they are frozen give the bag a sharp rap on the counter. The celery will splinter into a cascade of pieces. Celery crumbs can be used to season roast, add flavoring to soup, or any place you would normally use celery seed or celery salt.

To cut corn off the cob for freezing: Anchor the ear in the center stem of an angel-food cake pan. This holds the ear of corn secure and the pan catches the corn.

To freeze fruit: At the end of each batch there is always a certain amount that is imperfect. Instead of freezing "as is," put into popsicle molds with just a little extra sugar. The youngsters will love it.

Freeze applesauce in ice-cube trays. One cube is a nice accompaniment for the meat course. Two or three make dessert.

Freeze a can of fruit cocktail for a jiffy salad or dessert. Slice while still icy. Add a topping of whipped cream and it is a dessert. Add a topping of mayonnaise or fruit salad dressing and it is a salad.

Peaches and cream: If you serve this often, slice a few peaches into freezer containers, add sugar, a little cream, more peaches and more sugar and cream. Freeze as usual.

Christmas breads and cookies often call for lemon and orange juice and small amounts of grated rind. To avoid waste, freeze the left-over lemon and orange halves. You won't need to be in any hurry to use them. The rind grates easily while still partially frozen and the juice is just as potent in flavor as ever.

Variety bread loaf: Buy several kinds of day-old bread and repackage in mixed loaves. Freeze until needed. Gives variety to each meal.

Extra cake: If you have a cake that has gone begging, make it into crumbs. Add a little brown sugar and cinnamon and freeze. Can be used as crunchy topping for coffee cake or apple pie.

Bits of sweet bakery goods: Save and freeze. Soon you'll have a new and different bread pudding to make.

Whipped cream can be dropped from a teaspoon onto a cookie sheet and frozen. Package these "swirls" to be used later as toppings for pies and desserts.

Store brown sugar in the refrigerator. Moist cold prevents sugar from hardening.

If there is a baby in the house, cook several vegetables in quantity. Put through a sieve, or better still, use a blender. Freeze the puree in ice-cube trays. Store the vegetable cubes in plastic bags. These cubes are just right for baby.

Freeze Brazil nuts before you try to shell them. If frozen first, the whole nut meat will fall right out of the shell.

If your family likes to picnic, *a way to do it up in grand style on the spur of the moment is to keep two or three picnic meals packed ahead of time in your freezer. When you plan your menu for the coming week and do your grocery shopping, plan a picnic dinner or lunch that you can freeze. Make it up while you are putting away the groceries. This way you are all set to go whenever the family takes the notion.*

This method has another advantage: when you pack the picnic basket, the frozen food will keep the salad greens and other non-frozen foods at refrigerator temperature, right up to eating time.

SEASONINGS

In homestead days, spices were scarce items in most kitchens, but today's homemaker usually has a large variety of them because they are fairly inexpensive, easy to obtain, and have important taste value in the preparation of many foods. Thoughtful seasoning can turn a good dish into a memorable one. But the idea that each spice or herb has a specific dish or dishes in which it can be used is false. People's tastes differ as much as people themselves and what may be hot and spicy for one may be tame and bland for another. Read the directions and uses on the packages—but experiment for yourself—and you are on the road to gourmet cookery.

Select a good brand of spices and then stay with that brand. You become accustomed to the amount needed for your own recipes, and the spices in matching containers arranged alphabetically in a row on your spice shelf are a pretty sight.

There are so many wonderful new flavors and seasonings on the market, you might pick one out from time to time and learn all you can about it—when to use it and how much. In this way, each of your spices will become an old friend and be just as easy to use in the correct amount in the right place as salt and pepper.

Personally, I have never been what you would call a "spicy" cook because my family maintains there is nothing like meat, potatoes, and gravy; and if they could have only two seasonings, they would take salt and pepper. However, by purchasing a spice from time to time that we have never really become acquainted with and using it discreetly, we have learned to enjoy many spices that I never even used to keep on the spice shelf.

Oregano has now become a "must" in our family; we enjoy it in Pizza and have found that it works wonders for Spaghetti Sauce, if used sparingly. Prior to this, we had been convinced that the milder Basil was the only spice for our Spanish or Italian foods. Our most recent discovery is Pork Seasoning. Sprinkled lightly on sausage cakes or pork chops, it enhances their flavor considerably.

In trying out a new recipe, if you find it nonchalantly says "season to taste" . . . don't do it. I've spent the past 10 years testing and tasting such recipes and have come to the conclusion that if a recipe says "season to taste," I should just use 1 teaspoon of salt and ¼ teaspoon of pepper per pound of meat . . . there's no use eating your calorie quota in the testing and tasting. Let everyone season to suit his own taste. If properly used, a spice will not dominate, but enhance the flavor of the food. One-fourth teaspoon of seasoning to a serving of 4 is a good starter.

For those who like to explore new tastes and experiment with familiar ones, the world of spices and herbs has seemingly endless adaptations . . . a clove of garlic in a bottle of French dressing can add taste appeal; a bit of mace enhances seafood, especially Oyster Stew; a pinch of dried thyme added to fresh carrots improves the taste; a sprig of fresh mint cooked with green peas is tasty; cooked spinach, seasoned with butter and sprinkled lightly with Marjoram, is delightful.

You should check your supply of spices at least once a year for two main reasons: it is easy to gather an impressive collection yet be out of the very ones you need for a particular recipe; and old spices can lose their "zip." They have a way of reminding us how the years slip by . . . for example, when you find that you bought that dingy-looking box of allspice "way back when." When you make your annual "check," give your spices the "sniff" test. If they have a pungent odor, it is a safe bet they still retain their flavor. If the odor isn't good and strong, you might as well throw that spice out.

For a fascinating and useful hobby, grow an Herb Garden of your own. If you don't have a garden spot, grow them in pretty little flower pots on the window sill. They will add to the decor of your kitchen, make a good conversation piece, and do wonderful things for your cooking. Fresh or dried, their leaves and flowers and seeds make many dishes more interesting.

There are a number of seeds from which to choose. The first time around you might try sage, mint, marjoram, basil, chives, and parsley. Chives and parsley provide especially welcome winter cuttings. Occasionally you will see advertised a selected collection of herbs for planting, including such inviting names as rosemary, tarragon, and thyme.

Following is an alphabetical guide to seasoning with herbs and spices . . . with notes on their taste and use . . . to help you become better acquainted with the "wonderful world of spices" . . . .

Allspice: Like a mixture of cinnamon, cloves, and nutmeg— it's fine with soups, sauces, preserves, meats, apples.

Anise: A licorice flavor for iced drinks, candy, bread, pastry.

Basil Leaves: Like mint and very sweet smelling—excellent with game birds, duck, spaghetti sauce, cheese, and tomato dishes.

Bay Leaves: They have a strong, sweet-scented taste and are used in pickling solutions, stuffing for roast birds, tomato dishes, and fish sauces. Half a leaf only is necessary to flavor a quart of soup stock.

Capers: Pickled buds of a shrub of Spanish origin. Recommended for sauces, salad dressings, and meat.

Caraway Seed: Has a pleasant nut-like flavor and is recommended for pork, cabbage dishes, and mutton . . . it should be added before cooking.

Cardamom Seed: Somewhat like cinnamon. Use in Danish pastry, grape jelly—or add a single seed to a cup of coffee!

Cayenne Pepper: Hot, biting. Use sparingly but often in meat dishes, sea foods, salads, sauces, eggs.

Celery Salt, Flakes, and Seed: By-products of the familiar celery. Use in any recipe calling for celery. Good with salads, meats, and vegetable dishes.

Chili Powder: Hotter than cayenne. Gives Mexican dishes zip . . . but use discreetly!

Chives: A member of the onion family and one of the most popular of seasonings. Use in salads, especially potato salad, omelets, sauces, cheese, etc. Best when used fresh.

Cinnamon: Sweet with a tang. Primarily used with sweets, baked foods, fruits, pickles, sauces, sweet potatoes . . . and it accents chocolate.

Cloves: Warm and pungent. Use with baked goods, preserves, relishes, candy, fruits, and pork.

Curry Powder: Often referred to as the "salt of the Orient." Use with meats, vegetables, fish, and eggs.

Fennel: Like Anise, it has a licorice flavor. Makes a fine garnish for salads.

Garlic Salt and Garlic: Like onions, only more so. Use with salads, meats, vegetables, tomato dishes, spaghetti, soups, and cheese dishes.

Ginger: "To ginger" means "to put spirit into" and it does. Many like it in candies, cookies, cakes, (ginger) breads. Try rubbing pot roast with a piece of ginger before cooking . . . or add a tiny pinch of ground ginger to brown gravy.

Mace: A spice made from the outer coating of nutmeg and somewhat like nutmeg in flavor. Use in baking and in certain soups and stews.

Marjoram: Has spicy taste which is fine with lamb, poultry, eggs, stuffing, and bland vegetables.

Mint: There are many varieties, all used for flavorings, but spearmint is the most popular. Use to flavor pea soup, new potatoes, spinach, beverages, mint jelly, and in sauce for roast lamb.

Mustard Seed or Dry Mustard: Hot, pungent, tangy. Recommended for meat, pickle solutions, cream sauces, and egg and cheese dishes.

Nasturtium: Add chopped fresh leaves, stem, and flower to a green salad. Chop and mix with potted meat for sandwich fillings.

Nutmeg: Spicy. Its addition to fruits and desserts is ever so pleasant.

Oregano: This is really Wild Marjoram and is used the same way. It is quite pungent so is excellent in Italian and Mexican cookery. Recommended for use with pork and lamb, and in a variety of soups.

Paprika: Extremely mild. It decorates and enhances seafoods, meats, salads, and eggs.

Parsley: Stimulates the appetite. It is both a seasoning and a garnish for fish, meat, poultry, soups, stuffings, sauces and salads.

Pepper: Second only to salt as a basic seasoning. It is made from ground peppercorns. **Black Pepper** is made from the entire berry. **White Pepper** has the outer bark removed. Because heat reduces the flavoring value of Pepper, it is better not to keep it on shelf on stove. **Cayenne Pepper** is very strong . . . a little goes a long way.

Poppy Seed: Has a nut-like flavor. Use in canapes, baked goods, noodles, pickles, and preserves.

Pork Seasoning stimulates the taste buds and greatly enhances sausage cakes and pork chops.

Rosemary is piny in both flavor and fragrance. Rosemary wine can be made by packing ⅔ cup of Rosemary leaves in the bottom of a pint jar. Fill to the top with a dry, white wine. Seal tightly and store in the refrigerator for at least a week. Strain and keep in a sealed bottle in the refrigerator. Add one teaspoon to the liquid used in basting broiled fish or chicken . . . or the next time you make stew for six, add two teaspoons.

Sage: Said to aid the digestion . . . which was the original intent in using to season sausage, pork, and other rich meats. Generally speaking, there is a tendency to overdo when using sage. Never use so much that you actually taste the sage.

Salt: The one indispensable seasoning. Most cooking is nothing without it.

Sesame Seed: Similar to Poppy Seed, right down to the nut-like flavor.

Tarragon: Important in salads and sauces; also in chicken, veal, and stuffings.

Thyme: Has a delicate piny flavor. Use both fresh and dried leaves to flavor beef loaf, stews, soups, turkey, and stuffings.

INDEX